William H Stone

Familiar Instructions On The Sacraments

William H Stone

Familiar Instructions On The Sacraments

ISBN/EAN: 9783741156250

Manufactured in Europe, USA, Canada, Australia, Japa

Cover: Foto ©Thomas Meinert / pixelio.de

Manufactured and distributed by brebook publishing software
(www.brebook.com)

William H Stone

Familiar Instructions On The Sacraments

FAMILIAR
INSTRUCTIONS ON THE SACRAMENTS.

FAMILIAR INSTRUCTIONS

ON

THE SACRAMENTS.

BY REV. W. STONE,

SOUTHAMPTON.

"You shall draw waters with joy out of the Saviour's fountains."
Isaias xii. 3.

Dublin:
JAMES DUFFY & SONS, 15 WELLINGTON QUAY,
AND 14 PATERNOSTER ROW, LONDON.

PREFACE.

FOLLOWING the advice of my friends, whose opinion I am bound to respect, I have undertaken to publish a volume of "Familiar Instructions on the Sacraments." I know there are many persons who hold that we have already works enough on the subject, many of them by gifted authors, and this I am not willing to dispute, so far as *original* works are concerned. But when I explain that I make no pretension to originality—that I have freely used the works of others better qualified to write than I am, whose arguments and expressions I have intermixed with other matter—that I have put these Instructions together under the pressure of arduous missionary work, which rendered it impossible to devote sufficient time to give them that finish which may appear wanting—that I have had only one object in view, viz., to put the teaching of the Church, as explained by the best theologians, in simple language' suited to the intelligence of an ordinary congregation, it will be seen that my aim is a simple and unambitious one. Experience shows that *written* words are more easily understood and remembered than such as are merely spoken. Moreover, it is the only means of reaching those who, from whatever cause, are not able to be present at sermons or instructions. A glance at the Contents will show how the subjects are treated; and if this volume contribute in ever so small a degree to the glory of God, Who, in His goodness and mercy, has given us the Sacraments, and to the better use of the Sacraments as a result of more perfect knowledge, my labour will not have been in vain.

CONTENTS.

INSTRUCTIONS ON THE SACRAMENTS.

I.

ON THE SACRAMENTS IN GENERAL.

THE sacraments are so many channels by which sanctifying grace is infused into our souls, and certain especial helps are given us, so that we may practise virtue and persevere in good; or, as the Council of Trent says: "By which sanctification is acquired, preserved, and augmented, or, if lost, recovered." Of the sacraments it is my intention to speak, and in doing so I will begin by speaking of them in general, unfolding to you many things necessary for a Catholic to know. After which I shall proceed to treat of each sacrament in particular.

Beginning, then, with an explanation of the word *sacrament*, which, in particular, has various interpretations, but in common use signifies a sacred thing. In bygone times, when one person brought an action against another, a certain sum of money was placed by both in a sacred place, and when the case was decided, the person gaining the suit received back what he had deposited, and the other was condemned to lose the amount. For this reason, the money placed in a sacred place was called a *sacrament*. Secondly, the word *sacrament* has been used to signify an oath taken, which binds the person to the performance of some service. Thirdly, it is a word to express a sacred thing, but hidden or a mystery: thus the secrets of God, the mysteries of our holy religion, are sometimes called in

A

Scripture a *sacrament*.   Finally, it expresses every
sacred rite dedicated to the worship, honour, and service
of God.   Besides the meanings of this word given, there
is one which we, Catholics, understand.   The word
sacrament, by our holy Mother the Church, means " an
outward sign of inward grace, ordained by Jesus Christ,
by which grace is given to our souls."   Then a *sacrament* is a sign, that is to say, besides what it presents
to the senses, it constitutes also a medium through
which we arrive at the knowledge of something else.
For instance, when we see a thing, and we say that
that thing is a sign of this or that, we mean that that
thing brings to our minds the cognition of another.   So,
when we say a sacrament is a sign, we declare that it
brings to our minds something we do not see.   To
illustrate what I have just said : when a child is brought
to be baptised, the water poured upon its head and the
words said are a sign that by the power of the Holy
Ghost all the stain and defilement is inwardly washed
away, and that the soul of that child is enriched and
adorned with sanctifying grace.   You are not, however,
to suppose, when we say a sacrament is a sign, that we
mean a natural sign, as smoke denotes fire : no, but a
sign determined by God to signify a sacred thing ; for
it not only indicates, but produces at the same moment
what it signifies.   And this sign is also visible, that is,
something falls under our senses—something we feel,
touch, taste, and the like, as in baptism we see the
water and we hear the words: "I baptise thee in the name
of the Father, and of the Son, and of the Holy Ghost."
A *sacrament* is also a visible sign instituted by God;
if it were not so, it could not produce the effect.
Hence, it is necessary that the institution should be by
God ; for, if it were instituted by the Church it might
be a sacred thing as holy water, but not a sacrament.
Moreover, a *sacrament* is a visible sign instituted by
God, by which grace is given to our soul.   This is the
chief property of a sacrament—this is the end for which
sacraments were instituted, viz.: to adorn the soul with
sanctifying grace, or to increase it in those who have it.

Sanctifying grace cannot be received unless through the sacraments, if we are able to receive them—if we cannot receive them, we must have, at least, an ardent desire to do so. Thus, he who makes a perfect act of contrition obtains at once the grace of God—why? because he has perfect charity, and is willing to do all God requires of him, consequently there is an implicit desire to receive the sacraments. That God should be pleased to confer His grace by means of material and sensible things, such as the sacraments, when He could have given it to us directly by His omnipotent power, or at least through spiritual things, is not for us to investigate His motives for so doing. It is sufficient for us to know that God has so willed it. Nevertheless, St. John Chrysostom tells us: "It becomes God to communicate His grace to us by means of natural and sensible things, because we are not pure spirits, but composed of body and soul, and therefore He has appointed these external and natural means as best adapted to our weakness and to our nature." St. Thomas gives another reason, saying: "It is natural for us to arrive at the knowledge of intelligible things by means of sensible things." And St. Augustine: "God has been pleased to confer His grace by certain sensible signs, that by them we are distinguished; for no society of men, professing a true or false religion, can be knit, as it were, into one body unless they be united and held together by some federal bond of visible signs."

It is an article of our faith that the sacraments were instituted by Jesus Christ, God for evermore, and this truth has been revealed by God in Holy Scripture, and by means of tradition—a truth which the Church has always taught, and if anyone should say that the sacraments of the New Law were not all instituted by Jesus Christ, our Lord, let him be, saith the Council of Trent, anathema.

And not only did Jesus Christ institute the sacraments, but He destined and determined their matter and form. Thus He destined water for the Sacrament of Baptism, and He determined that it should be administered "In the name of the Father, and of the Son, and of the Holy Ghost." If Jesus Christ had not determined the matter and form of the sacraments, He would have left authority to the apostles or to the Church to do so; but to the apostles He has not left that authority, for they, far from calling themselves institutors of the sacraments, declare themselves to be ministers and dispensers of them. "Let a man so account of us as of the ministers of Christ and the dispensers of the mysteries of God." Neither has Jesus Christ left that authority to the Church; for had He left it to her to determine the matter and form of the sacraments, then the Church would have the power of changing them, which the Council of Trent declares she cannot do. Jesus Christ is then the institutor of the sacraments, and the number of them are seven, viz.: Baptism, Confirmation, Holy Eucharist, Penance, Extreme Unction, Holy Orders, and Matrimony. And this is also of faith, and we know it from Scripture, the Fathers, and the universal consent of the Church, so that should any one say they are more or less than seven, let him be anathema.

It may be asked if martyrdom is a sacrament, since it not only confers grace, but admits the person at once into heaven. No, it is not, for although it supplies the place of baptism in him who has not received that sacrament, gives sanctifying grace, and admits the person into heaven, yet, martyrdom was not instituted by God, nor has it those rites and necessary things to make it a sacrament. Again, should it be asked why Jesus Christ has instituted no more or less than seven sacraments, the best reply that can be given is, that God has done all things well. Nevertheless, an answer we will give in the words of St. Thomas: "Man is composed of body and soul, and has seven necessities for his corporeal life—public and private—and so seven sacraments are necessary for the public, private, and spiritual life of man." For in order to live and preserve life, and to contribute to his own and to the public good, these seven things are necessary, namely, to be born—to grow—to be matured—to be cured when sick—to be strengthened when weak; next, as regards the commonwealth, that magistrates, by whose authority and power it may be governed, be never wanting, and, finally, to perpetuate himself and his species by the propagation of legitimate offspring. In the same manner, for the spiritual life of man, both public and private, seven things are necessary, so that the soul may live to God. The first is Baptism, the gate, as it were, to all the rest, by which we are born again to Christ. The next is Confirmation, by virtue of which we grow up, and are strengthened in divine grace; for, as St. Augustine bears witness: to the Apostles, who had been already baptised, the Lord said: "Stay you in the city till you be endued with power from on high." The third is the Eucharist, by which, as by a truly celestial food, our spirit is nurtured; for, of it the Saviour has said: "My flesh is meat indeed and my blood is drink indeed." Penance follows in the fourth place, by the aid of which our health is restored, after we have received the wounds of sin. The fifth is Extreme Unction, by which the remains of sin are removed, and the energies of the soul invigorated; for, speaking of this sacrament, St. James has testified thus: "If he is in sins, they shall be forgiven him." Order follows, by which power is given to exercise perpetually in the Church the public ministry of the sacraments, and to perform all the sacred functions. Lastly is added Matrimony, that by the legitimate and holy union of man and woman, children may be procreated and religiously brought up in the worship of God and the conservation of the human race.

Though Jesus Christ instituted the seven sacraments, we are not, therefore, to conclude that there were not sacraments both under the law of nature and the Mosaic law; since it is certain that in the law of nature there was some sacrament—but what it was Scripture is silent, nor is it necessary for us to know. It is also certain that under the law of Moses there were sacraments, different, however, from ours. The sacraments of the New Law have a virtue more excellent and more efficacious than those of the Old Law, which, as "weak and poor elements, sanctified such as were defiled in the cleansing of the flesh, not of the spirit." The sacraments of the Old Law were instituted as signs only, sacred indeed, but signs of those things that were to be accomplished by our mysteries. Thus the Ark was a figure of the Catholic Church; the sacrifices of the Old Law were also a figure of that sacrifice which we offer of the Immaculate Lamb, Jesus Christ; but they had not the power to give grace to the soul—they were not able to cancel sin from the soul. The difference between the sacraments of the Old Law and those of the New is as great as that between a dream and the reality—a shadow and the substance. If, then, under the Old Law men were able to obtain sanctifying grace, it was through their faith, and not by the virtue of those sacraments. "For it is impossible that with the blood of oxen and goats sin should be taken away." How grateful, then, ought we to be to God for having given us such easy and efficacious means for the obtaining of our eternal salvation!

We have then seen what a *sacrament* is, how many, and by whom they were instituted; we will now see what is necessary for a sacrament. Three things are required for a sacrament—*matter, form,* and *minister.* The *matter* consists in the thing used, as water in baptism. The *form* is the words said by the minister, and these, united with the matter, form the sacrament. The matter of the sacraments is *remote* or *proximate, certain* or *doubtful.* The *remote matter* is that used for a sacrament, as water for baptism. The *proximate* matter is the use or application of it, as when the water is poured upon the child's head. Matter *certain* is that which is good and can be safely used, as natural water taken from a well, fountain, or river. *Doubtful* matter is that of which one is not certain that it is good for the sacrament, it may be and may not. For instance, water that has been mixed with other liquids—

wine and such like—is doubtful whether it will be good for baptism. Also the *form* of a sacrament may be *certain* or *doubtful.* If we use the words appointed for the sacrament, then the form is *certain ;* if we use words, not knowing for certain that they are the proper words used for the ministration of a sacrament, then the form is *doubtful.* Again, there is a form *absolute* and a form *conditional.* The form *absolute* is when the words are used without any condition being expressed. The form is *conditional* when the words necessary are pronounced, joining to them a condition, as if one were to say: "If you are not baptised, I baptise thee, &c." Finally, the form is *indicative* or *deprecative.* The *indicative* form simply indicates that which is done, as when the Confessor says: "I absolve thee, &c. ;" for by these words he truly absolves from sins. The *deprecative* form contains a prayer, by which the minister prays that God would deliver from evil the person to whom he administers the sacrament. For example, the form used in the ministration of the sacrament of Extreme Unction is *deprecative,* because the words used are a prayer for the deliverance of the sick person from the sins committed by the different senses.

The matter and form, unless they be united together, cannot make a sacrament. For example, when baptism is given, if whilst the water is being poured upon the head, the words are not pronounced, but a delay is made, the baptism is not valid, because the matter, which is the water, and the form, which is the words, were not united together. Therefore that there be a sacrament, the matter and form must be united together at the same time, either *physically,* as in the sacrament of the Eucharist, in which it is necessary that, whilst the priest pronounces the words of consecration, the bread and wine be really present, or *morally,* as in the other sacraments, in which it suffices that the matter and form be so united that it may be said, according to common estimation, that when the matter has been placed the form is also used. Leaving to another occasion to explain this more fully, in the mean time let me exhort you to attend these instructions on the sacraments, for I assure you they are more necessary than some suppose them to be. From ignorance scandal cometh, and many are to be found who know not what or how many are the sacraments, nor the effects of them, or the dispositions with which they ought to be received. And yet without knowing these things, in vain has Jesus Christ instituted the sacraments for them, since they are incapable of receiving them as they ought. Hence, in place of receiving the food of the soul, so that they may live in grace, it is converted into poison.

II.

In the preceding instruction, amongst the various things therein explained, I said a *sacrament* requires three things, *matter, form,* and *minister;* you were then told what is the *matter* and what is the *form* of a sacrament, and now I will in this instruction speak of the minister, leaving what remains to be said on the matter and form until I speak of the sacraments in particular.

Who is then the *minister* of a sacrament? It is he who uses the matter and form necessary for a sacrament and really administers it. For instance, the person who takes the water and pours it upon the head of the child, saying at the same time the words: " I baptise, &c.," he is the minister of the sacrament of baptism. The confessor who hears the sins of the penitent, and believing him truly contrite, absolves him; he is the minister of the sacrament of penance, and so with regard to the other sacraments.

There are two kinds of ministers, one *ordinary,* the other *extraordinary.* The *ordinary* minister is he who has been ordained by a Bishop, and who ordinarily and usually administers the sacraments. The *extraordinary* minister is one who has not been ordained by a bishop, and who only on certain extraordinary occasions and in extreme cases, administers a sacrament. And as only men can be ordained, it follows that only men can be ministers of the sacraments. Angels and souls that have left their bodies can be extraordinary ministers of the sacraments, for God, if He so wills, can make use of them, but they can never be the ordinary ministers.

That a minister may validly administer a sacrament

two things are required—*power* and *intention* to administer. It is of faith that power is required, for not every man has power to administer every sacrament, as asserted by some of the first so-called reformers, who had the audacity to say that all Christians are priests, having authority to administer every sacrament, which assertion was condemned by the Council of Trent, declaring: "If any one saith, that all Christians have power to administer the word and all the sacraments ; let him be anathema." Therefore to confer truly and validly a sacrament it is absolutely necessary that the minister should have power. Otherwise, whatever he does is null and void. So that should a layman bear a confession and pronounce the words of absolution over a person as often as he may choose, not one sin would be forgiven, for he has not power from God to confer the sacrament.

Moreover, besides *power* there is also required in the minister the *intention*, that is, of really and truly administering a sacrament—of doing what our holy Mother the Church does ; and this is defined by the Council of Trent : "If any one saith that in ministers, when they effect and confer the sacraments, there is not required the intention at least of doing what the Church does ; let him be anathema :" so that should a person use the matter required and pronounce the form of words used for a sacrament, but with his thoughts directed entirely towards something else, and without having the intention of doing what our holy Mother the Church does, it would not be a sacrament. For instance, a person takes water, pours it upon the head of the child, saying the words, "I baptise, &c.," having no intention of baptising, it would not be a sacrament. The person doing such a thing, could not be excused from sin, since it would show a want of reverence for the sacrament and for things sacred.

But should a person make use of the same rites and ceremonies used by the Church, and in his heart does not intend to administer the sacrament, and were you to ask me whether there would be a valid sacrament,

I should reply that it is a question, and the more common opinion is that it is not valid : for when one does a thing which can be done in different ways, it is necessary for such a one to have an *intention* which determines him to do it one way rather than another. For example, were I to pour water upon another, I may have various reasons for so doing ; to wash the head, or to remove some uncleanness, or to heal some disease, or in jest, or for a sacrament. Then the right intention is necessary to obtain the end : consequently there must be the *intention* of administering a sacrament, or at least of doing that which the Church does.

Now with regard to this intention we are not to be scrupulous, for when a person goes to baptise, we are not to suppose that his intention is entirely contrary to that, it is certain that he has the intention of administering the sacrament, or of doing what the Church does, so that it is not necessary that he should say within himself that he has the intention: nor is it necessary that he should have the *actual* intention, because we are all subject to distractions, it is quite sufficient to have a *virtual* intention, but not an intention that is only *habitual* and *interpretive* that neither knows or wants to know.

A minister, then, having the *power* and the *intention* of administering a sacrament, and having also mortal sin upon his soul, or having lost the faith, can he confer a sacrament ? If he baptises will it be a valid baptism ? Yes, it is of faith that that minister, having *power* and *intention* of doing what the Church does, although he be in mortal sin, nevertheless he administers the sacrament validly, and it produces all the good effects in him who receives it.

"If any one saith that a minister, being in mortal sin, neither effects nor confers the sacraments, or if any one saith that the baptism, which is even given by heretics in the name of the Father, and of the Son, and of the Holy Ghost, with the intention of doing what the Church does, is not true baptism; let him be anathema." And the reason is that the *virtue* and *efficacy* of the sacraments do not depend upon the sanctity of the minister, who is but an instrument in the hands of God, but immediately from Jesus Christ, who by His omnipotent power, causes the matter and form used by a lawful minister, to produce immediately a sacrament capable of conferring grace and sanctity to him who receives it. And although a minister, ordinarily speaking, ought not to administer any sacrament in a state of sin; and should he confer a sacrament in that state, he sins grievously, because holy things ought to be administered with a pure and good conscience. Hence it is that unless there is a grave reason, it is not lawful for a person to receive a sacrament from one, when he is positively certain that that person is in mortal sin, for that would be a co-operation in the evil he does.

At the same time, it is of faith, that however wicked the minister may be, the sacraments administered by him are valid, and produce. grace in him who receives them worthily.

After having spoken of the minister of the sacraments, I will now speak of those who receive them. Who are they that are capable of receiving the sacraments? With regard to baptism, every living human being in the world is capable of receiving that sacrament. The other sacraments can be received only by those who are baptised; because this sacrament is, as it were, the gate through which we enter into the fellowship of Christian life, and consequently are made capable of receiving other sacraments. Hence it is, should a bishop confer the sacrament of Orders upon an unbaptised person, it would be null and void, therefore it would be necessary to baptise that person first, and then re-ordain him. But should an unbaptised person receive holy communion, he would receive the sacrament, for it is not like the other sacraments that are made at the moment they are administered—nevertheless he would not obtain the grace or effect of that sacrament. Though baptism is necessary for the reception of the other sacraments, it does not follow from that, all are capable of receiving every other sacrament. Children, for instance, are not capable of receiving the sacrament of Penance, until they have arrived at the use of reason, or Extreme Unction, or Matrimony—neither can women receive Holy Orders.

What is required of a person in order that he may receive a sacrament validly? With regard to children that have not attained the use of reason, nothing is required of them, for the Church supplies the intention and faith in them: not so, however, with those who have the use of reason; for them *validly* to receive a sacrament there is required, in the first place, the *intention* to receive, or at least to receive that which the Church confers with a sacred rite—but an *habitual* intention will suffice, that is, they had the intention at one time and have never revoked it. For example, one desired to receive the sacrament of baptism, and afterwards lost his mind; now although he is in that unhappy state, he can be baptised, and that baptism is valid, because he had the intention of being baptised before the loss of his reason.

But if there is not, nor has been the intention of receiving that sacrament, then it is null and void. As for example, were I to baptise a person who *absolutely* declared his unwillingness to be baptised, it would not be a sacrament.

To receive a sacrament, at least an *habitual* intention is, I said, required. The sacrament of Penance, however, is an exception, for that requires three acts on the part of the penitent, viz.: contrition, confession, and satisfaction. Also Matrimony, which requires the consent of the contracting parties, and their intention, if not *actual*, must be at least *virtual*—that is, a consent that virtually perseveres.

There are other things required for the *validity* of a sacrament, and we will now proceed to consider them. For a right understanding of these things, we must make a distinction between what are called *living* and what are called *dead* sacraments. The sacraments of the *dead* are two, Baptism and Penance, and they are so called because they were primarily instituted for those who are dead to grace. The other five are sacraments of the living, because they are to be received only by such as are in a state of grace. Moreover, we must bear in mind that it is one thing to receive sacraments, and another to receive the grace and effects of them—in other words, the receiving of a sacrament, and the receiving it with profit and advantage to the soul.

If we speak of merely receiving the sacraments, except that of Penance, of which I said requires three acts on the part of the penitent, all the other sacraments, whether they be of the living or the dead, require nothing more of us than that we be subjects capable of having a firm intention. If we speak of receiving the sacraments, and of also receiving the graces annexed to them—that is, of receiving them with profit and advantage to the soul, for the receiving of the sacraments of the dead, Baptism and Penance, besides the capacity of the subject and the intention,—there is also required *faith*, and *sorrow* for sin in those who have arrived to the use of reason: because "without faith it is impossible to please God"—and without sorrow for sin it is impossible to obtain forgiveness. In order to receive *worthily* and with *advantage* to the soul, the sacraments of the living, besides the capacity and intention of the subject, purity of conscience is necessary—the soul free from mortal sin and in the grace of God; for the sacraments of the living were not *primarily* instituted to confer, but only to increase grace. Then, that these sacraments may so operate in us, it is necessary for their worthy reception that the soul be already in the possession of the grace of God. Consequently, whoever receives Confirmation in mortal sin, receives indeed the sacrament but not the grace of it, yea, he commits a sacrilege—one goes to Communion with mortal sin upon the soul and receives the sacrament, but not the grace, and he is guilty of sacrilege. One receives Extreme Unction, Holy Orders, or Matrimony in mortal sin, receiving indeed the sacrament, but not the grace of it, and he is guilty of sacrilege. And oh, how many sacrileges are committed by Christians known only to God who beholds the heart!

It now remains for me to speak of the *effects* the sacraments have in us, when we receive them with the proper dispositions. The first effect produced by them in us is, the giving of sanctifying grace—that grace which renders our soul beautiful as that of an angel, and it unites us with God, making us His friends. The sacraments of the dead, viz.: Baptism and Penance, confer sanctifying grace upon those who have it not; and should a person, before the reception of Baptism or Penance, have obtained sanctifying grace, by means of *perfect* contrition, then, these two sacraments by accident give an increase of grace.

The sacraments of the living give an increase of sanctifying grace to those who are in possession of it— but should a person receive the sacraments of the living, having a mortal sin on the soul without his knowledge, and believing himself well disposed, then the sacraments of the living, if he is sorry for all sins in general, will, in place of augmenting in him grace, confer *directly* upon him sanctifying grace, receiving forgiveness from God of the guilt of those sins that were upon his conscience without his knowledge.

Again, besides sanctifying grace, each of the sacraments gives another particular grace to those who receive them worthily, which grace is called by theologians *sacramental* grace. Thus baptism, besides giving sanctifying grace, gives that of despising the pleasure and vanity of this world, and also that of worthily receiving the other sacraments.

Confirmation gives the grace of professing openly our faith, even at the cost of our life. Eucharist infuses the grace of spiritual nourishment to the soul, and of increasing in us the love of God. Penance, the grace of hating sin, and doing penance for it. Extreme Unction communicates the grace of cancelling all the remains of sin, and of supporting patiently the pains of sickness and of resisting the temptations of the evil one, of making a happy death, and also of regaining the health of the body, should it be expedient for the soul. Holy Order gives grace to sacred ministers to discharge well their sacred functions, and of worthily administering the sacraments. Matrimony gives the grace of observing conjugal fidelity, of living in peace, and bringing up their children in the fear of God.

Finally, three of the sacraments—Baptism, Confirmation, and Order—besides the effects already explained, produce another effect upon the soul, which is called a character, that is, a spiritual sign impressed upon the soul, by which Christians are distinguished from those who are not—and a soldier of Christ from one who is not—and they who are ministers of God from those who are not. These three sacraments cannot be received more than once, because they give a mark to the soul, which mark can never be effaced.

Then, with these marks upon our soul, what confusion, what shame will be ours if we are lost, if we go to hell! To find ourselves in the company of Turks, infidels, and wicked spirits, with the sign of a Christian, a soldier of Jesus Christ, upon our soul! Oh, the confusion! Oh, the shame! "These," the damned will exclaim, "these are the followers, the brave soldiers of Jesus Christ, who deserted from the standard of their leader, and placed themselves under that of the devil, His enemy. We are lost, and it is our misfortune. We never heard of Jesus Christ or His law, but these professed themselves to be followers and soldiers of Him; these had from God so many graces, such wonderful helps through the sacraments, and yet they, like unto us, are eternally lost! Ah! they have been ungrateful to God a thousand times more than we, and they merit punishment a thousand times more than we!" Oh! what eternal shame will cover the face of a Christian if he is lost, having that character upon his soul, who had within his reach such powerful means as the sacraments, and to find himself now and for ever under the slavery of the devil and his ministers.

Nevertheless, how many Christians will suffer this eternal confusion! Jesus Christ has poured out His

blood for them—He has instituted the seven sacraments, that so they might have means most easy for all
their spiritual evils, and acquire grace and holiness.
And, alas, how many neglect these means for years and
years, how many now listening to me are negligent;
can they be good Christians, in the grace of God, in the
way of salvation ?　No, it is impossible for them to be
good Christians, to live in the grace of God and be
saved, whilst they neglect the means offered them.

Let me then exhort you to frequent the sacraments,
and approach them with the proper dispositions;
otherwise, in place of their giving life to the soul, they
will give death.

III.

ON THE EXCELLENCY OF THE SACRAMENT OF BAPTISM.

BAPTISM is the first and most necessary of all the sacraments; it is called by the Fathers of the Church the gate, and whosoever has not received this sacrament cannot receive any other. It is true, that by a special grace of God we have received this sacrament, and therefore we cannot again receive it; but that is not a reason why I should not speak of it. When we were baptised we were of an age incapable of knowing the dignity of this sacrament, or the excellency of the gift, or the wonderful effects it produced in our soul, or the strict obligations we have contracted by it. Then it behoveth us now to be fully instructed in them, and to reflect on them, and, if we have not done so before, a right consideration of the benefit bestowed by God upon us by this sacrament will move us to feelings of gratitude towards Him.

How true it is there are many Christians who have received the Sacrament of Baptism without scarcely knowing what is meant by being a Christian—what is meant by baptism. How many are ignorant of the blessing conferred upon them; and upon this great and important subject, so useful and so necessary to know, they neglect to be instructed, and from this negligence proceed errors and sin. Then the object of my present instruction will be the consideration of the excellency of the grace received in baptism; and this object will be obtained by explaining what baptism is, how great its necessity, and, finally, the singular happiness of those who have received it.

The word baptism is a Greek word, and it signifies

every kind of ablution; in the sense, however, we use
that word it denotes not every sort of ablution, but
only that which belongs to the sacrament, and which
is not administered without the prescribed form of
words; in that sense "Baptism is a sacrament which
cleanses us from original sin, makes us Christians, children of God, and members of the Church." St. Paul
calls Baptism the "laver of regeneration and renovation
of the Holy Ghost." As of all the other sacraments, so
likewise of this, we are bound to believe that it was
instituted by Jesus Christ. But when did He institute
this sacrament? Was it before or after His death and
resurrection? I answer: although it was not till after
His resurrection the command was given to the Apostles
of going to teach all nations, baptising them in the
name of the Father, and of the Son, and of the Holy
Ghost; nevertheless, it is the doctrine of the Fathers
and taught by the Church that Jesus Christ instituted
this sacrament when He was baptised by John at the
Jordan. Then it was Jesus Christ gave to the water
the virtue of generating spiritual life. From the
moment that Christ is immersed in water, from that
moment water washes away all sin. The Lord is
baptised, not having occasion to be cleansed, but that,
purifying the waters by the contact of His pure flesh,
they may have the power of cleansing. And a very
strong argument to that effect might be afforded by
the fact that the most Holy Trinity, in whose name
baptism is conferred, manifested their divine presence
on that occasion. For the voice of the Father was
heard, the person of the Son was present, and the Holy
Ghost descended in form of a dove; besides, the
heavens, whither we may now ascend by baptism, were
opened. Should any one desire to know how our Lord
gave to the waters a virtue so great, so divine, that,
indeed, transcends human comprehension; but that,
when our Lord received baptism, water, by contact
with His most holy and pure body, was consecrated to
the salutary use of baptism; that we can sufficiently
understand, with this observation, however, that, although

instituted before the passion, we must yet believe this sacrament to have derived all its force and efficacy from the passion, which was the consummation, as it were, of all the actions of Christ.

In the instruction on the sacraments in general you were told that every sacrament has its matter and form, and that both the one and the other have been expressly determined by Jesus Christ. What, then, is the matter of the Sacrament of Baptism? It is every kind of natural water, which, without any addition, is called water, be it sea-water, river-water, water from a marsh, or well, or fountain. But liquids taken from the vine, or from any tree, or water distilled from roses or any other flowers would not be matter for this sacrament, because it is not natural water. This is a most certain truth declared by Jesus Christ in the Gospel : "Unless a man be born again of water and the Holy Ghost, he cannot enter into the kingdom of heaven." These words have always been taken by the Church to express that natural water is the necessary matter of this sacrament. Now putting aside other reasons, the Council of Trent declares him a heretic who should say that "true and natural water is not of necessity for baptism, and, on that account, wrests, to some sort of metaphor, those words of our Lord Jesus Christ." And here we ought to be filled with sentiments of gratitude towards God for having willed that the matter of a sacrament so necessary should be water, a thing so easily obtained.

And how suitable it was to the nature and efficacy of baptism that water should have been instituted as its proper matter; for water explains the effect of baptism—as water washes away uncleanness, so does it also very well illustrate the virtue and efficacy of baptism, by which we are washed from the stains of sin. Moreover, water is extremely well adapted to cool bodies, so, by baptism, is—in a great measure—extinguished the ardour of the passions.

Although natural water, without any mixture, is the matter for this sacrament when necessity requires it to be administered, apart from necessity, in all other cases the water is to be taken from the baptismal font, in which sacred chrism has been mixed with it and blessed on Holy Saturday or on the Vigil of Pentecost, using, at the same time, all the sacred ceremonies prescribed by the Roman Ritual, and which, according to apostolical tradition, have been practised in the Catholic Church.

Having said all that is necessary regarding the matter of the Sacrament of Baptism, we will now speak of the form, which every one ought to know, since it often occurs that baptism requires to be administered by the laity, and very often by women ; hence, all the faithful indiscriminately ought to be well acquainted with what regards the substance of this sacrament. Now the perfect and absolute form of baptism is : " I baptise thee in the name of the Father, and of the Son, and of the Holy Ghost." In whatever language this form is said, nothing is taken from its value, or if the word Amen is left out, or should the name given be omitted. It would, however, be null if all three of the Divine Persons were not distinctly mentioned. Also should one pour the water upon the child and another say the form.

For the administration of a sacrament a minister is required, and that he must have the intention of doing, at least, what the Church does. Who is the minister of the Sacrament of Baptism ? The minister is the Bishop for his diocese ; and in the first ages of the Church almost all were baptised by the bishop. The parish priest for his parish, and these are called ordinary ministers, having, by reason of their office, jurisdiction over all their subjects in the administration of the sacraments. Other priests can also baptise with permission, using all the rites and ceremonies prescribed by the Ritual. If, however, we speak of the minister of this sacrament, in case of necessity, that is, when there is danger of death—in that case every one can be the minister, man or woman, Christian or infidel, providing there is the intention of doing what the Church intends to do. But even in this case of necessity, and several persons are present, a priest is to be preferred to a deacon—a deacon to a sub-deacon—a cleric to a layman—a man to a woman—a Christian to an infidel. Should any of you be called upon to baptise a child in a case of necessity, when a priest cannot be had, you have to use natural water—blessed water is not required—pour it upon the head of the child, and in case you cannot do that, you must pour it upon some other principal part of the body, and whilst you are pouring the water, say the words—"I baptise thee, &c.," having the intention of baptising, or of doing what the Church intends to do. And here admire the goodness of God, who is pleased to make everyone capable of administering this sacrament in case of necessity.

For our eternal salvation baptism is necessary, so much so that should any one, even without any fault on his part, die without baptism, such an one would be for ever excluded from heaven. It is necessary as a means for the infant just born, although born of Catholic parents; and the reason is, because all men have sinned in Adam, and are dead to grace; all are born children of wrath, and consequently under the power of the devil. Now, in the order of grace, to pass from a state of sin and damnation to a state of grace and salvation, which Jesus Christ has merited for us, no one can without the laver of regeneration, according to the expression of our Lord: "Unless a man be born again of water and the Holy Ghost, he cannot enter into the kingdom of God." Hence, the Church wishes children to be baptised as soon as possible after birth. And the Church has always taught that children dying without baptism cannot be saved, and will be eternally excluded from the vision of God. With what solicitude ought parents to procure for their offspring the reception of this sacrament, and the reason is manifest, because children have no other means but that for their salvation; whence it is parents, deferring their children's baptism longer than a convenient time are guilty of a grave sin, exposing their children to the danger of being deprived of the grace of baptism.

Again, the sacrament of baptism is necessary for every adult. Every pagan that has not the happiness of having put on Jesus Christ and of being incorporated with Him by means of this sacrament, is excluded from the fruit of His passion and death, and consequently, dying in sin, is eternally lost. Nevertheless, it is possible for an adult to be saved without having received the baptism of water, which can never be the case with children who die without it. The Church admits three kinds of baptism—that of water, that of blood, and that of desire. When, then, an adult cannot receive the baptism of water, if, for the love of Jesus Christ and in defence of the faith, he suffers martyrdom, he is, indeed, in his blood baptised, and the same effects will follow as if he had been baptised with water. The same may be said of one who desires baptism, and who is under instructions, should he die contrite and with this good desire, he will obtain the remission of his sins and be saved. That these two kinds of baptism of blood and of desire are sufficient for the obtaining of salvation has always been the doctrine of the Church, and of which there can be no doubt.

You have seen the indispensable necessity of baptism, both for infants and adults; that you may understand something of the excellency of the grace of baptism, it will be necessary to speak of its effects. For a fuller explanation of them I have reserved to another time; but it will not be out of place to make a passing notice of them.

The first and principal effect of baptism is the taking away the stains of original sin from the soul. This is not all; for, if the person baptised is an adult, and had committed many and great sins, they are, by the virtue of this sacrament, remitted. As God said by the Prophet: "I will pour upon you clean water, and you shall be cleansed from all your filthiness." And the Apostle, after enumerating the many and great sins committed by the Corinthians, says: "but you are washed, but you are sanctified." Nor is that all; not only are sins cancelled, but the punishment due to them is remitted, which is not done in the Sacrament of Penance, for there remains the temporal punishment to undergo in the present or future life. And the reason is, because by baptism we are made partakers not only of the passion and death of Jesus Christ, as in the other sacraments, but we are incorporated with Him, in Him we die, and in Him we are buried.

Whence it is the Council of Trent says that "in those who are born again, there is nothing that God hates;" and the Apostle, "there is no condemnation in those who are truly buried together with Christ by baptism into death." True it is that after baptism there remains in the baptised concupiscence, or an incentive to sin, which although not sin, is of sin, and inclines to sin, which is left for our exercise, but cannot injure those who consent not; yea, he who shall have striven lawfully shall be crowned.

These are not the only effects of baptism. For not only are we made free from all sin, but we are filled with the gifts of God. By means of baptism there is given to us that innocence which we lost in Adam. God comes to us—He dwells in us—the soul is born to a new life, filled with divine grace—this grace makes us children of God and heirs of heaven, and our soul to the eyes of God becomes beautiful and acceptable. By means of baptism there are infused into the soul the theological virtues, Faith, Hope, Charity, and the gifts of the Holy Ghost.

Also baptism, being one of the three sacraments which place a mark upon the soul, shows that the soul is impressed with a divine character, that it belongs to Christ, has become His member, distinguishes that soul from all who have not been baptised; and it is made capable of receiving the other sacraments.

From what has been said of the Sacrament of Baptism, we are constrained to exclaim, Oh, the singular grace God has deigned to confer upon us!—Grace, the excellency of which we can never sufficiently commend. This is that grace of which the writings of the Fathers

are filled with its praises. By some it is called the
sacrament of faith, because before receiving it the
Church requires us to make a profession of our faith,
and through it we are filled with the hope of entering
into eternal life; and by it God deigns to vivify and
purify our soul. By others it is called a "new planta-
tion," for by it we are taken from the parched desert of
infidelity and planted in the house of the Lord, and
there to fructify. It is a sacrament of a new life, a
second birth, and laver of regeneration. In a word,
baptism is a gift the greatest and most singular that
the almighty mercy of God could have conferred upon
man. And that it is so, it is sufficient to reflect that
by it God has drawn us from the shadow of death, and
made us to participate of the divine light, and of the
life of Jesus Christ. Of the excellency of the grace of
this sacrament no one has expressed it more beautifully
than the Apostle St. Peter: "He hath given us most
great and precious promises that by these you may be
made partakers of the divine nature." Oh! the singular
grace God has conferred upon us by baptism—grace,
the excellency of which is never thought of by the
greater number of Christians, nor is God sufficiently
thanked for His loving kindness towards us. A grace
the more signal and precious as it is an effect of the
divine mercy, and that not only we have not merited it,
but are unable ever to merit it—a grace given to us
and denied to the greater part of the human race!
Oh, yes! the mercy of God in giving us the grace of
baptism, "He hath not done in like manner to every
nation." Bring before your mind's eye the state of the
world, and you will see that the greater part of mankind are without the knowledge of God, without the
grace of baptism; and why are so many deprived of
this grace, why has God given it to us and denied it to
them? Why has He willed that we should be born in
the bosom of the Catholic Church and of Catholic
parents, and they not? Why do so many die in their
mother's womb? what merit have we that they have
not? None: it has been entirely the effect of the

mercy of God. If you read the ninth chapter of St. Paul's Epistle to the Romans, you will see that God will have mercy on whom He will have mercy, and whom He will He hardeneth. And the Apostle gives the example of Jacob and Esau, of whom before they were born or had done good or evil, the will of God had decreed that the elder should serve the younger—Jacob was loved, Esau was hated. That we have received the grace of baptism and so many have not is the mercy of God. Why a child born of Christian parents should receive the grace of baptism, and another belonging to the same should not, yea, sometimes the parents have made every preparation, and yet the child dies without this grace. Why the children of pagans should sometimes receive this grace, and children of Christian parents die without it? Oh, how inscrutable are the ways of God! But we who have had the happiness of receiving this precious grace, how have we corresponded with it, how have we, or in what manner have we shown our gratitude for the goodness and mercy of God towards us? Oh, my God, Thou hast hitherto had no other return for your loving kindness than that of ingratitude and injury!

But now let us detest our past forgetfulness of Thee and of Thy mercy, and never cease for the future to bless, praise, and thank Thee for the grace so great as that of baptism. Be you for ever blessed and praised, and as it has been through Thy mercy we have received the inestimable grace of baptism, grant us the grace that we may persevere to the end of our life, so that we may bless and praise Thee for ever in Thy kingdom.

IV.

FROM the consideration of the wonderful effects produced in the soul by the Sacrament of Baptism, which God in His mercy has caused you to receive, you are easily led to know the singular grace conferred upon you. That you may be moved to gratitude towards this good God, I will, for your instruction, propose two considerations. Firstly, the unhappy state from which you have been taken by baptism. Secondly, the happy state this grace has acquired for you. If you reflect and consider whose children you are, then you will understand from what a miserable and unhappy state you have been taken by the grace of baptism. Whose children are we? We are children of Adam, disobedient to God, for which he was driven out of the terrestrial paradise. We are inheritors of his sin, and consequently of his punishment. We were all contained in Adam, not only naturally but morally. When, therefore, he sinned through the suggestion of the infernal serpent, not only he did evil to himself, but to us, and to every one of his posterity that shall descend from him to the end of the world. I know not whether it be true or not, but it is said that there is a way of poisoning the fruit of a tree by poisoning its root. I know, however, that this has been done by the devil, when by his wicked suggestion he induced our first parent to sin. In him was, as it were the root, placed this powerful poison that has poisoned us, and this was original sin, a sin in which we are all born, and by which we are all miserably affected. Indeed, so poisoned are we by this original sin that there is nothing sound in us. The intellect, will, liberty, memory, and rational appetite are, by reason of that sin, disordered, tainted, and corrupted; as the Holy Ghost declares: "Error and darkness are created with sinners." Sometimes we hear it said of man that he has a powerful and great mind, wonderful talent, capable of doing anything, of acquiring wealth, of making a name for himself and family.

The wise men of Greece and Rome had great talent, but they were ignorant of Jesus Christ; a child baptised, knowing the mysteries of religion, is a thousand times more learned than they were.

A man deprived of the grace of being a Christian is in a state of darkness, illusion, and error. He may be likened to the world before the creation of light, when "darkness was upon the face of the deep." So the intellect of man before receiving the grace of baptism is nothing but ignorance and error.

The will has become so defective and wanting that without grace not only is it unable to do anything meritorious towards eternal life, but it is not able even to conceive a holy thought. God created man upright and just, free from all vice; but sin reduced him to a state most deplorable. He has become like a vessel fallen from the hands of the potter, dashed to pieces. In place of permitting himself to be governed by God, and of being subject to Him, he has rebelled against Him, nor does he wish to be any longer dependent upon Him. And God has abandoned him to his reprobate sense, and to his weakness and misery, that man might see that without Him he is unable to do good, but only evil. You may, perhaps, say that in spite of sin man is nevertheless free. True: but his liberty is so weak and so enfeebled that it may be likened to a leaf moved by every wind. The least encounter beats it down—a slight temptation causes it to fall; it submits itself to every passion; an unguarded look, a flattering object, the offering of a little gain, a momentary pleasure, some worldly honour, is alone sufficient to ruin it.

Then, again, what has the memory become after sin?

A receptacle and a sink of uncleanness and infection; a refuge of extravagance, folly, corruption, and filthiness, which made the Apostle exclaim: "Unhappy man that I am, who shall deliver me from the body of this death?"

Finally, what has our rational appetite become after sin? A perpetual rebellion of the inferior with the superior part of the soul; a continual opposition to virtue, and a disordinate affection for sensible things, such as vanity, riches, and the pleasures of this world, compared by the Holy Ghost to a horse not broken. It is carried away by passion and anger, the heart filled with a thousand inordinate desires, distracted by a multiplicity of cares, moved by curiosity; carried away by temptation, and filled with desperation and disgrace. Such, indeed, was man before baptism.

If, then, he was such with regard to himself, what was his state and condition before God?

The Apostle St. Paul applies to himself and to all men this most remarkable expression, that we "were by nature children of wrath," as if we were born by the anger of God, or, in other words, that we are by nature the scope and object of the wrath of God. If, then, we are by nature the children of wrath, it follows as a necessary consequence that we are also the scope and object of the Divine vengeance and of His chastisement. But God, is He not infinitely good and merciful? Of His mercy, the Prophet says, the "earth is filled;" and St. Paul that "He is rich in mercy." Is He not full of sweetness, charity, and love?

All this is true: nevertheless, God cannot love the man who is not baptised, having his soul infected with original sin. As such that man is always an object of His hatred, of His aversion, and consequently the object of His vengeance; and if he dies in that state, he will be for ever excluded from heaven. He belongs not to God, but to the devil; he is not a servant of God, but a slave of the devil, subject to him and in his power. Oh, the deplorable misery of the soul that has not received baptism! To be for ever the object of the wrath of God, and of His eternal chastisement! To be in the power of the devil and the slave of so great an enemy! And this is what we once were before we received the grace of baptism—we were then the scope and object of God's wrath, slaves of the devil, and victims of eternal punishment.

But to understand how miserable and unhappy was the state and condition of man before baptism, it is not sufficient to consider what man was in himself, or what he was in regard to God, for not less miserable and unhappy we perceive him to have been with regard to creatures, when as so many instruments they appear in the hands of God ready to execute vengeance against him, and remove him from the world. They, like the servants in the Gospel of whom St. Matthew speaks, knowing that their master had sown good seed in his field and that there appeared also the cockle, said: "Wilt thou that we go and gather it up?" In like manner irrational and insensible creatures, which as long as man was obedient and subject to God, were obedient and subject to man; but from the moment man rebelled against God and cast himself from Him, in punishment of his temerity and insolence, they wait only for the sign from their Creator to vindicate the outrage committed against Him. The beasts of the forest are ready to tear into pieces man by reason of his disobedience—the air to suffocate him—the earth to open and bury him—the sea to submerge him under its waves—the fire to consume him—"Wilt thou that we go?" Oh! then how miserable and unhappy is man both with regard to himself, to his God, and in regard to creatures, with the stain of original sin upon his soul? Perhaps we have never thought of the deplorable state out of which God has taken us by the grace of baptism—perhaps we have never shown our gratitude for the singular graces conferred upon us. If, in times past, we have neglected so necessary a duty, let us not do so in future.

Whilst we have life let us thank God for His mercy towards us. And indeed what would be our feelings of gratitude towards a physician who, by his skill, had cured us of some mortal malady ? What expressions of gratitude would we utter towards the person who had saved us from an ignominious death, and made us the friends of our sovereign ? How grateful would we show ourselves towards one who, when we were sur-rounded by enemies ready to put us to death, had delivered us from their hands, or taken us from a dun-geon to which we had been condemned to die ? Ah ! we should declare ourselves unable to express the great-ness of our sense of gratitude for the benefit done to us.

And yet they would have saved us only from some temporal misfortune, or obtained for us some earthly benefit ; but Jesus Christ, in conferring upon us the grace of baptism, has conferred a spiritual blessing to the soul, and consequently it is a thousand times more precious than all those temporal benefits. By this grace He has healed all our infirmities, cured the mortal wounds caused by sin—by this grace we have been freed from the slavery of the devil into which we had fallen, and He has drawn us from the eternal pri-son to which we had been condemned by God. And this is not all : for from the time we were cleansed by the sanctifying waters of baptism, God has been appeased, and in place of being what we were, enemies, we have been made His friends. How great, then, ought to be our gratitude towards Jesus Christ !

That our gratitude may be more hearty and effective, let us pass to the consideration of the happy state in which, by means of the grace of baptism, Jesus Christ has placed us. By baptism we have regained lost inno-cence—by it, after every stain had been cleansed from the soul, we received the inestimable gift of sanctifying grace, a gift which renders the soul beautiful to the eyes of God, and He becomes our friend. Oh ! that I had time, or rather words, to explain what is meant by the innocence which baptism restores to the soul, and the privileges that accompany this baptismal innocence ! Oh ! that I could explain to you what means sanctify-ing grace, how it beautifies and adorns the soul ! Oh !

that I could declare to you what it is to be loved by
God, and to have Him for a friend! Ah, were I able
to do that, I am certain that you would be persuaded
of the excellency of the grace of baptism, so as
never to allow a pearl so precious to be crushed under
your feet.

The grace that God confers upon you in baptism ought
always to fill your hearts with gratitude towards Him,
because of all graces this is the first God gives. It is
the first grace not only because it opens the gate to all
the other sacraments, but because it is the beginning
and the fountain from which flows all the other graces
that God goes on giving to the soul during the present
life, and in the future. Place before your eyes the wonderful and stupendous actions of the apostles, martyrs,
confessors, and virgins—recall to your mind the wonderful life of a St. Bernard, a Benedict, a Dominic, a
St. Francis, and other saints—consider their heavenly
intercourse, the knowledge, the transports, the ecstacies,
and the flames of burning love which sweetly consumed
them, and then ask yourselves from what source did
they derive those singular and wonderful graces ?
Without doubt from the grace of baptism. It was that
first grace from whence all those divine communications and heroic virtues had their origin, and which
made them so wonderful in the world. Again, raise
your thoughts above this earth, and fix your mental
gaze and contemplate those saints amongst the choirs
of angels, immersed in God and filled with the torrent
of delights, and ask yourselves—From whence had this
happy state its beginning ? What is the fount of that
torrent of pleasures and delights in which they are
inebriated ? The water of baptism, the grace they
received was the beginning of that blessed life. It was
that gift of God, of which Jesus Christ told the Samaritan woman, would become a fountain of water spring-
ing up into life everlasting.

Oh, the happiness of the soul that has received the
grace of baptism ! St. Gregory, reflecting on the wonderful effect baptism had produced in him, says: " I
am transformed into another man, I am no longer what

I was, I have become a new creature. In place of being what I was, human and corrupted, Jesus Christ has created in me a new being, all celestial and divine. Like a broken vessel, the pieces of which are taken by a skilful artist, melted in the furnace, and from them is formed a new one: so Jesus Christ has renewed me in the furnace of His divine love, and given me a new life, a life which is a participation of the life of God." The grace of baptism is the most noble, the most magnificent of all the gifts of God. It is the true light and splendour of the soul—the reparation of the defects of our origin—the most copious outpouring of the Holy Spirit. Oh! the grace and mercy of God that has called us to the grace of baptism to the exclusion of so many others!

But, oh! how monstrous has been our ingratitude towards God who has given us such a singular grace! Who amongst us has hitherto thought of it? Who amongst us has been penetrated with this truth? Who has given a moment's thought to the excellency and the greatness of the grace of baptism, or of the miseries from which it has delivered us, or the happy state in which it has put us in possession of? What has Jesus Christ done in order to merit for us this most singular grace? Ah! you have often heard. He became incarnate in the womb of the Blessed Virgin, and was made man, born in the midst of poverty and misery—led a life of want and inconvenience—derided, calumniated, scourged, crowned with thorns, and finally underwent the ignominious death upon the cross, after pouring out the last drop of His blood, so that He might merit for us this singular grace. And we think not of it; as yet we have not shown our gratitude! Should this last reflection unfold to your mind your obligation of gratitude, should your heart be inflamed with love towards the Divine Redeemer for the love He has borne you, let me entreat you by the mercy of God not to allow a day to pass without thanking the good God for the great grace conferred upon you by baptism, whilst so many, deprived of this grace, remain in the shadow of death.

C

In the "Lives of the Saints" I read how that many holy souls celebrated every year, with a particular devotion, the day on which they received the grace of baptism. And this they did in order to excite in themselves to feelings of gratitude towards God, and in examining themselves to see how they had corresponded by the sanctity of their lives to so great and so singular a benefit. How few are there who now-a-days practise this holy custom? How few remember the great benefit they have received? How few correspond to it by the sanctity of their lives? How many years have passed by since you were baptised, and how little the advance you have made in the practice of those virtues, which ought to be the continual occupation of a Christian. So little is the advance you have made in that sanctity your state requires, that perhaps many of you are leading a life opposed to your profession. What is the reason? I know that many of you blame the world, the occasions, the family cares, and your occupations. Although these things may have a part in it, but all will agree that if you had impressed upon your mind, and fixed in your heart the great truth that I have been trying to unfold to you, there would be seen in your life a greater conformity to the faith you profess. If, then, by these considerations brought before you to-day, your conscience accuse you of having neglected to lead a life conformable to the grace you received in baptism, and to the vocation of a Christian to which that grace has called you—oh, then, let me entreat of you to begin at once to occupy yourselves with the reflection on the excellency of the grace given you by Jesus Christ in making you members of His Church by baptism—grace which cures all your infirmities and heals all the wounds of your soul—grace that withdraws you from the wrath of God, from the slavery of the devil—grace that restores your lost innocence, and makes you a participator of all the other graces, gifts, and helps, to which, if you are faithful in this life, will procure for you happiness in the next.

V.

ON THE DIGNITY TO WHICH WE ARE RAISED BY BAPTISM.

BAPTISM makes man not only a new creature and a friend of God, bringing him into a participation of the same life of God, making him, as St. Peter says, a partaker of the divine nature; it goes further, for it brings him into fellowship with the divine Father, with His eternal Son, and with the Holy Ghost.

This is the motive which has led me to continue the same subject, and after having considered the grace of baptism in itself, and the wonderful effects that it produces in the soul, we will, in the present instruction, dwell on the nobility and dignity to which we have been raised by the grace of baptism.

The virtue of the grace of baptism is so great that it brings us into an alliance with the divine Father, and we become one of His beloved sons. Yes, from that happy moment in which we were washed with the sanctifying water of baptism, we became sons of God, for the Apostle says: "We have not received the spirit of bondage again in fear: but we have received the spirit of adoption of sons, whereby we cry, Abba (Father)." The written law was a law of fear—it was given by God on Mount Sina amidst thunder and lightning—it was promulgated by the prophets, and in expressions full of threats, and in itself contained severity and rigour—but by means of the grace of baptism we have been freed from this law of bondage and fear. Jesus Christ washes us with His most precious blood, and writes with his finger a new law upon our hearts—a law of love and grace, by which we are made adopted sons of the eternal Father, so that we can with all confidence exclaim: My God, you are my Father. Abba, Father. And this is what the same Apostle expresses in other words, that "God hath predestinated us unto the adoption of children through Jesus Christ." Oftentimes we hear of persons adopting children, but this is ordinarily done when they have not children of their own, or their children had died.

Now, what is done by those who have not children of their own. God has been pleased to do for us through the ardour of His love for us: not that He needs adopted children, having His only-begotten Son, who supplies an infinite number of others; nevertheless so great is His love towards us that He wishes to adopt us for His children by means of the grace of baptism.

You are not, however, to suppose that this adoption of the Eternal Father is only that of name, as is that made by men, and if even it were so, it would be a most singular honour and the highest glory. But it is a true and real adoption. And how is it so? I answer: The Eternal Word is by nature the Son of God, and we have become sons by grace. Listen to the words of the beloved disciple: "Behold what manner of charity the Father has bestowed upon us, that we should be called, and should be the sons of God."

Raise your mental eyes and enlarge your heart— why? That if possible you may conceive the excess of charity the Eternal Father has shown towards you, in making you not only in name but in reality and effect His sons: "that we should be called, and should be the sons of God." Had He said call me by the name of Father, although I am not, and say that you are my sons, this of itself would have infinitely honoured and raised us to what we could never have merited or aspired to.

But the love of the Eternal Father does not stop here—He is not contented that we should be called, or pretend to be His sons, but that we should be—not only does He wish us to have the honour, but He wishes us to have all the glory, and to possess all the rights and advantages of sons.

And this sonship of God, although adoptive, is more complete and perfect, and surpasses in honour every human sonship—our natural parent is not so much our father as God is by the grace of baptism : " From the paternity of God," says the Apostle, " all paternity in heaven and earth is named, and from that every other takes its idea and model." In comparing God as our Father by the grace of baptism with our natural parent who has given us nought but this mortal life, so full of misery and sin, He is more truly our Father, for He has given us life. We have, then, but one Father, who looks upon us with charity and tenderness. And this is the reason why our Blessed Lord has told us that one is our Father, who is in heaven, and to Him He tells us to direct our prayers, and to say, " Our Father, who art in heaven," because with Him alone we have those relations which the divine Son has.

That this theological truth may be explained to you with all possible clearness and exactness, you must know that holy Scripture, speaking of the second person of the Blessed Trinity, calls Him the Only-begotten Son, who is in the bosom of His Father—the Word of God—who is the image of the invisible God. He is the Son of the Father, because He is born of Him from all eternity—He is the word of the divine Father, because He has been begotten by way of understanding and knowledge—He is the image of the Eternal Father, because He has the same divine substance.

Now, every Christian participates in these sublime qualities of the Second Person of the Blessed Trinity through the grace of baptism. This grace is a participation and derivation of the divine Sonship, for, says the Apostle, " we glory in the hope of the glory of the Son of God." He is our Father, and we are His sons, " for of His own hath He begotten us by the word of truth ;" that is, by means of the sacramental words used in the administration of the Sacrament of Baptism. The Father begets His divine Son in the brightness of the saints, and that divine light which he necessarily communicates to His divine Son, passes freely into us, through the grace of His adoption. Finally, we are made to the image of God. The divine Son is the substantial image of the Eternal Father, and we, through baptism, are regenerated and formed to the image of this divine Son. Being washed by the waters of baptism, we no longer bear the image of earthly man, but celestial. And if this celestial man, who is Christ, is the image of the divine Father, and we bear the image of Him, it follows in truth that we are the image of God. We are then taken into a participation of the titles and qualities which the Eternal Father communicates to his Eternal Son—we are then sons of God.

Can it, then, be possible for us to conceive a dignity greater than that to which the grace of baptism raises us in making us sons of God ?

This dignity is greater than any dignity of this world, whatever it may be. All the titles and dignities of this world are nothing in comparison with that of the dignity of a Christian and of the son of God. You, then, who are here listening to me, and who have been by the wise providence of God placed in a condition humble and abject, raise yourselves up above your miseries and lowliness, and consider the sublime dignity of a Christian to which you have been raised, and which makes you sons of God, and envy no longer the false greatness of this earth, which dazzles the eyes of the vain and worldly ones.

You may say, "I have been born poor—by my condition of life I am condemned to labour, I am constrained to earn my bread by the sweat of my brow, and with all this I have scarcely sufficient to live upon; but what does that signify ? I am a Christian, and being a Christian I am a son of God. This is a dignity that infinitely surpasses the greatness of all earthly dignity and birth."

With reflections such as these you will find consolation in the midst of your poverty and low estate, as also you will conceive thoughts worthy of your

divine birth and sonship, which you have received
through holy baptism. A prince ought not to turn his
thoughts and affections towards anything but what is
great and noble, and such as are worthy of his birth.
As the prophet saith, a " prince will devise such things
as are worthy of a prince." What would you say of
the son of a king, were you to see him in the lowest
society in place of remaining amongst the nobles of
the court ? You would say that such an one is acting
in a manner unworthy of his high birth. And you,
from the moment you were made a Christian, were
made princes not of earthly blood, but divine, because
by the blood of Jesus Christ you have been regenerated
and washed by baptism. You have, in common with
Jesus [Christ, that excellent title of son of God, and
you have also the heavenly inheritance. " If sons,
heirs also: heirs indeed of God, and joint heirs with
Christ." That blessed kingdom is prepared for you,
and you are taught to ask it of the divine Father in the
Lord's Prayer: "Thy kingdom come." Why then do
we not direct all our thoughts and affections to spiritual
and heavenly things ? Why do we not lead a life holy
and perfect ? Ah, in this an infinite number of Christians are wanting.

True it is that many and many Christians, to their
eternal shame and dishonour, give all their thoughts
to the satisfying of their senses, and in following their
unbridled passions. And even amongst those who may
appear the most upright, we see some applying themselves to the amassing of riches in this world, and to
the acquiring of titles and worldly honours, forgetting
altogether the eminent dignity of a Christian, which is
the highest and most precious, but which, now-a-days,
is little cared for or esteemed. How many have been
ruined by lawsuits arising from an unwillingness to
forego a ridiculous precedence, or some foolish point of
ceremony.

To be worldly, rich, great, and to have the friendship
of the great ones of this earth, is what is sought after,
whilst the inestimable grace of the adopted sonship of

God is despised, undervalued, or not cared for. But
let it not be so with you, and if hitherto you have not
thought of the greatness and the dignity to which you
have been raised by the grace of baptism, begin now
to think seriously of it, and, in the words of St. Leo, I
say to you, "Acknowledge, O Christian, thy own dignity, and return no more to thy former baseness of an
unworthy life." Remember that you are sons of God,
brothers of Jesus Christ, members of His body. This
brings me to a second consideration of the dignity of
a Christian.

The Eternal Father sent His only-begotten Son into
this world that He might not be alone, but that He
should have many brethren, and by Him adopted sons.
When, therefore, the divine Father, by the grace of
baptism, adopted us for His sons, He made us brethren
of Jesus Christ. Yes, Jesus Christ, according to the
beautiful expression of St. Paul, has become our elder
brother: "That He might be the first-born amongst
many brethren." And Jesus Christ has, with His own
lips, called us His brethren, and "He is not ashamed,"
says the Apostle, "to call us brethren." Then from the
moment we received the grace of baptism, we became
brethren of Jesus Christ, and He acknowledges us as
such so long as we conform our life to His. Oh! what
honour, what glory and dignity is this!

But the glory and dignity of a Christian ends not in
this. By baptism he enters into the Church, which is
the mystical body of Jesus Christ, of which body Jesus
Christ is the Head, as St. Paul teaches, "He is the
Head of the body, the Church," and the Christian
becomes a member of Jesus Christ. Yes, Jesus Christ
is our Head, and we, by the grace of baptism, have the
honour of being, in quality of members, united with
Him our Head. This union between us as members
of this mystical body with Jesus Christ, is more intimate and perfect than that which exists between the
parts of our natural body. For these parts, although
united to themselves and make one body, yet one part
cannot be in another. The union, however, that we

have with Christ is essentially spiritual, and that makes us in Christ and Christ in us in a most wonderful manner, with, however, its proper proportion, by which He is in His Eternal Father.

This last expression might seem an exaggeration, if Jesus Christ had not Himself declared it to be so: "I am in my Father, and you in Me, and I in you." Oh, the honour and glory we receive through the grace of baptism! Oh! what a subject is this for our consideration, and worthy of our eternal gratitude to God. Of ourselves we are nothing, but by the grace of God we are united to Jesus Christ our Head, and we become His brethren and His members. We must, however, bear in mind that this noble quality and glory of being brethren and members of Jesus Christ require of us corresponding good works such as are becoming a name so venerable and so holy as that of a Christian. For a Christian who is made a member of Christ crucified ought to be firmly persuaded that he cannot be a true and living member of this divine Head, and receive from Him life, when he lives not according to the spirit Jesus Christ lived, or regulates himself according to the maxims He prescribed, loving what He loved, and hating what He hated. Now, what was the life and doctrine of Jesus Christ? It was that of a love for sufferings and humiliations, and a hatred for the pleasures of this world. A Christian, then, ought to labour with all his power to stir up in his heart a sincere love for sufferings and crosses; a hatred for the false and deceitful pleasures of this world. Woe to us if, after having been singled out by God as objects of His love, our life be not conformable to that of Jesus Christ— in vain will be our glory of a name so holy, if by our actions we profane it, we shall be more culpable than the pagan, and the religion we profess will reproach us for our disorderly lives.

That a misfortune so deplorable may not befall us, let us ever bear in mind the dignity to which we have been raised by the grace of baptism—let us ever remember the purity and holiness of our Head, Jesus

Christ, of whom we have the happiness of being members; "Acknowledge, O Christian, thy own dignity, remember your Head, and whose members you are." This holy thought will produce in your mind two most useful effects. It will humble us and make us ashamed of ourselves at the sight of the difference so great between a copy so defective and imperfect—between members so ill-shaped and deformed and a Head so pure and holy. Oh, my God, shall we have the boldness to call ourselves true Christians, whilst we are leading a life worldly and in direct opposition to that of Jesus Christ? A young artist blushes when he places his defective copy beside the original of a great master.

But this shame ought to give place to a noble desire, and a laudable emulation of imitating, as far as he is able, his master, and of conforming his works to the finished ones before him. So, likewise, this confronting ourselves with the divine Redeemer, who is our Master, our Model, ought to fill us with an heroic courage to imitate Him, and this is the second effect to be produced in us by this holy reflection. True it is that with all our exertions we shall never be able to come up entirely to this divine Model, nor shall we be perfectly conformable to Him. Nevertheless, with His assistance we shall be able to correct little by little our defects, and purify our hearts, so that we may arrive at that holiness of life that is required of a Christian.

Again, the grace of baptism has not only raised us to the dignity of the sonship of God, made us brethren and members of Jesus Christ, but it has also made us the temple of the Holy Ghost. Yes, the soul of a Christian sanctified by the grace of the Sacrament of Baptism, becomes the temple of the Holy Ghost. It takes up its habitation in the soul and dwells therein. But what ought to excite your greatest surprise and fill your mind with the highest conception of the excellency of this grace, is that not our soul only becomes the temple of the Holy Ghost, but also our body, that is, our eyes, ears, tongue, hands and feet. Yes, all these members, whilst we preserve the grace of baptism, are the temple of the Holy Ghost, and to Him they are consecrated. Few of you, perhaps, have ever reflected on this, and yet of its truth there is no room for doubt, for the Apostle has expressly declared it. " Know you not that your members are the temple of the Holy Ghost." Oh, the singular dignity of the grace of baptism!

" You," then the Apostle goes on to say, " you are not your own, but that of the Holy Ghost, Who is in you, Whom you have from God." This mysterious consecration is accomplished in us by means of the water and words used by the minister of the sacrament. You are then regenerated and renovated by the Holy Ghost. By Him you were made Christians, who sanctified the Blessed Virgin, and made her worthy to be the Mother of God. And as she had God in her womb, by the power of the Holy Ghost, so we, being the temple of the Holy Ghost, ought to glorify Him. Could then the dignity to which the grace of baptism has raised you be greater ? Could you receive more excellent graces and favours than you have through baptism ? For by it you have been made free from the slavery of the devil, and not only free but holy, not only holy, but sons of God, and not only sons but heirs of heaven —not only heirs, but brethren of Jesus Christ, and members of His body, and the temple of the Holy Ghost.

Then if you are raised to so great a dignity as to be sons of the Eternal Father by the grace of baptism, can it be possible that you should despise the sonship of God, and become by sin sons of the devil ? If by baptism you are made members of Jesus Christ, and His brethren, can it be possible that you should profane your body and soul by sinful and unworthy actions, renouncing that eternal happiness which God has prepared for you, by running after the false pleasures of this world? If by the grace of baptism you are made soul and body the temple of the Holy Ghost, can it be possible that you should make them, by iniquity and sin, the habitation of Satan ?—can it be possible

that you should allow those eyes, consecrated to the
Holy Ghost, to gaze upon the vanity of the world, and
upon unlawful objects ?—those ears that ought to listen
to the law of God and His divine mysteries, will you
permit them to listen to what ought not so much as be
named among Christians ?—that tongue that ought to
be employed in blessing and thanking God, will you
profane it by speaking irreverently of His holy name ?
those hands that ought to be extended towards works
of mercy, will you use them against your neighbour ?
Finally, those feet that ought to be directed towards
the Church and places of piety and devotion, will you
allow them to be moved to where your faith and morals
are in danger ? If unhappily in by-gone times we
have been wanting, let us not be so in future. Let us
now enter into ourselves, and since the grace of baptism has made us sons of God, brethren and members
of Jesus Christ, and the temple of the Holy Ghost, we
will lead a life worthy of the glorious qualities with
which we have been invested, so that we may have the
happiness of enjoying the fruit of them in heaven.

VI.

ALTHOUGH a knowledge of the ceremonies used in the administration of the Sacrament of Baptism is not absolutely necessary, yet the Catechism of the Council of Trent imposes upon us the obligation of instructing the faithful on the prayers, rites, and ceremonies of this sacrament, so that the inestimable gifts contained therein may be deeply impressed upon their minds. This is, then, what I propose to do in the present instruction, and I will, with the Catechism, divide these ceremonies into three parts. Firstly, those that are to be observed before baptism; secondly, such as are used at the font itself; thirdly, those that are added after baptism has been administered.

One of the principal things preceding baptism is the choosing of the sponsors. In case of necessity baptism can be administered without them, but they must be present when the Church solemnly administers this sacrament. The Council of Trent says that " one person only, whether male or female, or at most one male and one female, shall receive the individual baptised." This has been the custom of the Church from the most remote times. But since there is nothing, however holy it may be, which may not be subject to abuse, thus in our own days the choosing of sponsors is looked upon as a mere ceremony, having no signification, and persons are chosen for that office who know not the end for which they have been chosen, or the obligations they take upon themselves. Now, the end and reason why sponsors are chosen and admitted are, because they present to the Church him who is to be baptised, give a name to the child, and be witness of the baptism and answer the questions put to the person baptised, renouncing in his name the devil, his works and pomps, and finally to instruct him in the mysteries of our holy religion—that is to say, the Commandments of God and His Church, the sacraments and all that is necessary for a Christian to know, so that he may lead a life worthy of his vocation, should the parents neglect this duty or be removed by death. Hence, in the selection of sponsors a due regard ought to be had to their capacity for that office, and probity of life, and that they possess all those good qualities which render them commendable before God, and not what is done now-a-days by very many, who look only to friendship, wealth, authority, or some other temporal interest. The Church in her ritual prescribes that only those who have arrived to the years of puberty are to be admitted, which is the age of fourteen in man and twelve in woman, and that they have received the Sacrament of Confirmation.

The Church forbids also infidels, heretics, persons excommunicated, and public sinners. They must be also of sound mind, having a knowledge of the mysteries of religion, otherwise how can they instruct their spiritual children in things of which they are ignorant?

The Fathers of the Church called sponsors sometimes receivers and sureties. The Church has always willed that the baptised should have sureties, so as not to risk the grace of the sacrament, or expose it to the danger of being lost or despised. In this she acts with the caution of a prudent man, who lends his money or consigns his goods to one of whom he is not certain whether he will pay or not, and therefore he requires security of one whom he knows can do so. Now, the grace of baptism being the greatest of all the gifts of God, and the most precious of all His treasures, it is necessary that the Church should be assured of the good faith of those to whom it is administered. Therefore the Church, in the baptism both of adults and infants, wills that there be sponsors who become sureties for them, and promise that the baptised will lead lives

ON THE CEREMONIES USED IN BAPTISM.   47

as become true Christians, so that living in innocence
they may preserve to the end of their lives the grace
received in baptism.   This is the obligation of all who
take upon themselves the office of sponsors for children
in baptism.   On this subject let us hear what St. Denis
writes, speaking the language of the sponsor : " I promise by my assiduous exhortations to induce the child,
when he shall arrive at a knowledge of religion, to
renounce everything opposed to, and to profess and
perform the sacred promises which he makes."   St.
Angustine also : " I most especially admonish you,"
says he, " men and women, who have become sponsors,
to know that you stood sureties before God for those
whom you have been seen to receive at the sacred font."
Speaking of the same office of sponsors, St. Augustine
sums up, in a few words, the lessons of instructions
which ought to be impressed by them on their spiritual
children, for he says : " They ought to admonish them
to observe chastity, love justice, cherish charity ; and
above all, let them teach them the Creed, and the
Lord's Prayer, the Ten Commandments also, and what
are the first rudiments of the Christian religion."

Here we see confirmed the custom of admitting
sponsors, and St. Thomas gives a reason why it should
be so, and also the Catechism of the Council of Trent.
For baptism being a spiritual regeneration, by which
we are made sons of God, and become, as St. Peter
says, " as new born babes," it follows that he who is
born into this world has need of a nurse and master to
instruct him, so likewise is it necessary for those who
commence to live a life of grace by baptism, should be
confided to the care and prudence of a wise person,
from whom they may learn the precepts of religion and
Christian piety, so that by degrees putting on Jesus
Christ, they may, with the divine assistance, become
holy and perfect men.   Then, in the event of children
being deprived of this instruction so necessary, either
through the negligence or by the death of their parents,
the duty rests upon the sponsors to watch over those
whom they received at the sacred font.   They are the

spiritual children of the sponsors, and with them and with their parents they have contracted a spiritual relationship. Therefore they are bound to use all diligence in imparting to them a knowledge of those things that are necessary for salvation; and should they be in want, to render them assistance. Also should the sponsors perceive that their spiritual children walk not according to the law of God, they are to admonish and correct them.

Some of you may, perhaps, say, "If the obligations of sponsors are so great, we, henceforth, will be on our guard and not take upon ourselves an office that will be a burden upon our consciences." This is certainly not the consequence to be deduced from the doctrine explained, the object of which has been only that of instructing you, and to prevent you from undertaking an office without first understanding what are its obligations, and knowing them to fulfil them with exactness. To refuse to receive a child at the sacred font, you ought not without a sufficient reason. How can you refuse an office so pious, and thus set aside the order and discipline of the Church? Add to this the honour given to you and the merit you acquire by an act so charitable and so generous. For "he that showeth mercy lendeth to his neighbour," says the Holy Ghost. If this is done for a temporal benefit, how much more ought it to be done for the soul, so that it may be freed from the slavery of the devil and made a child of God. It has pleased God to become our surety, and in many places He is called such by the Psalmist. And "Jesus Christ," according to the Apostle, "is made our surety." Who, then, can refuse the office of sponsor?

After having, at some length, spoken of the obligations of sponsors, I will now speak of the other ceremonies preceding baptism. The child to be baptised is to remain in the porch of the church (the same is to be observed with regard to adults), because before being a Christian it is not worthy to enter, and since it has no right to heaven, so it is to be excluded from the church. The priest goes outside of the church to seek the child—this is done to signify the unhappy state it is in, and that being a child of Adam, disobedient to God, and for this reason driven out of the terrestial paradise, and having inherited his disobedience and sin is driven out of the heavenly paradise of God, had He not in His mercy opened the gate for him. A name is given to the child, and it ought to be the name of a saint, that the child may have a protector before God, and be moved to imitate the life and virtues of the saint. The priest then says to the child to be baptised: "What dost thou ask of the Church of God?" and it answers, "Faith," through which it hopes for life everlasting. The priest goes on to say, "If, then, thou desirest to enter into life, keep the Commandments. Thou shalt love the Lord thy God, with thy whole heart, with thy whole soul, and with thy whole mind: and thy neighbour as thyself." After this the priest breathes thrice upon the face of the child, commanding, at the same time, the devil to go out of him, and give place to the Holy Ghost. This sacred ceremony is very ancient, and was used by St. Augustine as an argument against the Pelagians, showing that new-born babes are infected with original sin, and are by reason of it under the tyranny and power of the devil, and that through that breathing, and by the command of the priest, they may be taken from that power, and transferred to the kingdom of Christ. See, then, what we were before baptism, slaves of the devil, children of wrath—see the power given by God to the priest of expelling the devil. This breath of the priest comes from what God did in the creation of man, breathing into his face the breath of life, and man became a living soul. In the regeneration which is made through baptism, there is given the life-giving spirit. Also this breathing is done in imitation of our Blessed Lord, who breathed upon the apostles, giving them the Holy Ghost, and it signifies the spiritual life the soul receives.

The sign of the cross is made with the thumb of the priest upon the forehead and on the breast of the child,

D

this is done to signify that baptism derives all its power and efficacy from the passion and death of our Divine Redeemer. Also that we are consecrated to Jesus Christ crucified, and that signed by this divine character, we are the sheep of this divine Pastor, whose voice we ought to hear, and in whose steps we ought to walk, never allowing ourselves to be " led away with various and strange doctrines."

The cross is made on the forehead to signify that a Christian ought to profess openly his faith, and never to be ashamed of it, or drawn away from the practice of it through human respect. It is made on the breast that a Christian should understand that his life is to be a continual warfare, and not one of worldly pleasures ; that he is to embrace the cross of Jesus Christ and carry it always in his body, mind, and heart, so that he may say with the Apostle : " God forbid that I should glory save in the cross of Jesus Christ, by whom the world is crucified in me, and I to the world."

The sign of the cross having been made, the priest lays his hand upon the head of the child to signify that he has now become a victim to be consecrated to God by baptism, and prays that God the Father of our Lord Jesus Christ would vouchsafe to look upon this child whom He has been pleased to call unto the rudiment of the faith, and to drive out of him all blindness of heart, break all the bonds of Satan wherewith he was tied, open unto him the gate of His mercy, that being imbued with the zeal of wisdom, he may be free from the abominations of all wicked desires, and, by the sweet odour of the divine precepts, may joyfully serve in the Church of God, and go forward from day to day.

The priest then puts a small quantity of the blessed salt into the mouth of the child, saying, " Receive the salt of wisdom ; let it be to thee a propitiation unto life everlasting." This is done to signify that by the grace of baptism is purged away all corruption of sin, and that God would preserve him from all vicious corruption, and dispose him for the reception of new and more abundant graces. Also it is to signify that he may have a taste for things spiritual, and that the word of God may not be insipid to him. Moreover, the salt signifies the wisdom given to the baptised, which is to guide a good Christian in all his actions, to the end that he may do nothing contrary to the law of God : finally, the salt denotes that by means of baptism he may hope one day to rise incorruptible.

The priest then goes on to exorcise and command the devil to depart from the servant of God in the name of the Father, and of the Son, and of the Holy Ghost, and this is done to make us the more and more convinced that before baptism we are all under the dominion of the devil, and that to chase him away there is required that divine virtue given to the priest. He speaks in the name of Jesus Christ, and tells the devil that He commands thee, who walked on foot upon the sea, and stretched out His right hand to Peter when sinking. Then the priest continues to exorcise the devil, saying, "Accursed devil, acknowledge thy sentence, and give honour to the living God, give honour to Jesus Christ His Son, and to the Holy Ghost; and depart from this servant of God, because God, even our Lord Jesus Christ, hath vouchsafed to call him to His holy grace and benediction, and to the font of baptism;" then making the sign of the cross with his thumb on the forehead, he commands the devil never again to violate the holy cross impressed on the forehead. This being done, the priest again places his hand upon the head of the child, and prays in behalf of this servant of God, that the Eternal Father, Author of Light and Truth, would vouchsafe to enlighten this child with the light of His wisdom, cleanse and sanctify him, give him true knowledge, that, being made worthy of the grace of His baptism, he may retain firm hope, right counsel, and holy doctrine. By this ceremony we are led to understand that from being slaves of the devil, we are made free, and are consecrated to the dominion of God, and are under His care, from whom we cannot be taken away or emancipated, unless by mortal sin. Whence it is that we no longer belong to the devil, but to God. Then the priest says to the child: "Come into the temple of God, that thou mayest have part with Christ unto life everlasting." The child having entered the church, the priest proceeds to the font, and recites along with the sponsors the Apostles' Creed. The reason for this ceremony is because the first thing required of him who draws near to God is that he " must believe that He is." True it is the child cannot speak, but in its name the sponsors do. After the Creed the Lord's Prayer is said, after which the priest again exorcises the devil. Then wetting his right thumb with spittle from his mouth, and touching therewith, in the form of a cross, the right ear of the child, and afterwards the left, says: " Ephphatha;" that is to say, be opened. This is done in imitation of our Blessed Lord when He gave hearing to the deaf man mentioned in the Gospel. Then touching the nostrils the priest adds, for a savour of sweetness, and then in a louder voice he adds these words: " But thou, Satan, fly, behold the God, great and mighty, draweth near: the God Who taketh away the prey from the strong one." This ceremony of touching the ears signifies that the internal eyes of the soul ought to be opened, so that they may not be deaf to the promises, the counsels, and commands of God, but may listen with attention to the divine Word; like sheep, simple and innocent, knowing the voice of their shepherd, and fleeing from that of the stranger. The touching of the nostrils is done to signify that we ought not to be sensible to the ill stench of the world, but only to the saving odour of God: " For we are the good odour of Christ unto God."

Then the person to be baptised is interrogated by name, saying, "Dost thou renounce Satan and all his works and all his pomps?"

But as I shall speak on a future occasion of this ceremony, and of the renunciation that every one makes in baptism, I will pass to the anointing made by the priest upon the breast and between the shoulders, say-

ing at the same time : "I anoint thee with the oil of
salvation in Christ Jesus our Lord, that thou mayest
have life everlasting." Oil has the virtue of healing
wounds and strengthening the limbs ; so the grace
signified by this anointing is the healing of the wounds
of the soul, and of rendering it strong to resist the
passions. "As of old the wrestler before entering upón
the struggle anointed himself that he might be strong,
and that he might the more easily escape from the
hands of his adversary ; thus the Christian is anointed
as a new wrestler of Christ, that he may be strengthened
against his enemies, the devil, the world, and the flesh.
Formerly the body was anointed, but now only the
breast and shoulders. The anointing of the breast
strengthens the mind and heart—the shoulders that
they may have courage to bear the yoke of Christ.
Finally, an explicit profession of faith in the mysteries
of the Trinity, the principal mysteries of Jesus Christ,
and a belief in the Catholic Church. Whence it is the
priest asks the person to be baptised by name : " Dost
thou believe in God the Father Almighty, Creator of
heaven and earth ? Dost thou believe in Jesus Christ,
His only Son our Lord, Who was born into this world
and suffered for us ? Dost thou believe in the Holy
Ghost, the holy Catholic Church, the communion of
saints, the forgiveness of sins, the resurrection of the
body, and life everlasting ?" And to each of these
interrogations the sponsors answer, "I do believe." By
this we are to understand that actual faith is required
in those who are capable, according to the teaching of
our Blessed Lord, Who has declared : "He that believeth
and is baptised shall be saved." And as we read in
the Acts of the Apostles, that St. Philip required this
belief in the eunuch before baptising him—"If thou
believest with all thy heart thou mayest ;" then, in
conformity with the ancient discipline of the Church,
according to which baptism was not given to an adult
unless it was desired (for baptism is not to be forced
upon a person, or a profession in the law of Christ), and
also in imitation of our Blessed Lord, Who, before

restoring to health those who came unto Him, required their express desire in these words: "Dost thou wish to be made whole? What dost thou wish that I should do unto thee?" And although the infant is unable to express its desire to receive this sacrament, the Church, however, wishes that this question be asked, saying: "Wilt thou be baptised?" and the sponsors answer: "I will." Then the priest pours the water on the head of the child, saying at the same time, "I baptise thee, &c."

The child being baptised, the top of the head is anointed with the holy chrism: this is done to signify that this child is now made a member of Christ, and also to signify that every Christian is, in a certain sense, a king and priest, according to the words in the Apocalypse: "Thou hast made us to our God a kingdom and priest." A white linen cloth, in place of the white garment anciently used and worn by the baptised for eight days, is placed upon the child. In placing this cloth the priest says: "Receive this white garment, and see thou carry it without stain before the judgment seat of our Lord Jesus Christ, that thou mayest have eternal life."

This ceremony signifies the purity of the soul, being clothed with sanctifying grace, and that the Christian ought to preserve his innocence till death. It also signifies the internal joy of the soul, as black signifies mourning. Lastly, the priest places a lighted candle in the hand of the sponsor, saying: "Receive this burning light, and keep thy baptism, so as to be without blame; keep the Commandments of God, that when the Lord shall come to the nuptials, thou mayest meet Him in the heavenly court, and have eternal life and live for ever."

This lighted candle has also its signification, which, according to St. Charles Borromeo, represents the theological virtues infused into the soul by baptism. Faith by the light, charity by its heat, and its erect position the virtue of hope, which leads us to aspire to heaven. The candle is placed in the hand to give us to understand that it will not suffice to have those virtues in our heart, but we ought to make them known by our works. Then the baptised is told to go in peace.

These are the sacred ceremonies used in baptism, full of mysteries and instructions. Oh, how much might be said upon these ceremonies, and how much might be learned; but as I shall touch upon them when I speak of the holy life a Christian ought to lead, I will confine myself to reminding all of their duty to lead an exemplary and irreprehensible life before all men, and to preserve with great care the grace of holy baptism, and to the observance of the Commandments of God, so that when the Lord comes to demand an account of your life and actions, He may find you good and faithful servants. You have heard that the Fathers of the Church called baptism "Illumination," and the baptised "Illuminated." If, then, you were once in darkness, but now children of light, walk as such. For the fruit of the light is in all goodness, and justice, and truth—doing only that which is well pleasing to God. And so let your light shine before men, that seeing your good works, they may glorify your Father who is in heaven. So that after having glorified Him here on earth by a good life, you may have the happiness of glorifying, blessing, and praising Him eternally in heaven.

VII.

ON THE PROMISES MADE AT BAPTISM.

IF the Jewish nation was at one time so glorious, so honoured, and so happy by reason of the covenant and alliance that God had made with it, making it the depository of His law and of His divine mysteries—if by every other nation they were called the chosen people of God, and prided themselves on this distinction, with greater reason ought we Christians to say that we are a chosen people, a holy nation, a purchased people, for such the Apostle St. Peter calls us, a people dear to God, and in whom He wishes to show forth His divine mercy, having called us out of darkness into His marvellous light. Under the law of grace we have been made the depositaries of treasures most precious, and of the highest mysteries. The covenant and alliance that God has made with us, has not been signed with the blood of oxen and of goats, but with the most precious blood of His Son Jesus Christ, the Lamb of God, who taketh away the sins of the world. But as the Jews of old frequently violated the sacred alliance God had made with them, degenerating from the glory of their vocation, and lived, as it were, in a continual prevarication of the law of God, for which the prophets upbraided them ; so in like manner very many Christians in our days lead a life unworthy of the name they bear, and contrary to the promises they made at baptism. I therefore propose in this discourse to direct my reproofs to such unworthy Christians, to the end that they may be brought to lead a life worthy of their vocation.

And since their disorderly life, ordinarily speaking,

proceeds from an imperfect knowledge of their duties and obligations, I will begin by showing the importance of the promises made to God in baptism; after which what these promises mean.

All the Fathers of the Church, who have spoken on the Sacrament of Baptism, declare that there is a species of contract between God and man, and between man and his God. God, through His infinite mercy, has been pleased to take us from the slavery of sin and the devil—from being rebels and enemies, He has made us friends and partakers of His gifts, conferring upon us His grace, to which if we are faithful unto death, He has promised to give us a crown of glory and life eternal. Man, on his part, has promised fidelity to his God—this promise is made in the face of heaven and earth, in the presence of God and His holy angels, declaring solemnly that he will belong to no one but to God, and Him alone will he serve. Consequently man has promised to renounce all that is contrary to God. And since there is nothing more opposed to God, no enemy more irreconcilable than the devil, and his works (which are sins), the pomps of the devil, which are those things by which the devil ensnares the sons of men, therefore, whosoever wishes to receive baptism, must make a solemn renunciation of these three things.

Amongst all the promises that man can possibly make, I affirm there is none of more importance, or that a Christian ought to be more faithful in fulfilling than those he makes to his God in baptism. The Fathers of the Church, enlightened by God, knew better than we do the strict obligation, and they used expressions both grave and stringent.

St. Ambrose calls these promises a contract of faith. For as men, when they enter into a contract, bind themselves by word and deed to submit to the penalty determined between them, should they fail to carry out the contract, so in baptism there is made a contract between God and man; and as in all contracts the obligations are mutual, so in baptism the condi-

tions and promises are reciprocal. God is faithful to
His promises, taking us from the miserable state of
sin, giving us His grace, and promising us eternal life.
Oh, how good is our God! Who are we, O Lord, that
Thou shouldst, by Thy grace, make us worthy to be
Thy sons and heirs of Thy kingdom? On our part we
take upon ourselves the obligation of renouncing the
devil, his works and his pomps, under the penalty of
eternal punishment should we fail to fulfil it. "Let
each one," says St. Ambrose, "consider and frequently
recall to his mind what he said and what be promised
when he came to the sacred font before being cleansed
by the sanctifying waters." What reply did you give
to the priest when he asked you, "Do you renounce
the devil, all his works and all his pomps?" Your
answer was: "I renounce them." Remember, then,
your word, let it not depart from your mind. And
indeed whosoever pledges his word to another, and fails
to fulfil it, burdens his conscience, and before God is
guilty of a sin—besides the sin he is subject to the
penalty of the law. With greater reason ought we to
say that the Christian, who fails to fulfil the promises
solemnly made in baptism, is guilty of a sin more
enormous, and brings upon himself the just anger of
his God, and exposes himself to the danger of His
eternal chastisements. Without doubt these promises
are more binding upon us than any we may make to
men. For by these promises we do not bind ourselves
to things temporal; but the soul, conscience, and faith,
which are certainly of infinitely more value than anything temporal. You, then, who have given your faith
to Jesus Christ, strive to keep it.

St. Paulinus and St. Jerome, speaking of these promises that are made in baptism, call them "the oath
of fidelity," which the creature makes to his Creator,
his Sovereign. You sometimes hear of her Majesty
conferring a title on one of her subjects. The first
condition sought for in the person thus honoured is
that he will never join himself with any of her majesty's
enemies, and he takes an oath of fidelity to his sove-

reign. Now, it is quite certain, as we have shown on a former occasion, that there is no dignity, however great it may be, to equal that of being a Christian. For it brings us into an alliance with the three divine Persons of the most holy Trinity, making us sons of the divine Father, brethren, heirs, and members of Jesus Christ, and the temple of the Holy Ghost. Therefore it is necessary that we be determined, and declare our fidelity to God, and to Him render our homage and service, and never to take part with His enemies, the devil, the world, and the flesh, that we always hate sin and fly from all those occasions that may lead us into it.

St. John Chrysostom calls the renunciation made in baptism "a confederation entered into with Jesus Christ." And it seems to me that this expression is most appropriate, when our works correspond to it. Jesus Christ in baptism deals with us as one would in purchasing a slave, first asking him if he will serve him; so Jesus Christ, who has purchased us with His most precious blood, first asks us if we are willing to abandon entirely the cruel tyrant and serve Him only; and then it is this confederation is entered into between God and us. St. Gregory declares that these promises form a compact which we make with God. From which we may deduce that if a confederation, a compact, entered into with man ought to be strictly observed, how much more so that between God and man? St. Thomas says the promises made in baptism are so many vows made by a Christian to God. What is a vow? It is "a deliberate promise made to God, to do something that is pleasing to Him." These promises made in baptism are made with a deliberate will to God, either by yourselves or by your sponsors. These vows bind you to an exact observance of the divine law, and to the renouncing of the devil, his works and his pomps: the doing of this is most pleasing to God. A Christian, therefore, is a religious, whose life ought to be regulated according to the religion instituted by Jesus Christ. The religion instituted by Jesus Christ is that which the holy apostles and all the true faithful professed and profess, and it has its foundation in the observance of the principles of a Christian life. This religion embraces every Catholic throughout the world, and it has for its rule the Gospel, and for its habit Jesus Christ. For St. Paul says: "As many of you as have been baptised in Christ, have put on Christ." See, then, the dignity, the greatness, and perfection of this religion which everyone professes, who makes the above promises and vows in holy baptism. See, then, the importance of those promises and vows and what care you ought to take in fulfilling them.

St. Augustine goes still further, and he says the promises made in baptism are not only vows, but they are the greatest of all vows. For all other vows can be dispensed with, but with these there is not a power in heaven or on earth that can dispense with them. We must therefore conclude from what has been said, that either the Fathers of the Church have been deceived in speaking with such gravity, or that the promises made in baptism are of greater importance than it is possible to conceive. And who can reflect upon the circumstances accompanying these promises and think otherwise?

These promises are not made to man, but to God, in the presence of those who hold His place—to God, who is not satisfied with words but requires deeds, and who punishes severely him who is wanting. These promises are made in the church, which is the house of God, in the face of heaven and earth, and in the presence of the angels, who will bear testimony of the words uttered. The observance of these promises will form the glory and felicity of the Christian in the present and in the life to come. Add to this, these promises are made by man who was a slave of the devil, and who has been redeemed by the most precious blood of his God, made man. It is then a slave who enters into a contract with his Deliverer—a servant with his Master—a creature with his Creator—this is a circumstance that increases, augments, and renders

our obligation more strict. If, then, this contract be
broken by the infidelity of a vile creature, by a miserable slave, his perfidy is more culpable. And this is
the reason why the Fathers, speaking of the gravity of
this sin, call it apostacy; that is, a denial of the Christian religion. In fact, an apostate is one who, entering
into religion, makes a promise never to abandon it, and
then, forsaking his profession, breaks his vows, puts
off the religious habit, and lives in the world as others.

Whence it is that such is the greatness and importance of these promises, that upon their observance or
transgression depends the salvation or damnation of
men. No human law can abolish them—there is not
a contract that may not be annulled—no oath or vow
that may not be dispensed with; but it is not so with
these promises, these vows that we make in baptism.
For these no dispensation can be granted, not even by
the vicar of Christ on earth. In the discipline of the
Church there may be variations and change, but never
in faith and morals. These have never changed, nor
will they ever change. In like manner having at our
baptism renounced the devil, the world, and the flesh,
which is a point of the moral law, it is absolutely necessary that we renounce them, and if we do not, for us
there is no salvation.

And this it was that forced St. Ephrem to say that
those Christians " who have not been faithful to their
vows and promises made in baptism, will hear from the
lips of Jesus Christ, both at the particular as well as at
the general judgment, those terrible words: 'Out of thy
own mouth I judge thee, thou wicked servant;' by the
promises you so solemnly made me, and which you
have so basely violated. Then without any other
examen the sentence of damnation will be pronounced."
If, then, it is thus, what will become of so many Christians who have neither observed, nor do they observe,
these promises, although upon them depend their
eternal salvation? What shall we say of those who
neither know or care to know what these promises are?
Of such we may say that they will be infallibly lost,

both for their transgressions so culpable, as well as for their ignorance. I will therefore try to remove this obstacle, and after having made known to you the importance of these promises, I will now explain to you their meaning, that knowing them you may be able to ratify them, and protest before God that if you have been hitherto wanting, from henceforth you will observe them with fidelity and exactness.

Three are the promises which every one is bound to make before receiving the Sacrament of Baptism, viz.: to renounce the devil, his works, and his pomps. This renunciation has always been considered so necessary by the Church that she would never admit anyone without it. For she knows well that maxim laid down by our blessed Lord: "No man can serve two masters." How could it be possible for one to be made a son of God and heir of heaven by baptism, without renouncing the devil, his works, and his pomps? No: it is not possible for one to be a brother of Jesus Christ, and at the same time a member and follower of the devil. In renouncing the devil we consecrate ourselves to God and are to live only for Him. To Him we have consecrated our mind, our heart, our will, and all the members of our body are to be employed only in doing His divine will and for His glory. This Jesus Christ has taught us, and He ought to be not only our Head, but our Master and Model, and His doctrine and example ought to be our guide in all our actions; for how can our heart become a témple consecrated to the most blessed Trinity, and at the same time a habitation for the infernal enemy? Our tongue, an organ of the Holy Ghost, and an instrument employed by Satan in blaspheming the most holy name of God and in speaking of things unbecoming Christians? "What concord hath Christ," says St. Paul, "with Belial, and what agreement hath the temple of God with idols?" How can light and darkness dwell together—grace and sin? This, then, is the reason why the Church, before conferring baptism, judges it necessary that a renunciation of the devil should be made.

Indeed, all the Fathers, who have spoken of this renunciation, represent it as of strict obligation, and that the violation of it is a sin greater than any committed by the infidel. What means this renouncing of the devil? It means the withdrawal of one's self from his tyranny and slavery, and the entering into the service of Jesus Christ our Master. It means that when the devil tries to draw near unto us by his wicked suggestions and temptations, we are to chase him away with promptness and courage. On these occasions we ought to say: "I renounce thee, O Satan; I belong to Jesus Christ!" Yes, my Jesus, You are my Saviour, my Lord and Master, and to You I am united! This sentiment ought to be deeply fixed in our heart, so that we may the more easily resist the attacks of the enemy of God and our salvation. These words we ought to say in the beginning of all our actions—when we leave the house, when we hear impious and wicked discourse, and when we see deceitful worldlings doing wicked actions, committing sins which are the works of the devil, and which, in the second place, are to be renounced.

After the priest has asked the person to be baptised if he renounce the devil, he advances further and he asks him if he renounce all his works? By the works of the devil the Fathers understand sin, for he, the devil, is the primary author of it, and he it is who continually tempts us to commit it. But if every sin is the work of the devil, that of pride is certainly one of his principal works; for it was that that changed him from an angel into a demon. "Pride is the beginning," says the Holy Ghost, "of all sin." It has been transmitted to us through Adam, it is a contagious and deadly pestilence which we have contracted by means of original sin, and which reigns in the world, and oftentimes infects and poisons even good works. And, as when a pestilence rages in a city, a larger number of persons are carried off by it than by the ordinary diseases; so, by means of pride a greater number of Christians are lost than by other sins. Let us, then, see if we have really renounced this work of the devil —pride; if we have put on the spirit of humility, for such is the spirit of Jesus Christ; if not our renunciation has been a mockery, and our profession a delusion. It is not, however, sufficient to root out pride from our heart, but all other sins that take their origin from it; that is to say, every thought, word, and action that has not God for its ultimate end. The works of the devil are all those false maxims that are put forward by the world: for example, not to allow an injury to go unpunished, that we should seek to raise ourselves above others and make a figure in the world, that to do so it is necessary to have means, and for the acquiring of which we are not to be over scrupulous as to the manner by which it is to be obtained. These, and such as these are the false maxims of the world, and the renunciation of them we were bound to make at our baptism, for St. Paul says, by baptism "we are dead to sin, how shall we live longer therein." Again the same Apostle says, by baptism the devil has been driven out of our heart, and that we are to keep a watch over ourselves, so as not to allow him again to enter. "Give not place to the devil." This enemy is so cunning, and we are so easily surprised, that should we give him the least encouragement he will enter into our heart and engage us to do his sinful works. It is, therefore, necessary to resist him in the beginning, and to be watchful lest he might induce us to consent to sin. This is the only evil in the world we have to fear—sin, this we must fly on all occasions. This is, then, what is meant by renouncing all the works of the devil.

In the third place, the priest asks the person to be baptised, " If he renounces all the pomps of the devil." The very name of the devil and sin ought to be sufficient to fill us with horror, and few there are who openly desire to traffic with the one or the other. Whence it is that perhaps there is not a Christian to be found who would not willingly declare by his words, if not by actions, that he will have no part with this enemy of God, and that, therefore, he has no difficulty in

ratifying the promises made in baptism of renouncing
the devil, sin, and his works. But it certainly is not
the same with regard to the pomps of the devil; for
how few are to be found among Christians who really
renounce them, and consequently few observe this
promise as the other two made in baptism.

You may ask what are the pomps of the devil? By
pomps the Fathers understand unlawful desires, vanity,
ambition, and that which is commonly practised by the
world, of which the devil, in the Gospel, is called prince
and master. Pomps of the devil are ostentation,
luxury, unnecessary expenditure in things for house
or table, when by it the poor are deprived of alms,
trades-people of their money, and servants of their just
hire. Pomps of the devil are profane balls, shows,
music halls, theatres; for in these representations the
pomps of the devil appear more than in anything else.

We must, however, confess that the pomps of the
devil show themselves principally in the sensuality,
grandeur, and superfluous luxury in dress and ornament. In fact, in our days men are not exempt from
that propensity by which women are carried away to
the ruin of soul and body. O my God, this luxury in
dress—this inclination to adorn one's self—to make an
appearance—to be seen and admired, has reached such
an extravagant excess that it seems impossible for it
to go further. Were I to form a judgment of the
position of a person from the mode of dress I should
fail to distinguish a servant from his master, or a
humble citizen from a nobleman. Now the wife and
daughter of an humble artizan dress and adorn themselves as if they were wives and daughters of princes
or merchants, and the wives and daughters of trades-
men as if they were so many princesses. The minister
of God may speak against this excess—this abuse of
dress, he may show by the doctrine of the Fathers that
it is contrary to the promises made in baptism, that
these are the pomps of the devil, and that whosoever
pretends to be a Christian must absolutely renounce
them; and yet neither men or women are moved to

E

compunction or amendment, nor is the mode of dress changed, so that unless God stretch forth His omnipotent hand and inflict some severe chastisement, it will remain an evil without remedy.

In fact, if so many men and women, who lead the course of life they do, had promised at their baptism to renounce Jesus Christ, His holy doctrine, and to follow the devil, world, and all its pomps, could it have been possible for them to have been more faithful to their word? Could they have shown greater fidelity to the devil and the world? Could you, sons of men, have given signs more certain to the world of your conformity to its maxims than by that of your own conduct? And you, daughters of Eve, could you have given a testimony greater to the devil and the world, that you follow their customs, manners, and caprices? And yet you call yourselves Christians, and glory in that name. But woe to you, if hitherto you have been lovers of the world and followers of its pomps, unless you now renounce them and observe with fidelity this promise! Without that you are not Christians, nor can you hope to receive the reward promised and given to the true Christian.

Perhaps some of you may say in your heart that you did not know baptism obliged you to so much; that you knew renunciations were made in baptism of the devil, his works, and his pomps, but that you looked upon them as a part of the ceremony and not as promises and vows: indeed we never supposed that we made a vow, besides we have always kept from taking vows, so that we might have our own liberty, and live in the world, and as we are in the world we live according to its customs. If these promises oblige us to all that has been explained, we must confess that hitherto we have not observed them. What, then, are we to do? I answer: we read that Esdras, a holy and learned priest of the old law, had the book of the law of God read to the people distinctly and plainly to be understood. When, then, the people had heard the holiness of the law of God, and reflected upon the transgressions committed against it, they were filled with compunction and wept aloud, so that Esdras was constrained to tell the people to cease weeping, and to ask of God mercy and forgiveness.

Would to God that the like were to happen to you who are now listening to me! You have heard how great the promises and vows are that you made in baptism; by them you bound yourselves to renounce the devil, his works, and his pomps, and on which, in times past, you have reflected so little; and, on the other hand, being filled with remorse of conscience for the many transgressions you have committed against these promises, may it please God to excite in you an inward sorrow, and move you to true repentance and a firm resolution to amend your broken promises and vows. Yes, renew now before this sign of your redemption the solemn contract you entered into with your God on the day of your baptism, and promise faithfully to observe it until death. Yes, Satan, I renounce you for ever—I resolve to have no part with thee—sins, which are the works of the devil, I now break off from you, and with the divine assistance I will sin no more. Profane shows, balls, music halls, theatres, and luxury of dress, which are the pomps of Satan, I renounce; and You alone, O Jesus, shall henceforth be my Master, my Lord, and my God; Your divine law shall in future be my rule in all my actions, so that I may one day come to the possession of Thee in heaven.

VIII

A CHRISTIAN AFTER BAPTISM OUGHT TO LEAD A HOLY AND PERFECT LIFE.

THE observance of the promises made in baptism is not the whole duty of a Christian. His chief obligation is to lead a life like to that of Jesus Christ, holy and perfect. This is a subject most necessary to be treated of, for many forget, or do not think themselves bound, to lead a life of holiness and perfection. Holiness is by them considered a state belonging only to those in heaven, or at most, to such persons who have embraced a religious life. Whence it is they look upon persons living in the world as having a right to lead a life according to the maxims and customs of the age in which they live. Therefore, I will try to remove this veil of deception from their eyes by showing them that every Christian is called to a state of holiness and perfection.

Oftentimes you may have heard expressions similar to these: "For me it is sufficient to be saved; I will be satisfied to reach heaven, and shall not trouble myself further; I content myself by leading an ordinary life; as to the practice of certain devotions, and giving myself to the exercise of heroic virtues I do not find myself called upon to perform, I leave the practice of them to the priest and religious, who have abandoned the world, and are bound to that sort of life."

Now let us reply to each of these excuses. "For me it is sufficient to be saved." Ordinarily speaking, one who limits his salvation to that of being saved is not saved, because such an one seldom does what is necessary for his salvation; for original sin has made us weak, and unless we take a very high aim, we can

scarcely reach the mark; how, then, can you suppose
you will reach it when you take an aim so low? " I
content myself by leading an ordinary life; as to the
practice of certain devotions and the exercise of heroic
virtues, I do not find myself called upon to perform, I
leave the practice of them to the priest and religious."
I answer: then you will not attain to an ordinary life,
neither will you practise the more common virtues,
unless you aspire to the more eminent and heroic.
How many souls have fixed in their mind the exercise
of the highest and most eminent virtues, and drawn
down by the weight of their corruptible body and by
the continual warfare against their passions, have
scarcely, and that with great labour, attained to the
observance of things essentially necessary; do you
think you can be saved when you content yourselves with
so little? You say the practice of these virtues and
holiness you leave to religious. You are deceived in
thus reasoning, for every one is bound, if not actually
to be perfect, at least to strive to attain to holiness.
Whoever makes a profession of a state of life, says St.
Thomas, he is bound to fulfil all the obligations of that
state. You have embraced the state and life of a
Christian, which has annexed to it perfection; to this
you are bound and effectually to aspire after. I do not
deny but that it belongs to the religious to lead a life
more perfect, by reason of their profession, and woe to
them if they do not aim and aspire to it. Woe to
them if they do not strive to acquire that perfection to
which they are bound by vow. At the same time you
must know that it is incumbent upon you to seek and
aspire after perfection, and that by reason of your
baptism. The obligation is upon all, both religious
and laity, to do all the good they can. To all the Holy
Ghost has said: "Whatsoever thy hand is able to do,
do it earnestly." To all Jesus Christ has prescribed
holiness: "Be you, therefore, perfect, as also your
heavenly Father is perfect." We are then bound not
only to root out vice, but to plant virtues that make
the saint.

You may say that it is quite sufficient to be a Christian, as to become saints that we leave to others. If so, why not leave it to others to be Christians, renounce the grace of baptism, and have your names erased from the baptismal register? Perhaps you are scandalised at this expression, and yet it is based on truth. A Christian life is a holy life, therefore to be a Christian you must necessarily be a saint, or to holiness you must aspire. For what is a Christian? He is one who, by the infinite mercy of God, has been called and placed in the highest state, and raised to the most eminent dignity—he is one called, as you have before heard, to a participation of the divine nature, and to the marvellous society of the Eternal Father, by which he is made a son, a member and brother of Jesus Christ, and the temple of the Holy Ghost. A Christian is one signed with the arms and seal of the Divinity in his baptism, and he bears impressed upon his soul a sacred character that can never be effaced, and if saved, it will be for him his glory in heaven, if lost, his eternal ignominy and confusion in hell. A Christian is one who ceases to be what he was before—he is dead and crucified to the world, and the world to him. How can we imagine him to be otherwise than holy and perfect? The first Christians were fully persuaded of this truth; they knew well that the grace of baptism and the name of Christian imposed upon them the strict obligation of being holy and perfect. In the first ages of the Church no distinction was made between being a Christian and being a saint, for every Christian was considered a saint, and he that was not did not receive the honourable name of a Christian. This is the reason why St. Paul many times in his Epistles calls the faithful saints. "Salute Philologus and Julia, and all the saints that are with them." "But now I shall go to Jerusalem, to minister unto the saints." "To all the saints who are at Ephesus." Now, tell me were St. Paul to write to the Catholics of this place, do you think he would use the same expressions towards them? I leave it to each one to ask himself the question, and according to the reply the conscience gives, to answer. I perceive you are confused; this I say not by way of reproof, for to all the conscience has replied sanctity is far from them; and yet, if you are not saints, or, at least, trying to become saints, you cannot call yourselves true Christians, since the name of saint and Christian is one and the same thing. Again, a Christian is one consecrated to God and destined to His worship and service, therefore he is bound to do always what is well pleasing to the divine will, that is, to be perfect, consequently holy. In the old law the Jews were the chosen people of God, and for this reason they were bound to be holy. "You shall be holy men to me," and "Be ye holy, because I, the Lord your God, am holy." Now, if God required the Jews to be holy, and if He bound them by such grave precepts, how much the more so ought we Christians to believe ourselves bound to lead a life of holiness, when God has given us more abundant graces. For it is not from the bondage of Egypt He has delivered us, but from that of sin and the devil—He has led us not to the promised land, but to the glory of heaven—He has fed us not with manna, but with His own most precious body and blood—He has made Himself our Brother, our Redeemer, our Reward. To us, then, are the words to be applied: "Be ye holy, because I, the Lord your God, am holy," and because from all the infidel nations He has chosen and destined us for His divine worship.

And that these words are especially addressed to us, and that after baptism we ought to lead a life holy and perfect, listen to the words of St. Peter: "According to God that hath called you, Who is holy, be you also in all manner of conversation holy: because it is written, "You shall be holy, for I am holy." As if he were to say, if God has chosen us in preference to so many others, and given us the inestimable grace of baptism, raised us to the august dignity of Christians, that we might be consecrated to His worship; if after giving so many proofs of His love, it is but just that we should give corresponding proofs of our love by leading a life

holy and perfect, that it may be known that the choice
God has made of us is one worthy of Him. Such, according to St. Peter, is the will of God that we be holy,
a holiness that regards all times and seeks in all our
actions to honour and glorify Him. "Were a sculptor,"
says St. Augustine, "able to give a heart and communicate life to a statue that he himself had formed, to
whom ought it to direct its thoughts, give its homage and
affections, if not to the sculptor ?" Now, God has not
only given us our being, our life, but He has given us
understanding to know Him, a heart and will to love
Him. This is not all. He has separated us from an
immense multitude of beings whom He has permitted
to remain in the darkness of infidelity and heresy—He
has "called us," says St. Peter, "out of darkness into
His marvellous light ;" into the bosom of the Catholic
Church. For whom then ought we to live, if not
for the good God ! For whom shall be our intellect,
our will, our heart, if not to know and love Him, Who
has loved us so much ! Yes, to God ought to be directed
all our thoughts and affections, to Him all our worship and service. This is the end for which we were
created, that we should be holy, and by the practice of
every virtue strive to be so, this is our obligation. That
such is the will of God St. Paul expressly declares.
These are his words : " Blessed be the God and Father
of our Lord Jesus Christ, Who hath blessed us with
spiritual blessings in heavenly places in Christ, as
He chose us in Him before the foundation of the
world." And why has He chosen us ? "That we
should be holy and unspotted in His sight." The
Apostle says: " Before the creation of the world ; because
God had the intention that we should be holy—He has
chosen us in Jesus Christ, because Jesus Christ is the Holy
of Holies, and He is the source and beginning of all
sanctity." He has chosen us to " be holy and unspotted
in His sight ;" for it is not sufficient to have an external holiness, but we must have an internal holiness,
and that it be such in the eyes of God, Who sees and
penetrates the heart.
   But what I wish you principally to reflect upon is

that the Apostle is not satisfied with any kind of holiness, but that which is perfect, "holy, and unspotted, and blameless." And the Apostle makes this reflection to remove the false pretext of some Christians of being just and holy only by halves. No; it is necessary that you be entirely holy and perfect. Upon this point, however, understand me rightly. When I say that by reason of baptism you are bound to lead a life holy, unspotted, and blameless, I do not mean a life exempt from all venial faults (for this cannot be unless by a special assistance from God), nor do I mean that you are to work miracles, or that you are to be in a continual state of contemplation, ecstacies, or that you are to practise virtues the most eminent and heroic, which are to be found only in some special chosen souls. But I do mean that a Christian, by virtue of the promises made in baptism, is bound to renounce the devil, his works and his pomps, is bound to perform good and holy works, honour God, and to Him direct all his actions, loving Him above all things, with his whole heart, mind, and strength, and his neighbour as himself. And this not by words only, but in deed and in truth. In one word not to be wanting in those essential things prescribed by the divine and evangelical law. In these, with the grace of God, every one can, and ought to be holy, perfect, and blameless, and this cannot be, as some erroneously suppose, by observing one thing and transgressing in another.

And since this is a subject of great importance, the Apostle St. James has treated it with words most appropriate. He proposes, then, what I ought to say to him who observes all the law and breaks one of its precepts: "Whosoever shall keep the whole law, but offend in one point, is become guilty of all." Here the Apostle takes away all hope for those who think themselves good Christians, when they break the law in one particular point, providing they observe the rest. It is frequently said by persons in our days: "I have no difficulty in observing all the precepts of the law, but I cannot bring myself to the observance of the seventh—

not to steal. Necessity, and also that I may lead a life more suitable to my station, obliges me sometimes to make use of what belongs to others." There is not a precept more beautiful nor more holy than that which forbids us to take revenge of our enemy, and commands us to love those that hate us; and we hear persons declaring themselves unable to keep this precept. " I," another will say, " do no murder, and he who commits it must be a brute." " I do not steal," says another; " I do not dishonour God by profaning His holy name; but the Sixth Commandment, and that alone, I do not observe with exactness. Ah ! we are made of flesh and blood, and God will have compassion on me if I fail to observe this." No, He will condemn you with all the workers of iniquity. The words of the Apostle are clear and distinct. He speaks of a man that offends in one point, as you offend, and declares you guilty of all. True it is that if you break more than one precept you commit a greater number of sins, and are more culpable before God, and consequently your punishment will be greater in hell. But it is also true, that one mortal sin alone is sufficient to deprive us of the grace of God, make us His enemies, and we shall be punished for all eternity, even as those who had broken all God's precepts. You, then, being baptised, and wishing to bear worthily the name of a Christian, ought to lead a holy and perfect life, and one blameless before God; all, without any exception, are bound to observe the entire moral law. The obligation of leading a holy, perfect, and blameless life before God may be shown from your having been baptised, and from the motive and design God had in calling you to so eminent a state. With what greater facility can it be also shown from the character you have acquired by baptism ! Many times since I began these discourses on baptism, you have heard what this character of a Christian brings with it, nor will it be out of place to repeat it again. You have been made children of God, brothers of Jesus Christ, and the temple of the Holy Ghost. You are sons of God, and God is your Father, and you call Him by this endear-

ing name every day—" Our Father who art in heaven,"
and to Him you have recourse in all your wants. And
can it be possible that you do not wish to lead a life
holy and blameless, when it is possible for you to conform yourselves and imitate Him ? Oh, yes : " Be
perfect, as your heavenly Father is perfect." " Be ye
therefore followers of God, as most dear children."
You are brothers of Christ, and what purity of morals
and holiness of life ought you to lead so as not to
degenerate from so illustrious a character.

Finally, you are the temple of the Holy Ghost, and
oh ! that I had time to make known to you the excellency of this dignity, this illustrious character, this
nobility of your soul and body, in which the divine
spirit deigns to dwell. If I had time to place before
you what holiness ought necessarily to be in you that
you might in some way correspond to a privilege so
illustrious! But you ought to be convinced that
no thought or affection should be in you unworthy
of that God, Who dwells within you, and Who has
given you this distinctive character of being His sons,
brothers and temple, and Who has adorned your soul
with His grace, clothing you with the white robe of
baptismal innocence, and this you ought to carry without stain before the tribunal of Jesus Christ. Whence
it is your life ought to be pure and holy until death.

But tell me, have you up to the present time led a
life holy and blameless, as you promised to do at the
sacred font ? When death comes you will have to
present yourselves before Jesus Christ at the particular
judgment, accompanied by your works, be they good or
bad, as the Apostle says: " For their works follow them ;"
also accompanied by your guardian angel and the devil.
The former will present your good works ; the latter,
your evil deeds, of which he will have kept an exact
and faithful account. When this shall come to pass,
tell me what does your conscience say ? will you be
able to present a number of works good and meritorious ? or an immense number of evil and sinful
ones ? Will you carry before that dread tribunal the

white robe of your baptismal innocence, without spot or
stain, or covered with filthiness and defilement. The
brethren of Joseph having taken his coat and dipped it
in the blood of a kid, sent it to their father, saying :
" This we have found, see whether it be thy son's coat
or not." What Joseph's brethren did to deceive their
father, Jacob, the devil will do to induce Jesus Christ
to condemn the soul to hell. "Most just Judge," he
will say, "see whether it be Thy son's coat or not. This
garment so filthy, so defiled ; see if this is the white
robe You clothed him with in baptism, with the obligation of presenting it to You without stain. You gave
him the white and beautiful garment, and he has dyed
and defiled it with the blood of the oppressed poor—
robbed so many of their innocence by detraction and
calumny. Behold it defiled with immodesties, in which
he has lived immersed ; can You distinguish by these
marks the garment adorned with Thy grace, and which
every Christian ought to possess ? The wicked and
immoral life he has led ; is that the pure and holy life
which an adopted son ought to lead ? Is that the
obedience he has shown to Your commands ? Is that
the fidelity with which he has kept those promises?
He promised to renounce me, Your and his enemy, and
yet he has been most prompt and ready to obey my
commands. It suffced me to give the least sign by my
suggestions, and he immediately complied with my
wish. He promised to renounce my works and my
pomps, and yet I have had a most faithful follower of
them in him. There has not been a maxim of the
corrupt world which he did not willingly embrace. He
was always to be found in the midst of those whose
conversation was dangerous, and who had gone wrong
in faith and in morals. His mind was filled with the
thought of unlawful objects ; his will carried away by
unchaste desires ; in a word, his whole life has been a
continual chain of offences against Thy divine majesty.
Condemn him, then, most just Judge, to hell, for such
his offences deserve."

Should there be any one present whose conscience

accuses him either in part or in all of these reprehensions made by the devil before the judgment seat of Jesus Christ, what else can he expect but the pronouncing of the sentence of eternal damnation for having been grievously wanting in his profession of a Christian, and for having so degenerated from being a son of God, and for having so often violated the promises so solemnly made ? But if, now your conscience reproves you for having led a perverse life, do you wish to persevere in that course until death, and then go forth to receive that sentence of woe ?. Ah, no. "Enter not into judgment with thy servant, O Lord." Before thou callest us, O Lord, to give an account of our mis-spent life, deign to show us Thy mercy, and grant us pardon and forgiveness. "Judge of justice, hear my prayer; spare me, Lord, in mercy spare, ere the reckoning day appear." We confess, O Lord, that we have too often been wanting in our profession as Christians; too often have we led a life wholly unworthy of the name of Thy sons; too often have we violated the promises which we made to Thee, and thus merited Thy just chastisements ; but You are a God of mercy and goodness, and, therefore, cannot reject a contrite and humble heart; hear us then, and turn not away Thy face from us, since we now resolve, with Thine assistance, to lead a holy and perfect life, such as becomes Christians, and to wash away the stains from our souls in Thy precious blood by a sorrowful confession ; so that we may appear before Thy tribunal cleansed, and receive the reward given to the clean of heart.

IX.

WHAT A CHRISTIAN OUGHT TO DO TO LEAD A HOLY AND PERFECT LIFE.

THOUGH many things have been said in the instructions I have given you on baptism regarding the obligations of a Christian, and the holy life he ought to lead after baptism, nothing, however, has yet been said on what the one or the other implies. Therefore I will endeavour in this instruction to explain with all possible exactness and clearness what the obligations of a Christian are, and how they are to be fulfilled, so that he may lead a holy and perfect life. Three things, according to holy Scripture, are laid down for the Christian to do. The first regards Jesus Christ; the second, our neighbour; and the third, ourselves.

"As many of you," says St. Paul, "as have been baptised in Christ, have put on Christ." The interior and spiritual life of a Christian should be a copy and a continual imitation of that of Jesus Christ. He is our Model, and our life ought to be conformable to His if we desire to be saints. You have been told that holiness should be the character of every true Christian. Holiness is not only for him who has embraced a state of life, of which much consideration should be given before making the choice, since our salvation may depend upon it. No: holiness is necessary for every state of life, as explained in the former instruction. Now as we have to choose some one as a model for our imitation, it would be impossible for us to take one more excellent than that of Jesus Christ. He is the beloved Son in Whom the Father is well pleased, and He it is Whom the Eternal Father has proposed as a model for our imitation. " This is my beloved Son in Whom I am well pleased."

Jesus Christ being then the Pattern Man Whom we ought to imitate, and to Whom we ought to conform our lives, it remains for us to see in what way this is to be done. Man has three principal faculties—that of thinking, speaking, and doing. A Christian, then, should conform himself to Jesus Christ in these three things. He must, then, think and have the same sentiments and form the same judgments that Jesus Christ had with regard to those things that are profitable to the soul, and reject those that are injurious. This is what the Apostle St. Paul teaches, and his words are: " Let this mind be in you which was also in Jesus Christ, in Whom are hid all the treasures of wisdom and knowledge." Now what did Jesus Christ think of the things the world esteems so much? What were His sentiments—His judgments in regard of those things called by the world riches, glory, dignities, and honours? He declared them to be vanity, emptiness, and nothingness, and that all these united together are incapable of satisfying the heart of man. If we speak of pleasure and delights, of joys and gladness, such as worldlings seek after with so much eagerness, the sentiments and judgment of Jesus Christ were the same as He formed of the things of this world. He looked upon them as so many fatal enchantments, employed by the devil to amuse the souls of miserable mortals; like a sweet but deadly poison they corrupt the heart and cause it to lose all relish for things spiritual. Whence it was He pronounced a malediction against the rich: " Woe to you that are rich." On the other hand, a blessing to the poor and to those who are detached from the world: " Blessed are the poor." Whence it was He uttered those terrible words against all who pass their time in vain delights: " Woe to you that laugh, for you shall mourn and weep." To those who weep and are afflicted He says: " Blessed are they that weep now, for they shall laugh." These were the sentiments of Jesus Christ—how different from those of the followers of the world! By the world it is esteemed as folly and weakness of mind the placing of glory in humiliation, riches in poverty, and joy in affliction and sorrow. The world calls those happy whose birth, title, position, and wealth afford them an opportunity of being over others, and of making a display in the world; nor can it be induced to believe that poverty, humiliation, and affliction are profitable to a Christian. Moreover, the followers of this world submit with difficulty to the ordinary condition in which they are placed, and sometimes accuse providence of partiality towards others whom they see raised above themselves. Such are the sentiments and judgments of worldlings, and they are entirely different from those of Jesus Christ.

From which we must conclude that the one or the other is deceived. That Jesus Christ could be deceived would be the greatest blasphemy a Christian could possibly be guilty of, in Whom is the wisdom of the eternal Father, Who cannot deceive or be deceived. Therefore His sentiments and judgments are just. If, then, you think as worldlings think, your sentiments are false; and if so, why do you not abandon them, and embrace those of Jesus Christ? Why do you judge things profitable to you which He declared injurious? Change your sentiments, and if at baptism you put on Jesus Christ, and, as it is your duty, propose to imitate Him: "Let this mind be in you which was also in Jesus Christ."

But for a Christian to be holy and perfect, he must not only think as Jesus Christ thought, but he must also speak as He spoke. If we, according to the Gospel, are to be judged or condemned by our words: "For by thy words thou shalt be justified, and by thy words thou shalt be condemned,"—you will see how important it is to regulate them according to the divine model.

But what were the conversations and words of Jesus Christ? It will suffice to read the Gospel in which they are recorded, and you will see that they were in accordance with the sentiments of His heart. His whole occupation was in seeking the glory of His Eternal Father and the salvation of souls, for which end He came into the world, and to this holy end He directed all His discourses. If you follow Him to the Synagogue or Temple, places appointed to explain the law and the prophets, you will see that He spoke only of things spiritual and divine. Follow Him into the desert or upon the mount when He was instructing the people and His disciples, and you will hear from His lips only words of eternal life. What more? Enter into those houses where He went to eat bread, and you will find that then He took an occasion of giving instruction. In the house of Martha, so divine was His discourse, that her sister Mary was filled with the love of God, and rapt in ecstacy, so that she was unable to separate herself from Him. In a word, His words and conversation were, at all times and in all places, holy.

From this fact you have to learn that your conversation, your words, ought to be edifying, if you wish to imitate your divine Master.

You have to avoid those conversations, those circles where are uttered the most pernicious maxims—where religion and piety are derided—where modesty and bashfulness are jeered at.

You have to avoid those "evil communications," which, says St. Paul, "corrupt good manners." For it is not lawful for a Christian to listen to or speak of things disedifying or unprofitable. The first Christians never spoke of things profane, unless to despise them. Occupied, as they were, in the important affair of their salvation, they never met together unless to consult upon the means most opportune for that end. They were penetrated with a most lively sense of the grace of faith and baptism, which they had received, and ceased not to proclaim the infinite mercy of God for having deigned to do so much for them, and their conversation was one continual act of praise and thanksgiving, "teaching," says the Apostle, "and admonishing one another in psalms, hymns, and spiritual canticles."

F

The imitation of Jesus Christ to Whom we ought to conform ourselves ends not in thinking and speaking as Jesus Christ thought and spoke, but we must also work as He worked, that is to say, with the same end and spirit. This is the command He gave to the Apostles just before His death: " I have given you an example, that as I have done to you so you do also." Since, then, every thought and every word of our blessed Lord were directed to the one end, the glory of His Eternal Father, and the bringing back to the right path all who·had unhappily gone astray—to the same end tended all His works—to this all His anxieties, journeys, fatigues, preaching, and miracles. Having fixed in His mind these two great objects, He sought not His own esteem or advantage—He did not desire the punishment of His enemies, but their pardon—He amassed not riches, but despised them. In a word humility, sweetness, and charity was the soul of all His. operations. These are the examples Jesus Christ has left us, and these we ought to imitate, working according to the impulse of His spirit, and according to His holy end. We are not to imitate, I do not say those false Christians whose actions are manifestly culpable, or those actions that are approved of by the world and its followers, which can never be directed to the glory of God ; as, for example, balls, theatres, and other such dangerous amusements, but the actions of those who have no other end in view than that of their own interest, vanity, and ambition. True the labourer works and fatigues himself, but has no other end than that of gaining his daily bread—the tradesman applies himself to his business but that he may better his position and amass wealth—the courtier serves with assiduity his prince that he may gain favours and be rewarded. Now, as in these actions neither religion or God has any part, for each one works according to the impulse of the passion that rules and governs him, this alone he consults, this alone he has for his object and end. All these works are lost, the reward of them they receive in this world, but they cannot hope for any in the next.

If, then, you wish your works to be meritorious for
eternal life, you must be animated with the spirit of
Jesus Christ, and like Him you must direct them to
the divine glory. Thus you will be fulfilling your obligation, which is to imitate Jesus Christ in thoughts,
words, and works.

The second thing to be done by a Christian in order
that he may lead a holy life, and which the grace of
baptism requires, is that which regards his neighbour,
towards whom he ought to have the spirit of charity.
This charity, this fraternal love, is the true character
and proper virtue of a Christian. This the Apostles,
instructed by Jesus Christ, went forth to preach with
such zeal the union of hearts and the charity of all the
followers of Christ as most necessary. St. Paul com-
pares the union that ought to exist among Christians
to that of the members of the human body. See the
union there is between the members of the body, how
one assists the other, so ought there to be a union and
charity between us. The Apostle goes further and says
that we ought to have the greatest concern in keeping
"the unity of the spirit in the bond of peace," in holy
charity—because the religion is one—"one body, one
spirit, and one hope, one Lord, one faith, one baptism,
one God, Who is the Father of all." According, then,
to the Apostle fraternal unity and charity are necessary
for the obtaining of that happiness which is the hope
and consolation of the true Christian. Woe to us if we
break it : we cannot then have a firm hope—we cannot
participate in the benefits of baptism—we are no longer
living members of the mystical body of the Church, of
which Christ is the Head—we have not God for our
Father. From this you will see how prejudicial is the
want of charity.

The beautiful character and effects of charity the Apostle
St. Paul describes: "It is," he says, "patient, kind, envieth
not, dealeth not perversely, is not puffed up, not ambitious, seeketh not her own, is not provoked to anger,
thinketh no evil, rejoiceth not in iniquity, but rejoiceth
with the truth, beareth all things, endureth all things."

How beautiful is the character and how holy are the effects of charity. And, indeed, show me a Christian in whom charity reigns and you will see in him all the above-named qualities; he is not harsh with anyone, nor proud, but to all he will be humble and kind; he will not seek his own interest, nor will he envy the good of another; he will not judge evil of anyone, but good of all, and will assist all in as much as he is able. Such ought we to be towards our neighbour, if we desire to be perfect, and fulfil our obligations as Christians.

In the third place, a Christian, in order to lead a holy life, which the grace of baptism imposes upon him, must have the spirit of mortification and penance. This is what gives the finishing touch, and terminates the great work of a Christian life—it assimilates the Christian to Jesus Christ, Who was a man of sorrows and acquainted with grief, and whose life on earth was one of continual suffering. He commenced at the stable of Bethlehem, and terminated it on Calvary, to teach us that mortification and suffering is the foundation of His religion, without which we are not Christians. This glorious title is not obtained unless by subduing the passions, curbing the liberty of the senses, and crucifying the flesh—"Always bearing about in our body the mortification of Jesus, that the life also of Jesus may be made manifest in our mortal flesh." All that forms the false joy, pleasure, and diversion of worldlings ought to be far removed from a follower of Christ, and afflictions and crosses ought to be his joy and contentment. This, according to the teaching of the Fathers, is what is signified by the making of the crosses upon the child in the ceremony of baptism—they are intended to give us to understand that the life of a Christian is one of mortification and trial. The cross is also made upon the head of the baptised, because the head is the seat of reason and judgment, by which things are esteemed or despised, and that he ought not to value or love aught but the cross. "God forbid," says the Apostle, "that I should glory, save in the cross of our Lord Jesus

Christ, in Whom the world is crucified in me, and I to the world." Yes, the object of our delight, our joy, and our glory is to be the cross, for everything else that is in the world is nothing but vanity and vexation of spirit. The cross is made upon the shoulders of the Christian to teach him that he must always carry it, and in it he is to put all his strength and courage. If misfortunes overtake you, if death deprives you of your dearest friends, if sickness obliges you to keep your bed, if the unfaithfulness of a friend, or an accident, deprive you of your substance, and bring ruin upon your home, where can you find strength to support yourselves under so great an adversity, or to bear it with patience and resignation? In the cross, and there it will be found.

Perhaps some of you say in your heart that this doctrine exacts too much from you, and that the following of it would oblige you to lead a life too austere and severe. To which I reply: you must undeceive yourselves and be fully persuaded that the life of a Christian ought not to be any other than that of mortification, a denial of himself, and a continual warfare. He must bear the cross upon his tongue, so that it speaks nothing unseemly, slanderous, or blasphemous; upon his eyes, that they be not fixed upon the vanity of this world, nor upon unlawful objects; upon his mouth, that it be not given to gluttony or intemperance. A cross, in a word, upon all the senses of the body and the powers of the soul, so that the disorderly passions be restrained. And here I speak not of an external cross, but internal, that rejoices in sufferings and afflictions. The greatest happiness that can be conferred upon a Christian in this life is to have a cross and to know how to make good use of it. God cannot confer upon us a more singular grace than that of making us partakers of His sufferings; this is a means most efficacious in sanctifying and leading us to the possession of eternal glory. God has made the cross a bridge over which His elect pass to heaven. The glory of heaven is the fruit of the cross of Jesus Christ. He has gained that glory by His passion and death, and the right of gaining the same glory He has made over to us; and God will give it to us if we imitate His divine Son in mortification and in the carrying of the cross.

You have now heard what a Christian ought to do so that he may lead a holy life. It consists in imitating Jesus Christ in His thoughts, words, and actions, in a love for his neighbour, and in embracing mortification and self-denial. And it now behoveth you to examine your conscience, that you may know whether hitherto you have fulfilled the obligations imposed upon you as Christians; and, if by the light given you from above, you see that you have been wanting, strive henceforth, with the assistance of the divine grace, to conform your thoughts, words, and actions to those of Jesus Christ; to have a love for your neighbour, and to embrace with courage a life of mortification and penance, so that after having led a holy life on earth, you may be made worthy of the reward in heaven.

X.

THE practice of our holy mother the Church has always been to administer the Sacrament of Confirmation to the faithful after baptism. On that sacrament I intend to instruct you.

That Confirmation is one of the seven sacraments instituted by Jesus Christ for the benefit of our soul, it is not necessary to occupy your time in adducing arguments to prove, because it is a Catholic truth, registered in holy Scripture, proved by the constant tradition of the Fathers, and confirmed by the Council of Trent, declaring: that "if any one saith that the confirmation of those who have been baptised is an idle ceremony, and not rather a true and proper sacrament; or, that of old it was nothing more than a kind of catechism, whereby they who were near adolescence, gave an account of their faith in the face of the Church; let him be anathema." Therefore, my instruction will be confined to the explanation of the Sacrament of Confirmation; what the effects are that it produces in our soul; the desire every Christian ought to have to receive it: lastly, the dispositions required in us that we may receive it with profit.

"Confirmation is a sacrament of the New Law, instituted by Jesus Christ, in which, by the imposition of hands, the anointing with the sacred chrism, and by the words said by the bishop, we receive an increase of grace and power—a particular strength; so that we may confess, defend, and sustain the faith of Jesus Christ on all occasions in spite of every obstacle, temptation, or danger." For the validity of every sacrament three things are required, viz.: matter, form, and minister. With regard to the minister, it is certain that a bishop only is the ordinary minister of this sacrament. In some urgent and extraordinary cases, by a special permission and delegation of the holy See, a priest may be the extraordinary minister. Should, however, a person receive this sacrament from a priest who has not received this special faculty from the holy See to administer it, the sacrament would be null and void.

The matter for this sacrament is the imposition of hands and the anointing with chrism; the form, the words used by the bishop in administering this sacrament. There are many theological questions concerning the matter and form of this sacrament, the deciding of which belongs not to me, but only that of instructing you. The rule for all who have not been confirmed is —that they should know what is required for the validity of this sacrament, that they ought not to satisfy themselves by coming before the bishop and having their foreheads anointed with the sacred chrism and the form of words said over them, but they ought to be present at the beginning of the imposition of hands, when the bishop imposes hands over those to be confirmed, and prays that God would send down upon them His divine Spirit and Its sevenfold gifts; also they ought to remain in the church until the bishop has finished the prayers after the anointing and given the solemn blessing.

I said the matter of this Sacrament of Confirmation is the imposition of hands and the anointing with chrism. It will be good for you to know from whence the word chrism is derived. It is a word borrowed from the Greeks, and it is composed of oil of olives and balsam, and it is consecrated on Holy Thursday by the bishop. The oil of olives expresses the plenitude of grace, through the Holy Ghost, which is poured into others from Christ the Head; and the balsam is a substance the odour of which is most agreeable, and it has the property of preserving whatever is anointed with it from corruption; and it signifies two things: firstly, the fragrance which every Christian ought to diffuse by the practice of virtues, so that the sweet odour of Jesus Christ may be to the edification of our neighbour, according to the Apostle "We are unto God the good odour of Jesus Christ;" secondly, it expresses the incorruption of morals which ought to shine forth in every Christian, who, being dead to the world through baptism, is embalmed with the sacred chrism that he may be protected from the contagion of sin, and never allow himself to be corrupted by disorderly passions or by the world and its false maxims.

The anointing with chrism on the forehead by the bishop in the form of a cross is because it is that part of the body that presents itself to everyone, and it is that we should bear in mind that the cross of Jesus Christ ought to be inseparable from us and that it ought to be our sign, our glory, and never to be deterred by shame or fear from professing ourselves openly to be followers of Jesus Christ crucified. "For he that shall be ashamed of me and of my words, of him the Son of Man shall be ashamed when He shall come in His majesty."

Finally, the person confirmed, when he is anointed receives a slap on the cheek from the hand of the bishop, who says at the same time: "Peace be with you." This is done to express what every Christian should be prepared to do, viz.: to suffer with a spirit unconquerable whatever injury, affront, suffering, or adversity he may have to endure for the name of Jesus Christ and the love of His faith ; and by doing so that peace will be given such as the world cannot give— that true peace and tranquillity of spirit which will be an earnest of that eternal peace that God has promised in heaven.

This now brings me to speak of the wonderful effects produced in our soul by the Sacrament of Confirmation. These effects are two: it impresses a character upon the soul and increases sanctifying grace, giving the soul a special strength, so that it may fulfil all the duties of a good Christian, and on all occasions make a good confession of the faith of Jesus Christ.

The character impressed upon the soul by this sacrament is a sign, a mark which can never be effaced. In baptism we receive a character, a sign that we are Christians. In confirmation the character given is a mark that distinguishes the Christian from all others, and it is a sign that we are soldiers of Jesus Christ, always prepared to confess openly, defend, and maintain the faith and His sacred name. And since this character is indelible, it cannot, therefore, be ever effaced from the soul; nor can confirmation be received more than once, so that whosoever should presume to receive it a second time would sin grievously.

The second effect produced by confirmation, not, however by its nature, but by an ecclesiastical precept, is a spiritual affinity, which consists in a certain spiritual relationship between him who confirms, the person confirmed, his father and mother, and him who places his hand upon him. For this reason, a father or mother ought not to be sponsors for their own children, a husband for his wife, or a wife for her husband, for there would arise a spiritual affinity that would immediately cause a matrimonial impediment. Neither is it advisable to have young people for sponsors at confirmation.

But the effect most wonderful and most advantageous to us is that confirmation produces an increase of sanctifying grace in our soul, giving us power and strength, so that we may overcome every difficulty, every obstacle that we may encounter in the leading of a true Christian life, especially that of confessing the faith and name of Jesus Christ, by which alone we can be saved. For the better understanding of this effect, represent to yourself a child just born. What has this child acquired by its birth? Existence, and nothing more. This existence requires food, an increase of strength, so that by degrees the child may grow to man's estate, have sufficient strength to support, defend, and maintain itself. Now unless the child receive nourishment it will not increase, but will always remain small, weak, delicate, incapable of supporting and defending itself, and in danger of premature death.

The same may be said of us with regard to the spiritual life of the soul. When we are baptised we are regenerated in Jesus Christ, that is, we are born to grace and regain the spiritual life of the soul lost by sin. If, after baptism, we lose this spiritual life, we regain it through the sacrament of penance by a good confession. But what are we after baptism or penance? We are children just born, according to the words of St. Peter, "as new-born babes;" we have simply acquired spiritual life, and this is a great benefit conferred on us by God; but if this spiritual life receives no increase, no strength, how can it be preserved? We shall continue to be, as the Apostle says, weak children, exposed to the danger of being tossed about by every wind of doctrine, and lose the life of the soul. On the other hand, if we receive an increase of strength, by degrees we grow to be perfect Christians, imitators of Jesus Christ, capable of defending ourselves from every danger until we all meet into the unity of faith, and of the knowledge of the Son of God, unto a perfect man, unto the measure of the age of the fulness of Christ.

The Council of Florence, speaking of confirmation, says: in this sacrament is given the Holy Ghost, as given to the apostles on the day of Pentecost, in order that Christians may be strengthened and fully confirmed in the faith, to confess and glorify the name of Jesus Christ, whence also, no doubt, originated the very name of confirmation. The words of the council are worthy of our consideration, for it says, the Holy Ghost is given to the faithful as it was to the apostles. Then to understand the effect produced in us by this sacrament it will be sufficient to consider what it did for the apostles. We know that before the coming down of the Holy Ghost upon them the apostles were timid, weak, even at the time of our Lord's Passion they immediately fled away in place of defending Him, and St. Peter, terrified at the voice of a weak woman, denied, not once, nor twice only, but a third time, that he was a disciple of our Lord Jesus Christ. After the resurrection they all remained shut up at home for fear of the Jews. But on the day of Pentecost, so great was the virtue of the Holy Ghost, with which they were all replenished, that they went forth from the upper chamber with a courage invincible, and far from being afraid of the Jews, preached the gospel of Jesus Christ with such energy and in so many different tongues that St. Peter alone at his first sermon converted three thousand; at his second, five thousand; and despising every threat, every danger of imprisonment and death, the apostles went forth to preach the faith, not only in Jerusalem, but to the whole world, and converted not only the poor and ignorant, but the learned and great ones of the earth. Far from being afraid or vacillating for one moment, they counted it their glory to suffer for the love of Jesus Christ, and give, as they did afterwards, their lives for the faith.

These are some of the wonderful effects wrought by the Holy Ghost in the apostles, and these are the effects the Sacrament of Confirmation can produce in us; for this sacrament increases in us the grace of God, strengthens our faith, enables us to live as Christians ought to live; it fortifies us so that we may easily overcome temptation and endure every torment, even death itself, without wavering in the faith. The only difference is that the apostles received visibly the Holy Ghost, in the form of parted tongues, and we receive it invisibly. Nevertheless, we receive it with its manifold gifts, viz.: Wisdom, Understanding, Counsel, Fortitude, Knowledge, Piety, and the Fear of the Lord. Who, then, is there amongst us that will not hold in great esteem this Sacrament of Confirmation? Who is there amongst us who has received it will refuse to thank God for so great a benefit? Who is there who has not received it, and who ought to do so, will not be filled with the desire of receiving it? True it is, the necessity of this sacrament is not so great that without receiving it we cannot obtain salvation, at the same time it is true that should anyone wilfully neglect to receive it, it would be difficult to excuse such an one from mortal sin, since such negligence could scarcely be separated from a contempt of the sacrament.

A Christian not confirmed, although he has the grace

of God, is like a soldier without arms, and if he goes into battle he runs the risk of being wounded or killed, for he has not wherewith to defend himself. So one may be in the grace of God, but as man's life on earth is a continual warfare, if he goes into the battle of life unarmed, it is extremely difficult for him to defend himself from the three great enemies—the devil, the world, and the flesh. A traveller may enjoy the friendship of his sovereign, but if he is overtaken by robbers unarmed, it will not be easy for him to save his money or preserve his life. So a Christian may be in the grace of God, but if in the way of his eternal salvation he is overtaken by his enemies unarmed, not having been confirmed, it will be easy for them to deprive him of the spiritual life of his soul. In the history of the Church we read of one Novatus who neglected confirmation, the enemy took such a possession of him that in the time of persecution he became weak and apostatised.

True, there is not in our day the persecution like that of the first ages of the Church; there are not now tyrants to force us to deny the faith under the pain of martyrdom; but it is true there are in these our days persecutions and persecutors of another kind, equally dangerous as those in bygone days. In our time we have a diabolical literature—books scattered broadcast, filled with the poison of error and licentiousness, lending all their enchanting powers to destroy faith and religion; we have philosophers, libertines, without morals, without shame, whose whole study is to corrupt the mind and morals of others by deriding piety and devotion, by speaking against the frequentation of the sacraments, and thus they seek to draw people from the practice of religion, and by their despising the word of God and by reviling the truths of religion, sacred things, the Church and its ministers, they hope to engender contempt of them, and disbelief in all. Besides these we have the world persecuting us with its false maxims, its corrupt customs, its bad example; we have the devil who persecutes us with his wicked suggestions, going about like a roaring lion, seeking to devour. Now we shall not be able to resist him, says St. Peter, without being well strengthened in the faith. Finally, we have the flesh, and our corrupt passions and inclinations persecuting us in a thousand different ways. And without great grace, without that assistance, that particular strength; without those spiritual arms which God gives in the Sacrament of Confirmation, how shall we be able as good soldiers to fight and defend ourselves from so many persecutions, so many enemies, external and internal? How shall we be able to resist so many temptations—to overcome human respect, and keep ourselves firm in faith and morals? Oh, then, put on the armour of God, that you may be able to stand against the deceits of the devil!

Amongst those who have received confirmation, some may be found who say how is it we have not discovered the good effects represented; yea, after confirmation we find ourselves as we were before, that is, weak, vicious, and miserable? Alas! know you not the reason! It is because you have received confirmation without the proper dispositions, or, after you had them, you have been careless and negligent of the grace of that sacrament. This is the reason why so many persons confirmed have so little faith and religion, and their morals are so bad. If good seed is strewn upon bad ground, or ground badly tilled, or neglected by the sower, it will not produce good fruit; the fault is not the seed, but the negligence of the sower. So it is with the grace of this sacrament. If it does not produce the good effect, the fault is not the sacrament's, but his who receives it.

With regard to those who have received this sacrament with bad dispositions, and perhaps with mortal sin upon the soul, or who have been careless and neglectful, and since none of these can receive this sacrament again, is there no hope or remedy for them? Oh, yes, there is a remedy for them. If they received confirmation in bad dispositions, it is for them to dispose themselves for a good confession, a true conversion to God, and then the grace of the sacrament will spring up and produce in them the good effects that it would have done at the time it was received. If they have been careless, let them be so no longer ; but take the advice of the Apostle, " Neglect not the grace that is in them, which was given them by the imposition of hands ;" and this grace well preserved will produce all its good effects. To those who are not confirmed, that they may be properly disposed to receive the sacrament, I will say a few words on the dispositions they ought to have with respect to both body and soul.

As to the body, you ought to be present in the church with reverence and respect, dressed as it becomes decency and propriety, in all simplicity and modesty, without pride, vanity, or ambition, and especially with the forehead clean and uncovered, putting back the hair so that it may not impede the anointing.

Of the soul, the first disposition is baptism, because this sacrament is the door that opens to us the other sacraments. Then it is necessary to be in the state of grace, that is, without mortal sin upon the soul, for confirmation is one of the living sacraments, and therefore to receive it in mortal sin is a sacrilege. Thirdly, prayer, after the example of the apostles, who, waiting the coming down of the Holy Ghost, persevered in prayer. Also, you must know the articles of faith, the principal mysteries, the Lord's Prayer, Hail Mary, and I Believe, the Commandments of God and the Church, the effects of this sacrament, and the more important obligations of a Christian. For this reason children ought not to be confirmed before they are seven years of age, that is, the use of reason. For it is difficult for a child of too tender an age to dispose itself as it ought, and also for the danger there is of a child forgetting that it has been confirmed, and so receive it a second time. We except the case when there is a legitimate reason, as there would be when a child is in danger of death, or when living at a great distance from the bishop, and might have to remain a long time before receiving the sacrament—then it would not be necessary to have completed seven years.

These are the dispositions to receive with fruit the Sacrament of Confirmation, to the end that we may be confirmed in·faith, live as Christians ought to live, and obtain our eternal salvation. Let us remember that this sacrament, like that of baptism, places an indelible character upon our souls; if, then, we should have the misfortune to be lost, and placed in the company of the wicked angels, of so many infidels, who received not from God the graces we have received with these marks upon our soul, these signs of Christians and soldiers of Jesus Christ, they will be for us an eternal confusion; therefore let us so live as to avoid so great an evil by profiting by the grace of God and placing our soul in security.

XI

ON THE INSTITUTION OF THE HOLY EUCHARIST.

I NOW undertake to explain the Sacrament of the Eucharist, destined to strengthen in us the spiritual life received by means of confession—a Sacrament the most august, the most holy—a Sacrament that contains the most abstruse mysteries of the divine wisdom of God— the greatest device of His omnipotence—the most loving pledge of His goodness—a Sacrament, in fine, in which Jesus Christ has, according to the expression of the Prophet, " made a remembrance of His wonderful works, being a merciful and gracious Lord, He hath given food to them that fear Him." And this we shall see in this and in the instructions that follow.

What is the Sacrament of the Eucharist ? The Sacrament of the Holy Eucharist is the true Body and Blood of Jesus Christ, under the appearances of bread and wine. This Sacrament, as you know, was instituted by Jesus Christ at the Last Supper, which, the day before His passion, He made with His disciples. The Evangelists tell us that Jesus Christ, after having eaten of the paschal lamb, which was a figure of this Sacrament, arose from the table to wash the apostles' feet, then He sat down at the table, took bread and blessed, and broke, and gave to His disciples, and said : " Take ye, and eat : This is My Body." And taking the chalice, He gave thanks, and gave to them, saying : " Drink ye all of this, for this is My Blood." Then it was that the consecration of the Holy Eucharist first took place. The words pronounced by Jesus Christ wrought invisibly the great miracle of changing the bread and wine into His own Body and Blood. And since this miracle was to be perpetuated in the Church, Jesus Christ gave to the apostles,

G

and in their person the bishops and priests, the power to do what He had done to the end of the world, saying to them: "Do this in commemoration of Me." That is, I give you the power to do what you have seen Me do; bless in My name the bread and wine, say the words I have said, and these words which you will pronounce in My name, will have in your mouth the same power they have in Mine. Thus Jesus Christ commanded the apostles, ordaining them, at the same moment, priests of the New Testament, and prescribing the matter and form to be used. Hence in the same manner in which this Sacrament was instituted, it is done also at the time of the holy Mass. The priest takes the same matter as used by Jesus Christ, that is, bread and wine—pronounces the same words used by Jesus Christ, which constitute the form of the Sacrament. This is My body, this is My blood, and in virtue of these words is renewed every day upon our altars this adorable Mystery. Mystery called in Scripture and by the Fathers: Mystery of Faith. And with great reason, because there is not another mystery that exercises our faith so much as this by the union of so many wonders that are united in it. Call to mind, in the brief explanation that I am about to give, all the truths this Sacrament proposes to our belief: to believe, I say, not to discuss and examine them.

The first truth is the real presence of Jesus Christ in the Eucharist; in virtue of the words of consecration, pronounced by the priest over the bread and wine, there is present not metaphorically or in figure, but truly, really, corporally, and substantially Jesus Christ, Son of God, true God and true Man. Yes, that same Jesus, born from the womb of Mary, died on the cross and rose again, Who now sits at the right hand of the divine Father. Of that we may be certain, both by the words Jesus Christ expressed, promising to institute this Sacrament, and by the words He used when in the act of instituting it.

I said in the first place, Jesus Christ promised to institute the Blessed Sacrament. After the miracle of the multiplying the loaves in the desert, He took an occasion of directing the minds of the multitude, filled with astonishment at the miracle they had witnessed, to the consideration of a more wonderful prodigy, to another bread, not corporal, but spiritual and divine that He intended to give them, and this bread was Himself. "I am," He says, "the Living Bread which came down from heaven : and the bread that I will give, is My Flesh for the life of the world." These words were so taken to the letter, that they said one to the other: "How can this man give us His flesh to eat ?" But Jesus Christ, far from saying that His words were to be taken in a figurative and not in a literal sense, which would have removed every difficulty, He insisted and used greater force to what He had already said, adding: "Amen, amen, I say unto you : Except you eat the Flesh of the Son of Man, and drink His Blood, you shall not have life in you." And immediately after He repeats and reaffirms the same thing several times—" He that eateth My Flesh, and drinketh My Blood, hath everlasting life, and I will raise him up in the last day. For My Flesh is meat indeed, and My Blood is drink indeed." Thus inculcating and repeating the self-same truth.

Again, the words used by Jesus Christ in the act of instituting the Blessed Sacrament are clear and precise. He does not say, Take and eat: this is the figure of My body ; but He said : This is My body. And then He gives a greater declaration, saying to them that He gives the same body that was about to be sacrificed, and the blood that was to be shed for them. Now, without doubt the true and real body and blood of Jesus Christ were offered on the cross, so also true and real is the body and blood of Jesus Christ given to us in the most holy Eucharist. Neither was He able to express more clearly the real presence in the Blessed Sacrament, nor was He able to express Himself in terms more significant in manifesting a real intention of establishing it.

From this first truth you can infer the pre-eminence of this Sacrament over all others. For the other sacraments contain the grace of Jesus Christ differently modified, according to the different ends of the same sacraments; but in this the Author of grace is Himself contained.. The others are channels of grace, this the Fount and Source of grace.

You must not, however, suppose, according to the error of the Lutherans condemned by the Church, that the bread and wine, after the consecration, exist together with the Body and Blood of Jesus Christ. No; this, then, is the second truth regarding the mystery faith proposes to us to believe; that is, the whole substance of the bread and wine is changed into the Body and Blood of Jesus Christ. After the consecration there remain only the appearances—the sensible qualities, such as the form, smell, colour, and taste of bread and wine. If we consult our senses of sight, touch, taste, and smell there appear to us bread and wine; but faith tells us that what appears to our eyes bread and wine is no longer bread and wine, but the Body of Jesus Christ. This is that wonderful conversion properly called by the Church Transubstantiation, by which there is a conversion of one substance into another, a conversion declared by the words of Jesus Christ, Who did not say: In this bread or with this bread is My Body— but He said: " This is My body."

Neither ought this to appear to us impossible. For if God was able to change the wife of Lot into a statue of salt, the rod of Aaron into a serpent, the waters of Egypt into blood, and the water into wine at the marriage feast of Cana of Galilee, why should He not be able to make a similar conversion ? · If we believe that God was able to make all things out of nothing, we ought to believe that He can more easily change one substance into another. If bread and wine, by a natural power unknown to us, be daily converted into the flesh and blood of him who eats and drinks thereof, why should we not believe them to be changed by a divine power into the Body and Blood of Jesus Christ ? This second truth of faith leads us to mention the two-fold diversity between this and the other sacraments.

The first is, that in the other sacraments the matter is
not changed, but remains always the same ; for example,
water in Baptism, oil in Extreme Unction, and so on ;
in this Sacrament, however, the matter is changed into
the Body and Blood of Jesus Christ, nothing remaining
of the bread and wine but their sensible qualities.   The
second difference between this and the other sacraments is that they do not properly exist except in the
act of their being administered and received, whilst this
Sacrament is permanent ; since the substance of the
bread and wine being changed into the Body and Blood
of Jesus Christ at the moment the words of consecration are pronounced by the priest, this conversion being
once made Jesus Christ remains under the appearances
of bread and wine as long as these appearances last.
From this permanent presence of Jesus Christ in the
holy Eucharist under the sacramental species follows
the obligation of paying Him divine worship, internal
and external.   And in fact, if by us Jesus Christ is to
be adored and worshipped on the cross, with reason
ought we to adore Him in the Eucharist, where He
truly dwells with all the fulness of His divinity ; bearing well in mind that our adoration refers not to the
sacramental species, but to Jesus Christ Who is hidden
under them.

The third truth is that Jesus Christ is Whole and
Entire both in the host and in the chalice—both under
the appearance of bread as well as that of wine, though
for a different reason.   I will explain myself: in virtue of
the words of consecration, which operate only what they
signify, the bread is changed into the Body, the wine
into the Blood.   But Jesus Christ is living, glorious and
immortal, in the holy Eucharist, so that by a natural
concomitance there is united to the Body in the host
the Blood and Soul ; united to the Blood in the chalice
is the Body and the Soul, and finally, by the hypostatic
union with the humanity there is also the divinity, so
that Jesus Christ is there as God and Man, Whole and
Entire.   Yea, not only is Jesus Christ Whole and Entire
under either kind, but He is also under the smallest

particle of each kind, and like our soul, which is entire and indivisible in the whole body and in every part of it. This is clear from the Gospel, for Jesus Christ did not consecrate separately all the different portions with which He communicated the apostles, but consecrated at one time such a quantity as would suffice to communicate all of them ; and yet He said to each one that he received His divine Person. Whence it follows that dividing the host, the species only are divided, not the Body of Jesus Christ, which remains always equally entire, even when receiving only the smallest part of the consecrated host.

Oh, what an abyss of prodigies is contained in this divine Sacrament! It is justly called by the Church a Mystery of faith. In the other mysteries we believe what our eyes do not behold, and here we have not only to believe what we see not, but also the contrary to what we appear to see. We must believe what I will now state in a few words.

1. That the whole substance of the bread and wine is converted without there being made any change in their accidents.

2. That these accidents exist without the support of their substance, and they effect all the effects of the same substance which is no longer present—we see bread and it is not there—we taste wine and it is not there.

3. That to the substance of bread and wine the substance of the Body and Blood of Jesus Christ, true God and true Man, takes its place.

4. That the Body of Christ without being lessened is contained in the small host, yea, in every part of the consecrated host and wine.

5. Finally, that the same and only Body of Christ, without multiplying Itself, is at the same time both in heaven and in the host, and in every place where there are consecrated particles.

This is such a group of miracles that although they are certain to our faith, they are also above our understanding. But what matters that ? Shall we dare to call in doubt or disbelieve what God Himself has proposed to us to be believed ? What idea can we have of God, of His wisdom, of His veracity, of His omnipotence, of what He is, if we do so ?

If the difficulties that our poor weak reason meet with in this Mystery be a legitimate title for refusing our belief, then there are many other articles of our faith equally as incomprehensible, as the Trinity, Incarnation, the Resurrection of the body. Also there are many natural truths that are most certain, and yet cannot be explained. We must, then, either disbelieve everything that is above our understanding, and that would be the renunciation of so many things that cannot be denied, though they cannot be explained—this would be placing a limit to the divine power, that can do all things, and which could do but very little were it able to do only what is within the reach of our understanding, or we must bow ourselves down to the weight of divine authority.

Thus it is : from the moment God has revealed to us a truth, understanding, or not understanding it, there remains no other course for us than that of believing it. This is the only reasonable course to follow : for if the things revealed to us are obscure and impenetrable in themselves, they are clear and luminous in the support they have upon the divine revelation, upon the divine word, the resistance of which is a temerity and an abuse of our reason. That which emanates from God must be true, and the divine omnipotence is able to do more than we can imagine.

Let us, then, renew our faith and protest before God that though our senses and our understanding oppose themselves, we firmly believe with our intellect and will the most august Mystery of the Eucharist, as it has always been believed in the Church. Although the Jews murmured among themselves and were incredulous when this truth was proposed to them, Jesus Christ did not wish to satisfy their curiosity, and to all He made known the belief required ; this He did to teach us that in the divine mysteries we ought not to seek the how or why, but to rely upon His divine word,—in that consists the merit of faith.

I am convinced that you, Catholics, believe in this Mystery, but you ought also to have at heart the maintenance of your faith by a conduct corresponding to the belief you profess, so as not to give an occasion to heretics to be obstinate in their misbelief. All the difficulties and objections made by heretics against this Mystery of the holy Eucharist can be refuted. There is, however, one difficulty to which I know not how to answer, and that one ought to fill us with confusion; they charge us Catholics with a disbelief in this Mystery, but upon what foundation? Upon this, that they observe so much irreverence, profanation, and scandal in our churches. "How is it possible," they say, "looking at the external appearance of Catholics in their churches, there is nothing that can lead us to suppose that they really believe in the real presence of Jesus Christ Himself, true God and true Man, under the sacramental species? The conduct of those who do not believe in this Mystery could not be worse." Here you see is a direct contradiction between belief and behaviour, which redounds to the injury of religion, the dishonour of our faith, and serves to keep heretics obstinate in their errors; and thus the name of the Lord is continually blasphemed all the day long. On the one hand, by the force of reasoning, supported by divine authority, we draw heretics; and on the other hand, we drive them away from the Church by the force of bad example. Let us, then, strive to cause to shine forth in us the belief we profess of this august Mystery of the Eucharist, and thus put to confusion the misbelief of others, appearing always in presence of Jesus Christ in the Blessed Sacrament with that respect, modesty, and devotion that will make known to all our faith. So much the more ought we to do so since it is through the excessive love of Jesus Christ that He remains hidden under the sacramental species, as we will show in the next instruction.

XII.

THE Holy Eucharist, as we have seen in the former instruction, is a Mystery of faith, because it forms that complication of prodigies and marvels which it contains in itself. It is also the greatest excess of the divine love for us, called by the Fathers the Sacrament of love. That you may the better understand the immense love of Jesus Christ for us in the Eucharist, I will place before you reasons most clear and adapted to the intelligence of all, that being persuaded and convinced of the great love of Jesus Christ, you may be led to love Him and profit by the great benefits offered to you.

So great is the love that Jesus Christ has shown and shows towards us in this Sacrament of the Eucharist that the sacred Council of Trent says that "Jesus Christ has poured forth the riches of His divine love towards us." And, indeed, observe what love is able to do when once it takes full possession of the heart. We have nothing, then, of our own ; it suffices to know that the person loved has need of something, that we can assist or do him some good, and we are immediately ready to give that assistance within our power with great pleasure, though we hold most dear the object required. In fine, true love makes us generous in our gifts, that we may be able to do a favour even at our own personal inconvenience. What greater generosity and liberality—what greater gift was Jesus Christ able to give us than that which He continually gives us in the most holy Sacrament of the Eucharist. To us two kinds of food are necessary—one material for the life of the body, and one spiritual for the life of the soul. With the material food for the life of the body we were already provided by the fruits of the earth; the spiritual food for the life of the soul was wanting to us, and since Jesus Christ knew that the best food He could give us for this life was that of Himself, He has given, and continues to give us, in the holy Eucharist, His Body, His Blood, His Soul, His Divinity, and to all without distinction—not only to the bishops and priests—not only to kings and princes, but to the poor and needy. Oh, unspeakable goodness! If faith had not taught us, if God had not said so, who could have thought that the love of Jesus Christ towards us would have reached so far? If Jesus Christ had given us His permission to ask of Him all that could be of benefit to our soul, to whose mind would it have entered to ask of Him for the food of his soul His Body, Blood, Soul, and Divinity? Who would have presumed to have asked for so much? Yet He, knowing that this would be for us the best food, the most useful, and the most advantageous for our soul, was moved by His love to give it. The holy Scripture, to make known to us the ardent love that Jonathan had for David, says: "The soul of Jonathan was knit with the soul of David." Now what did Jonathan do for David? On a certain occasion he "stripped himself of the coat with which he was clothed, and gave it to David, and the rest of his garments, even to his sword, and to his bow, and to his girdle." If, then, Jonathan, for having given to David nothing but his garments and arms; yet, for having given them under such circumstances, he gave him all that he possessed, testified his ardent love, loving him as he loved his own soul, who can measure, who can fathom the love Jesus Christ has towards us, when, in the Sacrament of the Eucharist, He gives us, not things perishable, but His own Body, Blood, Soul, and Divinity—all that He is able to give us? He gives us most generously all that is in His power to give as man, because He gives us His Body, His Blood, His Soul; all that He has as

God, because He gives us His Divinity, His holiness; all that He possesses as God and Man, because He gives us all that belongs to Him as God and Man—His Divinity, His Humanity, His virtues, His graces, His merits, His satisfactions. So that Jesus Christ, although omnipotent, cannot give us more—although He is infinitely wise He cannot give us more—although He is infinitely rich He has nothing more to give. If, then, Jesus Christ in giving us Himself, all His Humanity, all His Divinity, has given us all that is most rare, most precious that is in His power, He has given us a gift that holds in astonishment all the angels in heaven, it is an evident sign that He loves us with a love the most tender and most affectionate, and it is most manifest that Jesus Christ has a love so great that it surpasses our understanding.

Ah! this truth that Jesus Christ in the Sacrament of the Eucharist in the most holy communion gives Himself for the food of our soul, is a truth that we all know, that we frequently hear repeated, that we have, so to speak, continually under our eyes; for this reason many make no account of it, nor does it produce in them the effects and impression that it ought; but now let us reflect seriously, with a spirit animated with a lively faith. Ah! the thought that God made man has made us, miserable creatures, participators of His most sacred Humanity, of His Divinity for the spiritual food of our soul, ought to fill us with wonder, and make us convinced of the love and the goodness of God towards us, and bring us to know that in the Sacrament of the Eucharist He has not only given us His love, but He has poured forth the riches of His divine love towards us.

That we may be the more convinced of this great truth, let us continue to consider what love does when it has taken possession of the heart. Love induces one to remain willingly in the company of the person loved, and desires nothing else; so that when the person is present there is joy and contentment; when absent, affliction and sorrow. Thus Eliseus loved so much the

108 FAMILIAR INSTRUCTIONS ON THE SACRAMENTS.

prophet Elias that he wished to be always with him, though the prophet frequently told him to leave him, he, nevertheless, said to the prophet: "As the Lord liveth, and as thy soul liveth, I will not leave thee." So we see that when two persons have a great love for each other, be it for good or be it for evil, they always seek to be together, and when separated, oh, how bitter is the separation! Now let us consider the conduct of Jesus Christ towards us. After being on this earth for thirty-three years, He had to finish the work of the Redemption, to leave this world and return to His Eternal Father. On the one hand He willed to do the will of His Father; on the other, it grieved Him to abandon us, His dear children. And since love is solicitous, ingenious, and knows how to find a way of being with the object loved, so Jesus Christ, seeing the time of His departure was at hand, what does He? That He might not be separated from us, that He might be with us always, Body, Blood, Soul, and Divinity, He institutes the Sacrament of the Eucharist. After this wonderful institution He says to His apostles: "With desire I have desired to eat this pasch with you." And now that I have instituted it, behold I am with you all days, even to the consummation of the world. Now I shall have the consolation of being always in the company of My dear children, for My delight is to be with the children of men. Could it be possible to have a greater proof of the love Jesus Christ has towards us? If a king were to come and visit one of us, and were he to say—Your company pleases me so much that I wish to be always with you, enjoying and making you to participate in my delights, in my riches, should we not look upon such a declaration as a sign of most ardent love and of great goodness? Should we not be filled with wonder and astonishment at the sight of such love and goodness of a sovereign towards a subject? And Jesus Christ, King of kings, Supreme Monarch of heaven and earth, God of infinite Majesty, declares that He has instituted the Sacrament of the Eucharist in order that He may be always with us, in our company, to assist and comfort us in all our wants, to preserve in us the spiritual life of the soul, to enjoy His graces and His favours : an evident proof of the immense love of Jesus Christ towards us—a love that surpasses our imagination. Yet this is not all.

Jesus Christ has instituted the Eucharist, not only that He may remain always with us, Body, Blood, Soul, and Divinity, to the end that we may visit Him in the church, remain with Him, speak confidently to Him, make known to Him our wants, present to Him our supplications, obtain His graces ; but more, He has instituted It that He may dwell within us, making our breast a living tabernacle for His Body, Soul, and Divinity—to unite Himself with us, making Himself one with us, forming of His own Flesh and Blood the spiritual food of our soul. Oh, holy faith ! What can there be in the world more wonderful ? A God comes to unite Himself to a loathsome humanity, dwells within us, in a breast full of impurities, makes His Body, His Blood, our spiritual food. Oh ! this is a love, a degradation that holds in astonishment the angels in heaven. It was a great condescension on the part of Jesus Christ in permitting Magdalen to kiss His feet, also that of allowing St. Thomas to touch His hands and His side, and the beloved disciple to lay his head upon Jesus' breast. Yes, all these were wonderful condescensions ; but they are not to be compared to that He does for us in the holy Eucharist, in virtue of which each one of us, after communion, can say : Now God, that God, is with me, I have Him within me. King Solomon, after having built the most magnificent temple, said : " Is it, then, credible that God should dwell with men on the earth ?" The Church never ceases to express her astonishment that Jesus Christ should have deigned to remain hidden in the womb of the immaculate Virgin for the space of nine months : "When Thou tookest upon Thee to deliver man : Thou didst not abhor the Virgin's womb." And we, ought not we to be amazed, and wrapt in admiration and delight at the immense goodness of Jesus Christ, Who comes and dwells within us, Body, Soul, and Divinity, becoming our food, our spiritual nourishment? And yet the love of Jesus Christ ends not here.

Let us here observe in the third place what love is able to do when it takes possession of the heart. Oh, then one willingly undergoes sufferings for the person loved. An example of this we have in Holy Writ. Jacob conceived an ardent love for Rachel; he asked her of her father for wife, and he promised to give her to him on the condition that Jacob would remain as a servant in his house for the space of seven years, submitting himself to every kind of fatigue; but his love was able to endure all that, for Jacob loved Rachel most tenderly, and served the seven years. When that time had passed, Laban, in place of giving Rachel, by deception, gave Lia, her sister, to him. And when Jacob discovered the deception, he told Laban that he wished to marry Rachel, to which Laban replied, Then you must serve me another seven years. Imagine, if you can, what must have been the grief of Jacob on hearing this. And yet so great was his love for Rachel that he willingly yielded to the pleasure of Laban, and served him another seven years. See, then, the power of love. And experience proves that oftentimes persons, through love, undergo every kind of suffering, expense, and hardships, day and night, which, if only the half had been done for God, they would have become great saints. Let us now consider what Jesus Christ has suffered and continues to suffer in the Sacrament of the Eucharist, and we shall be more convinced of the immense love of Jesus Christ for us. In the Incarnation, Jesus Christ, by becoming man, so humbled Himself, that the Scripture tells us: "He emptied Himself, taking the form of a servant." In the holy Eucharist He humbles Himself yet more, for He not only takes the form of a servant, but of a material thing, such as bread and wine. In the Incarnation His divinity was hidden under the mantle of our humanity, in the holy Eucharist He conceals not only His divinity but also His Humanity, under the appearances of bread and wine. In the Incarnation Jesus Christ so humbled Himself as to appear like unto ourselves—in the Eucharist He so humbles Himself as to become our food. Oh, wonderful humiliation! Who can declare the insults, the injuries, endured by Jesus Christ in the Sacrament of the Eucharist? How many receive Him in a state of mortal sin, constraining Him to remain in company with His enemy the devil? How many make use of the sacred species for superstitious purposes, which is the only celestial food, and only comfort and salvation of the soul? How many, whilst Jesus Christ is exposed upon our altars to listen to our supplications and hear our prayers, enter into the church, t lled with pride and vanity, without respect and veneration, insulting Him under His own eyes? And Jesus Christ, through love for us and for our good, tolerates, endures, all these insults. When He instituted this blessed Sacrament He foresaw all this ingratitude, everything was present to His mind, but it did not lessen His love or prevent Him from instituting it, as if He should say: Let it cost what it may, come whatever insult, as long as I may be always with My dear children, Body, Blood, Soul, and Divinity, to comfort and assist them. Jesus Christ could, at the sight of so many and so great insults, have deprived us of so great a benefit as that of the Sacrament of the Eucharist; but He would not, that He might, to our great advantage, remain with us to the end of the world. Oh! if our faith were a lively faith, we should be convinced of the immense love of Jesus Christ in the Sacrament of the Eucharist, and filled with admiration.

But if Jesus Christ has given and continues to give us so many proofs of His love, whence is it that we love Him not as we ought—that we are tepid and cold? The Apostle says: " He that loves not the Lord Jesus, let him be anathema." Whence is it that we are without a sentiment of gratitude for the great benefits received from Him, particularly in the holy Sacrament of the Eucharist, and that we do not think to say to Him with St. Bernard: "O my God, I thank You for the great benefit You have conferred upon me, and I beg of the angels and saints to thank You for me. I offer to you all their adorations in thanksgiving for this august Sacrament." Whence is it that so many have no relish for this spiritual food, although Jesus Christ promises them through it, an abundance of graces and favours: "Whosoever eateth of this bread shall live for ever," and He threatens those who do not receive it: "Unless you eat of the flesh of the Son of Man, you shall have no life in you." Whence is it that Jesus Christ being so filled with love and goodness towards us, remains hidden in the tabernacle, exposed upon our altars to receive our visits, to hear our prayers, to receive our adorations, to communicate to us His graces, and yet so few present themselves? Oh, where is our faith? Of many Christians we are constrained to say of them that either they do not believe what faith teaches them regarding the Sacrament of the Eucharist, or they are false to their faith, to their God, and to their own souls. But what will happen after to those who have betrayed their faith—after they have been, by their ingratitude, false to a God Who has given so many proofs of His love and goodness—after having been false to their own souls, depriving them of those graces and benefits which they could have received from the Sacrament of the Eucharist? It will come to pass that they will have to suffer for all eternity the terrible rigours of the divine justice, in place of entering into heaven, there to enjoy the glory of God, for the obtaining of which He has left the most holy Sacrament a sure pledge.

Let us, then, be grateful to God for having instituted this divine Sacrament; let us profit of the advantage we have of possessing Him, honouring Him by frequently visiting and receiving Him.

It will not be possible for us to be without love and devotion towards Jesus Christ in the Eucharist, if we bring before our mind, and before our mind we ought always to have that this same Jesus, made our food during life, wishes to be also our Viaticum at the end of our sojourn on earth—Who will come to our bedside in our last illness to accompany us in our passage from this life to eternity.

Oh! will He, then, come to us in the quality of a Father and a Saviour, recalling to His mind the homage we had given Him, and desiring to repay us by supporting and comforting us in the midst of the terrible anguish of body and soul; or will He come in the quality of a Judge to avenge our coldness and indifference for Him, and thus make us feel beforehand our condemnation?

What reply can I make for you, what reply can I give for myself?

From the treatment we show towards Him during our time of probation, we may be able to declare with every probability what kind of treatment we shall receive from Him at that moment.

Let us, then, well reflect and make good use of the acceptable time, remembering always that He stands not in need of our homage, but we stand continually in need of Him during our life, and more particularly at the hour of death.

XIII

ON FREQUENT COMMUNION.

Is it not a subject of much surprise, if God forbids a thing as injurious, pernicious, capable of causing our death, nevertheless, we desire to do that very thing; if He commands us to do something that is advantageous to us, capable of producing in us every good, it is that we precisely neglect and are unwilling to do. Let us see if it is not so, and be filled with astonishment. God, in the terrestrial paradise, forbade Adam and Eve to eat of the fruit of the tree, signifying to them that should they eat thereof they would surely die; and, notwithstanding that, they saw that the fruit was fair to the eyes and delightful to behold, took of the fruit and did eat, without regard to the evils they were bringing upon themselves and upon their posterity. God commands us to eat of the Eucharistic bread, to eat of the bread of angels—a bread that comes down from heaven—a bread, not like the manna in the desert that was eaten, and they who eat it died, but a bread that whosoever eat thereof shall live for ever—a bread, in fine, that has every kind of virtue—it has that of vivifying the soul and of increasing in it more and more the grace of God—it has the power to cure all our evils and procure for us the perfect health of the soul—that of fortifying us against the disorderly passions, wicked inclinations, temptations, and the assaults of our three enemies—the devil, the world, and the flesh—that of rendering virtue easy to us, of illuminating our mind, obscured by errors, deceits, and prejudices, and of causing us to know the truth—that of inflaming with fervour our hearts to love God and serve Him faithfully, in spite of every obstacle and difficulty; it has the power of cancelling in us venial sin, and of preserving us from mortal sin, of diminishing the temporal punishment due to our sins, the virtue of uniting us closely .to .God, to His Divinity, of enriching us with most abundant graces, giving us assistance, light, favours, benefits, filling us with sweetness and consolations as a pledge of that eternal glory He has prepared for us. And God commands us to eat of this heavenly food; He exhorts, invites us to eat of it, He begs and entreats us to partake of it. "Come, eat my bread, and drink the wine which I have mingled for you." That we may be the more animated and moved, God, after having assured us that we shall find in this bread every good and eternal life, threatens those who refuse to partake of it every kind of evil; that they will meet with eternal death : "Amen, amen, I say unto you, Unless you eat the Flesh of the Son of Man, and drink His Blood, you shall have no life in you." And notwithstanding all this, who could believe it, if he did not continually witness it—the greater part of Christians do not care for this celestial bread, neglect, despise it, and remain not only for months but years without receiving it. Oh, what base ingratitude they show towards a God so good! What affront, what insult, what outrage they offer to a God of majesty! He gives Himself for the spiritual nourishment of their souls, offering them His Divinity, His graces, His assistance, His favours, His benefits—every kind of good, spiritual and eternal; in one word, He offers them all that is most rare and precious, and they show themselves utterly regardless of Him and of His gifts. Is it possible to imagine anything more ungrateful? What should we say of one were he invited by his sovereign to sit frequently at the table with him, to partake of his pleasures, offer him his favour, his friendship, his protection, with all that could be possibly desired; and should that one show that he has no wish for them, that he cares neither for the king or his favours, yea, should he despise and refuse them?

Would you not say that such an one is wanting in respect? Is it not true also that the king would be offended and angry with conduct so ungrateful? From this you may argue how enormous is the ingratitude of those who refuse the gracious invitation of Jesus Christ, not caring for the immense graces which He desires to bestow upon them in the holy Eucharist, you may judge how their conduct offends and irritates Him. The parable in the gospel of St. Luke is very expressive of His anger. "A certain man made a great supper, and invited many. And he sent his servant at the hour of supper to say to them that were invited that they should come, for now all things are ready. And they began all at once to make excuse. The first said to him: I have bought a farm, and I must needs go out and see it; I pray thee, hold me excused.. And another said: I have bought five yoke of oxen, and I go to try them; I pray thee, hold me excused. And another said: I have married a wife, and therefore I cannot come." Finally, one with one excuse and one with another, all refused the gracious invitation. "Then the master of the house, being angry, said to his servant: Go out quickly into the streets and lanes of the city, and bring in hither the poor and the feeble, and the blind and the lame.... But I say unto you, that none of those men that were invited shall taste of my supper." Ah! the time will come when they will desire my supper, but they shall not be admitted; the time will come when they shall desire my favours, but I will be no longer disposed to grant them. The parable, up to this, is very clear; the application of it to ourselves only remains. The supper is the Holy Communion; Jesus Christ invites us to it through His sacred ministers; the invited are all of us. Woe to us if, for one excuse or another, we remain deaf to the invitation of Jesus Christ! Woe to us if we refuse the graces and favours He desires to give us in the holy communion! All the excuses that we are able to make are inconsistent and frivolous. Jesus Christ, being angry with us, will turn His back upon us, will consider us

unworthy of His graces and of His benefits, and when
we shall desire them, He will no longer give them.
"None of those men that were invited shall taste of my
supper."

It seems to me that many there are who suppose the
receiving of Holy Communion is not of obligation, that
it is only of counsel, of supererogation, or of simple
devotion, to be practised by him who wishes, and
nothing more. They are, however, deceived; it is a
command—a precept expressed by Jesus Christ—a
precept which, if we do not observe, we cannot be
saved. Is it not true that Jesus Christ commands us
to preserve the spiritual life of the soul, that is, to live
always in the grace of God? Is it not true that the
Sacrament of the Eucharist has been instituted by
Jesus Christ that the spiritual life of the soul may be
preserved? That is of faith. It is then manifest that
whilst Jesus Christ commands us to preserve the
spiritual life of the soul, He also commands us to
receive holy communion. Moreover, is it not true, that
punishment presupposes guilt? If, then, Jesus Christ
declares that He will punish with eternal death those
who do not receive Holy Communion—who do not eat
of His Body, and drink of His Blood—it is an evident
sign that such are guilty of a grievous sin, and that
they transgress a precept—a command of God. But
this precept of receiving holy communion, when does it
oblige, when ought we to observe it, or when is the
Christian obliged to receive it?

This precept obliges a Christian to receive it when
there is danger of death in the time of sickness; and
with regard to women, when given child-birth there is
that danger; before departing on a dangerous voyage,
and on all other occasions in which we find ourselves in
danger of death, because then it is we stand in greater
need of the grace and assistance of God, to resist the
temptations which ordinarily beset us, and that we may
pass happily from this to eternal life. And yet, how
many, in the midst of these dangers, never give a
thought of receiving the Sacraments of Penance and
Communion.

It seems as if it gave them pain to be converted to God, and to profit of His mercy; it seems as if it were a great affliction to them the giving of the few moments of life that remain, after having spent their lives in the service of the world, the flesh, and the devil. They are advised to think of their souls and adjust the affairs of their consciences by confessing and communicating, thus dispose themselves for a good death, and they turn the conversation, showing themselves annoyed at such remarks, and sometimes give sharp replies. The minister of God exhorts them, and I assure you that it distresses him to see people so badly disposed, so badly inclined. And what can be hoped for of such people? It is a sign that they are without faith, without fear of God, or the least regard for their souls; it is a sign they never were, or are, or wish to be, good Christians; for if they were they would be eager to reconcile themselves to God and procure His grace, His assistance, His favours, which He desires to impart to them. Whence it is the terrible threat of Jesus Christ is verified in them: "None of those men that were invited shall taste of my supper." In the whole course of their life Jesus Christ had invited them to receive His sacraments, His benefits, but they refused; therefore they do not deserve to receive them at their death; in their greatest need God permits them either to die without the sacraments, or that they commit a sacrilege by receiving them unworthily, and thus crown a bad life which they had always led.

In the second place, we are bound to receive Holy Communion, because this Sacrament is necessary to acquire strength to bear with the afflictions, tribulations, and to resist the temptations to which we are exposed, and render our victory over them more easy. And who is without tribulations and temptations?

Finally, we are bound to receive Holy Communion many times during our life. This many times formerly signified to go frequently to communion; but afterwards holy Church, seeing that Christian piety and fervour had grown cold, reduced the precept of receiving Communion, or the obligation of it, to three times in the year; the Nativity, Easter, and Pentecost; finally, in the Council of Lateran and that of Trent, the Church restricted this obligation to once a year, and that at Easter. And with all that, there are Christians to whom it seems too much for them even once a year, and they absent themselves from it for years, quite unconcerned about the number of mortal sins they commit during those years, by the transgression of this precept. And are they good Catholics? No; though they were to remain in the church all day in prayer, though they were to inflict upon themselves every kind of penance, practise every kind of imaginable devotion, unless they comply with their Easter duty they are not good Catholics—they are only so in name; because if they were really such, they would never allow their consciences to be burdened with so many mortal sins, and live on in that state with the danger of being at any moment eternally lost.

Though the Church obliges us to receive Holy Communion but once a year, we are not to conclude that it is not necessary to receive more frequently. The Church commands us to receive communion once a year, and that at Easter; but she does not say that we are to do so but once, but she says: "At least once." This word "at least" signifies a great deal. To understand rightly its meaning: let us suppose a mother has a sick child; we can imagine her thus speaking to that child: Though you do not wish to eat anything, take this "at least," and eat it to please me—what does this expression mean? Does it mean that the child is only to eat that small quantity offered by its mother? No, it means that the mother's desire and pleasure would be that the health of her child were such, that it might be able to eat more; but being unwell and having no desire for food, she hopes that the child, by partaking of at least that little, the life may be preserved. So the Church, our mother, in commanding her children to receive at least once a year, has the intention and desire that we should commmunicate more frequently;

but suppose that we are tepid, cold, and without relish for this spiritual food, she commands us to communicate at least once a year, so that the life of the soul may not altogether perish. In fact, the Church speaks plainly, for the Fathers of the Council of Trent, after having declared the desire of the Church is, that the fervour of the first Christians, who communicated daily, might return, go on to say: We beg, exhort, and beseech, through the bowels of the mercy of God, that all and each of those who bear the name of Christian, would, with such devotion of soul, with such piety and worship, receive frequently that supersubstantial bread, and that it may be to them truly the life of the soul, and the perpetual health of the mind. And speaking of the sacrifice of the Mass, they say: The Church would fain, indeed, that, at each Mass, the faithful who are present should communicate, not only in spiritual desire, but also by the sacramental participation of the Eucharist, that thereby a more abundant fruit might be derived to them from this most holy Sacrifice. The Doctors of the Church speak the same language, exhorting, recommending, and inculcating upon Christians frequent communion, not only as useful, but necessary, that they may live well.

And since example has more force than words, the Church, to move us to receive frequently Holy Communion, places before our eyes the example of the first Christians. We know from Scripture that the faithful in the time of the apostles met together daily to participate in the most precious Body and Blood of Jesus Christ; and why? because they were convinced that as material food is necessary for the life of the body, so also spiritual food is necessary for the life of the soul—because they knew that that Eucharistic bread is that daily bread, which Jesus Christ has taught us to ask of His heavenly Father—that is, that supersubstantial bread of which whosoever eat shall live for ever, and whosoever shall refuse shall perish eternally; because they knew that that bread gives all force, assistance, courage, and grace to resist every torment and cruelty of tyrants—that it imparts strength for the curbing of our passions, the overcoming temptations, the overcoming every difficulty, every obstacle, and enabling us to walk in the path of virtue and holiness. Such were the primitive Christians. They were convinced that their eternal salvation depended upon frequent Communion—upon frequently receiving the Body and Blood of Jesus Christ—that their greatest affliction was the deprivation of it. And oh! what shall we say now, seeing that Christians have so great a repugnance, so great an unwillingness, so great negligence in receiving holy communion? What shall we say, seeing that many are not only without desire to receive, but seek by a thousand excuses to absent themselves from it, and who would never receive if the Church did not command it? We are constrained to say that they are Christians only in name.

Ah! it is too true we observe the terrible change that has taken place from time to time in Christians, regarding the Sacrament of the Eucharist. What wonder, then, that there should be such a difference between Christians of our day and those of the first ages? What wonder, then, that they lead a life different from that led by the first Christians? What wonder, then, that vice now reigns everywhere, whilst then there was everywhere virtue? And the principal reason for this difference is, that the Christians of that time received frequently the Body and Blood of Jesus Christ, and from this spiritual food received all the graces, assistance, and light they stood in need of; and on the other hand, Christians now-a-days neglect this spiritual food. For this reason they pass from bad to worse.

Oh, that the custom of frequent Communion could be introduced among Christians; but not through mere use, vain glory, human respect; not simply to gain an indulgence, or because it is the feast of some saint; but willingly, with great purity of conscience, with a hatred for sin, with a right end in view, with a true devotion, and with all the necessary dispositions. Ah! then the whole face of Christianity would be changed—

then we should soon see vice and scandals banished, and in their place would everywhere appear piety, good example, virtue and holiness.

From what I have just said some may say that to live as Christians, and to make progress in the way salvation, it will be required of us to go to Communion every day, or at least frequently. I did not mean that, because with regard to frequent communion no general rule can be given that may serve for every one. For the needs of each one, as also the dispositions of each one, are different, so also for each one the frequency must be different. One ought to go frequently, another less frequently. The sentiment of St. Augustine has been adopted by St. Francis of Sales. The practice of daily Communion I neither praise nor dispraise. Let us understand well these words. St. Augustine does not praise the practice of communicating every day, because very many have not that purity of conscience, nor dispositions, nor that ardent desire for the Eucharist, which is required for those who daily receive ; consequently, such he neither approves or praises. Nor does the saint disapprove of daily communion ; because there are souls of such purity, of dispositions, of fervour, that it is praiseworthy that they should daily receive this spiritual food. But to receive Communion, continues the saint to say, every Sunday, or every eight days, is a practice that he counsels all to do, providing they be so converted to God as to be without any affection to mortal and venial sin.

The general rule which will serve for all regarding the frequency of Communion, is that laid down by St. Francis of Sales, that we ought to manifest to our confessor both our internal and external dispositions— our profession and our state of life, and then follow his advice. Another general rule given by the same saint is that those who desire to serve God faithfully, ought not to remain more than one month from one Communion to another, following, however, always the advice given by the confessor.

In my next instruction I shall speak of the excuses

given by those who absent themselves from Holy Communion—these excuses are, for the most part, frivolous, but they are such as lead God to deprive us of partaking of that heavenly banquet which He has prepared for them—as He deprived those that were invited in the Gospel, and refused His gracious invitation : "None of those men that were invited shall taste of My supper."

XIV.

ON THE EXCUSES GIVEN BY THOSE WHO NEGLECT HOLY COMMUNION.

THAT you might be animated with the desire of receiving frequently the Sacrament of the holy Eucharist, in my last instruction I brought before you reasons clear and urgent. Now to take away every cause for negligence, I will briefly employ myself in combating the excuses and pretences that are usually made by those who absent themselves from Communion. The first excuse is that of the great respect and reverence due to this most august Sacrament. Ah! they say: "It is a thing of great importance that of receiving in our breast a God, King of heaven and earth; we are poor sinners, full of vices and sins; we are unworthy to receive Him so frequently; we remember the words of St. Paul declaring to us, that a man is to prove himself, and so let him eat of that bread and drink of the chalice; for he that eateth and drinketh unworthily, eateth and drinketh judgment to himself, not discerning the Body of the Lord." Very good; tell me: If you are unworthy to receive Communion every eight, or fifteen days, or once a month, by reason of your sins, will you be worthy to receive after the sins of two or three months, or of one year? The more numerous are your sins, the less worthy you are to receive. For, as St. Augustine says, if you are not worthy to receive frequently, neither will you be worthy to receive but seldom; if you are unworthy to receive once a month, so much the more unworthy will you be to receive once a year. Consequently, the staying away from Communion brings you to that state that you no longer merit to receive, and thus you permit your soul to languish and die. True it is we are all unworthy to receive Holy Communion, and of this we ought to be fully convinced, and we ought to humble ourselves; for the believing of ourselves worthy, renders us absolutely unworthy. But because we are all unworthy, in a certain sense, is it for this that we ought to absent ourselves from receiving? No: it is better, says St. Thomas, to go to communion through humility than to keep from it through fear. Let us examine this thing a little, and you will see what it really is.

In three ways a soul may consider itself worthy to receive Jesus Christ in Holy Communion. The first is, if the soul should have a purity corresponding to the infinite purity of Jesus Christ. But such a purity it is not possible to find in anyone. Even the greatest saints did not possess it, nor are the angels capable of having it; for however great may be the purity of a creature it will always be limited, whilst the purity of Jesus Christ is infinite; consequently it is impossible to equal it. Therefore, it being impossible for us to arrive to such a purity of conscience, corresponding to that of Jesus Christ, it is clear that God does not require that in us; and if He does not expect it, then, without doubt, it is not necessary for receiving.

The second way of being worthy of the Holy Communion is, to have that good disposition, which, with the assistance of God, the souls most pure, most holy, most inflamed with charity, strove to have. To understand to what degree this good disposition can attain, it would be necessary to penetrate into the heart of a St. Augustin, of a St. Francis, of a St. Philip Neri, of a St. Teresa, and of so many other saints, and there to see the acts of profound humility, of faith, of hope, of sorrow, of the most fervent love of God, of the most ardent desire with which they strove to render themselves worthy of receiving Jesus Christ in Holy Communion. But this disposition, since it is extraordinary, and cannot be obtained by all, so God does not require that in us, neither is it necessary for receiving Holy Communion, nor is it necessary to be worthy of it in this way.

The third way of being worthy of Holy Communion consists in having the soul pure and free from all mortal sin, in having the grace of God, and in having put aside all will, all affection towards that horrible monster, mortal sin. This is the worthiness, this is the necessary and sufficient disposition for receiving Holy Communion. If, however, we speak of receiving communion frequently every eight days, according to the teaching of St. Francis de Sales it is not sufficient to have laid aside all will and affection to every mortal sin, but it is also necessary to lay aside all will and affection towards all venial sin, and to have an ardent desire to receive Jesus Christ and His graces. And does it require much to render us worthy to receive Him in this manner? Does it require much of us to put ourselves in the grace of God by a good confession? Does it require much of us to lay aside all will, all affection, not only to mortal sin, but also to venial sin, so that we may be worthy to receive frequently the celestial food? After the assistance of God, which He denies to no one that asks it, nothing else is required on our part but a little good will, a little real devotion, a little care for our souls.

I am prepared to hear what some may say, that this good will—this true devotion—this fervour of spirit is precisely what we want. We are tepid, dry, undesirous, we do not feel ourselves animated with that inclination to good, to devotion, neither do we experience pleasure or consolation in things spiritual. How, then, can we be worthy to go to Communion? This is not a sufficient excuse to keep us from Communion. In fact this tepidity, this dryness, this undesiring of spiritual things proceeds either from ourselves or from God. If it comes from us, that we have by degrees relaxed in the service of God, it is sufficient to try by prayer, by mortification and penance, by meditating especially on the eternal truths; these have a wonderful efficacy in undeceiving and in making us enter into ourselves; it is sufficient, I say, to try and arouse ourselves from our lethargy, excite and rekindle in us our first fervour; and then soon we will become worthy, soon will we be disposed to frequent Communion. On the other hand, if God permits in us this dryness, this desolation of spirit, this little or no pleasure in spiritual things, in order to prove our virtue, our constancy, to exercise our patience, giving us thereby an occasion of increasing our merit, and that we may serve Him through love; in that case, in place of keeping from Communion, we ought to approach it more frequently, that so we may obtain from God the assistance, grace, and comfort necessary, so that we may not succumb, that we may not abandon devotion, that we may be firm and con- stant in the practice of virtue. Thus the saints did, as we read in their lives; they were tried by God with dryness of spirit, with most painful desolation, so that they had no sentiment of pleasure or consolation in spiritual things; and they were tried, not for a short time, but for years; nevertheless, they always fre- quented Communion, and in it they found comfort in their affliction—in it they experienced assistance and strength, so as not to succumb, until God, in reward of their firmness and constancy, gave them tranquillity and a most abundant consolation of spirit.

There are some who may say that should they go to Communion frequently they would become so familiar with it that they would cease to think of the greatness of the benefit, and that they would receive Jesus Christ through custom, without that reverence and respect due to so great a Sacrament. On the contrary, when one has been a long time without tasting a food that gives pleasure to the palate, he enjoys it the more, and he has a greater relish for it; so, when one has been a long time from Communion, he approaches it with greater devotion, with more desire and pleasure, and derives more spiritual fruit from it.

This is a deception. The spiritual food of the Eucharist is likened to the material food in this—that the material food preserves and prolongs the life of the body; so the spiritual food of the Eucharist is that which preserves, prolongs, and increases more and more the life of the soul. In other things there is a great difference between these two; because, if one eats a great deal of material food, he is satisfied, and the desire for it is taken away, neither does he desire to eat more of it; but spiritual food never satisfies, nor does it ever take away the desire of eating thereof—yea, as Jesus Christ has said: "They that eat Me, shall yet hunger: and they that drink Me shall yet thirst." There is a great difference between dealing with God and dealing with creatures of this world. The more familiar we are with a person, the more we know of that person's weakness, his defects, his imperfections, and consequently by degrees we lose that esteem for him, and his company becomes, as it were, wearisome to us. But with God it is not so. The more familiar a soul is with God, the more the soul treats with Him, especially in the Holy Communion, so much the more the soul learns to know Him for that great God—so much the more it honours and esteems Him, and so much the more it is enraptured with Him. It happens to the soul precisely what took place with the Samaritan woman recorded in the Gospel. This woman came to draw water from the well, where she found Jesus Christ sitting. Jesus Christ took an occasion of asking her to give Him water to drink; she ramained, discoursing familiarly with Him, and oh, what a fortunate conversation was that for her! She knew nothing of Jesus Christ, and for having remained a short time with Him, commenced to know Him to be a Prophet, and then finally for the Messiah—for the Son of God, Who had come into this world to redeem mankind, and she departed filled with consolation, esteem, respect, veneration, and love for Him. The same takes place with the soul that receives worthily Holy Communion, and the more frequently it receives, so much the more it learns to know, esteem, respect, and love Him. Listen to what St. Francis of Sales says on this subject: "Should anyone ask you why you go frequently to Communion, tell him that you do so to learn how to love God, to purify your soul from imperfections, to free it from its miseries, to console you in your afflictions, and to have support in your weakness; tell him that two classes of people ought frequently to receive : the perfect, that they may preserve their perfection ; the imperfect, that they may advance in perfection—the strong that they may not become weak— the sick that they may be cured of their spiritual infirmities—the healthy that they may not become infirm, and that as to yourself, precisely because you are imperfect, weak, infirm, you have need of frequent communion ; therefore you unite yourself with Jesus Christ, Who is holiness itself, Who is your strength, your Physician. Finally, tell him that you frequently receive Jesus Christ that you may learn to receive Him worthily, because it is difficult to do a thing well, when it is seldom done." After what the Saint has said, it seems to me that there remains nothing more to urge against the excuses made by those who seldom receive communion. No, it is good to go frequently to communion, and for many it is absolutely necessary. All that is required, before receiving, is to purify well the soul from sin, particularly that of mortal sin, by a good confession— lay aside all affection, all attachment to sin, both mortal and venial—and with the advice of your director go frequently to the altar, doubt not you will receive great advantages from it, providing you do so after a good preparation.

It is true that sometimes you receive communion without feeling all the great advantages, the good effects ; but it is also true that they are received without your knowing it. How many graces, how much assistance, light, and how many inspirations are given us by God, which He would not have given us if we had not frequented communion ? How many more sins might have been committed, and were not ? How much good would have remained undone, which was done by frequenting communion ? All these advantages, all these good effects, are not ordinarily seen, but by frequenting communion are known in time. To those who receive frequently it happens what takes place in a child, when he tries on the clothes worn by

I

him during the last winter, he then discovers them to be too small, and that he has outgrown them.

It may be urged by some against what has been said that they have so many occupations and so many affairs to attend to, that it is impossible for them to go to the church every day to receive.

To give this excuse all the merit it deserves, it is necessary that we should consider two classes of persons—those that are depending upon others, as wives with regard to their husbands, children to their parents, servants to their masters—and then there are those who are not in that state of dependence upon others. Now, with regard to the first class of persons; if, by going frequently to communion, they are unable to attend to the duties at home, or fulfil their obligations, then it would be better for them to follow the advice of their director, and go less frequently. But if these persons are able so to regulate their duties, and thus find time to go frequently, without causing inconvenience or displeasure to others;—when, however, they really cannot go frequently, let them make a spiritual communion, especially when they hear mass. What is this spiritual communion? It is an ardent desire to receive Jesus Christ, to unite one's-self intimately with Him, to obtain His grace to love and serve Him more faithfully. And this spiritual communion has so great a virtue and efficacy that, spiritual writers say, sometimes it is more useful and more advantageous than sacramental communion. That this ardent desire to receive Jesus Christ be a true spiritual communion, it is necessary, says the Council of Trent, that beforehand there be a living faith, animated by charity—of that faith, the Apostle says, which worketh by charity.

If, however, we speak of that class of persons who are not depending upon anyone, who can do whatever they wish, and who make an excuse for not frequenting communion that of their affairs and temporal occupations,—to such I reply that the welfare and care of their souls ought to be their first occupation—that the affair of their eternal salvation is the most important, to which everything else is vanity and vexation of spirit, and without attending to the soul it is not possible to be saved. "Seek first the kingdom of God." Seek the things that are above, not the things that are upon the earth. In the second place, we know from history that many had immense occupations, affairs of the most important character, and nevertheless they found time for them, never losing sight of their souls, and often receiving the sacraments. The chief reason for which they do not receive frequently communion, is not so much on account of their occupations, as that of the little or no care they have for their souls—for the little or no fear of God—the little or no will to amend their lives. Before going to communion it is necessary to make a good confession ; to do this it is necessary to be truly repentant of sins committed—to have a firm will to amend—a firm will to eradicate bad habits—to destroy vices and defects—a firm will to abandon that friendship, that occasion of sin, to change life, to live as true Christians, to imitate Jesus Christ in His virtue and in His example—and this is what gives them pain —this is what they do not wish to do. This is the reason why so many do not frequent communion. As long as it is a question of hearing Mass, of reciting the Rosary, of being present at benediction, of performing some work of piety and devotion, which can be done without going to confession, yea, with sin upon the soul ; these things they easily perform ; but when it is a question of communion, knowing that a good confession ought to precede it, knowing that communion and sin cannot exist together, they absent themselves from it. But woe to them : That terrible threat of the Holy Ghost is upon them : "They that go far from Thee shall perish," a threat confirmed by Jesus Christ : "Unless you eat the Flesh of the Son of Man, and drink His Blood, you shall have no life in you." Therefore, have a little care, a little concern for your soul—if you have a soul stained with sin, wash it in the bath prepared for you by Jesus Christ in the Sacrament of Penance, by a true repentance and a good confession, and by a change of life dispose yourself to receive Jesus Christ in the holy communion, and having received Him worthily, receive Him frequently—if you do this you will live always in the grace of God, and living in His grace you will live eternally with Him in His glory. "If any man eat of this bread, he shall live for ever."

XV.

ON THE REMOTE AND PROXIMATE DISPOSITIONS FOR
HOLY COMMUNION.

WHENCE is it in the holy communion we receive within
us the God of holiness and we are not sanctified—we
receive the divinity and we are not made divine—we receive the Author of grace, virtue, and perfection, and yet
we remain always so weak, so defective, and so vicious ?
Ah ! the fault is not the communion, which is in itself
most efficacious, capable of producing in us the most
wonderful effects : the fault is ours, because we do not
approach it with those dispositions that are required ;
yea, sometimes without the necessary dispositions.
These dispositions some regard the body, others the
soul—some are remote, others are proximate. Give
me your attention and I will briefly explain them.
   The first disposition of the body consists in having
it so disposed that in receiving communion, the sacred
host can be retained in the stomach without the danger of being rejected. Consequently, when one has
an obstinate cough, an irritation that produces vomit,
he is not disposed for receiving, even should he be in
danger of death, by reason of the danger of irreverence
to the Blessed Sacrament.
   The second disposition of the body is exterior devotion, which consists in coming to the altar dressed
modestly and decently, and with such comportment of
the body that shows piety and breathes devotion.
Hence it is, when one goes to communion he should
go with a decent dress, that is, not filthy, ragged, or
in tatters, but that it be proper and clean, as well as it
can be, each one according to his condition ; at the
same time, though it is proper that the dress be modest,

there ought not to be anything like pomp, vanity, or
ambition about it; women ought to have the neck and
arms covered, otherwise they are not dressed according
to modesty and sobriety, becoming persons presenting
themselves for communion. Also when one goes to the
altar he ought to go there with such behaviour of the
body, the eyes cast down, with step not hasty, but
grave ; in fine, with such a deportment that shows
nothing in our exterior but what testifies piety, devotion, respect and reverence. The third disposition of
the body is a natural fast. When one is going to communion he is not to eat or drink anything from mid-
night, so that should he receive communion without
having observed this natural fast, he would be guilty of
mortal sin, except in the case of danger of death by sickness, or of one condemned to death; in these two cases
communion can be given, though the natural fast has not
been observed. But to take away doubts, and to remove
scruples that may arise regarding this natural fast to
be observed before receiving communion, it may be
necessary that I should explain what is meant by breaking the natural fast. To break the fast, the thing taken
and swallowed must come from without, so that should
one swallow some blood, coming from the gums, he
would not have broken the fast, and could therefore
go to communion. It is not sufficient that what is
swallowed should come from without, but it must be
what is capable of giving nourishment, and that it be
taken by way of food or drink. Let us suppose that a
person inadvertently allowed some food, that had remained between the teeth from the day previous, to
pass into the stomach—another whilst washing his
teeth allowed inadvertently a drop of water to go down
his throat—another has tasted a little soup, simply for
the purpose of knowing whether it is palatable or not,
and as soon as it has been tasted, rejects it, or, without
perceiving it, swallowed a small quantity. Now, in the
three given cases has the natural fast been broken ?
No, certainly not ; because that which had been taken
had not been taken by way of food or drink, but by

way of saliva; consequently they can receive communion.

Another swallows a small stone or a piece of metal of any kind, is the natural fast broken? No, for there is nothing in their nature that could give nourishment. Should, however, one swallow a thing that can be digested, such, for example, as paper, wax, seed, or any sort of herb, in this case the fast would be broken, because these things contain a sort of sugar, and what gives nourishment. But should the wind cause some rain, snow, or sand to enter into the mouth, or should a fly, an insect, enter therein and pass into the stomach, the natural fast would not be broken. Again, though without a legitimate cause one ought not to smoke or masticate tobacco before receiving communion, yet by doing so the fast is not broken. Hence one can abstain from them through mortification, but not through any obligation.

Having now explained the dispositions of the body, we pass to those regarding the soul, so that we may receive worthily holy communion. The first disposition of the soul consists in it being free from all censure, either that of excommunication or interdict, which is an impediment to the receiving of the sacraments.

Secondly, the soul to be free from all mortal sin, and if one knows or doubts whether he has, he ought to procure the removing of it by a good confession, and place himself in the state of grace. Woe to him who receives in mortal sin, approaching that sacred table without the nuptial garment, which is the grace of God! Woe to him who blends together light and darkness—Jesus Christ with the devil; for he that eateth and drinketh unworthily, eateth and drinketh judgment to himself!

But before receiving communion is it necessary to purify the soul also from all venial sin? Ah! however we may purify the soul, believe me it will never be sufficiently purified to receive a God of infinite sanctity and holiness; therefore, no diligence will be too great for a work of such great importance. Jesus Christ wished us to understand that when, before communicating His apostles, He washed the disciples' feet, though they were pure; and He intimated to St. Peter that unless he allowed Him to do so, he could have no part with Him. He wished to signify to us the great purity of body and soul with which we ought to approach holy communion. When God, in the wilderness, caused the Manna to come down (a figure of the Eucharistic food), that it might not be soiled He did not permit it to fall upon the earth until it had been covered with a dew, and thus the earth purified and cleansed, the Manna came down upon it. This, also, was to give us to understand the great diligence we ought to use in purifying our soul before uniting it with Jesus Christ in the holy Eucharist. Then, for your guidance, as regards the purifying of your soul from venial sins, that is to say, of those from which no one in this world is exempted, not even the souls of the most just, such are those defects, those imperfections, those small faults, which are committed without full advertence, and, as it were, imprudently through human weakness and frailty, providing one repents of them in general—providing he abhors them, and has the will to amend; these, I say, do not prevent the receiving of communion; yea, this is precisely the way to cancel them more quickly, and obtain from God the light to know them, and the grace to amend more easily. But if we speak of venial sins voluntarily committed, although, rigorously speaking, these are not an obstacle to communion, because they do not deprive us of the grace of God; nevertheless, if one does not repent of them—if he does not try to cancel them by a good confession, or by penance and prayer to amend himself, they are an obstacle to frequent communion, and render him unworthy to receive it frequently; because it shows a want of respect to God to receive Him without trying to purify the soul from all stains of venial sins. And although these sins do not entirely deprive the soul of the fruit of communion, yet they always prevent it from producing all the good effects

which it would otherwise; this is the reason why, after
so many communions, we are always what we were,
without having worked any reformation in our lives,
without having made any advance in piety and in virtue.
There are those who eat and drink as others do, yet
are always weak and infirm, and why? Because they
have within them bad humours, which prevent the
food from giving them the nourishment that it
would otherwise give ; for that reason they are always
indisposed.

The same thing takes place with those who receive
the food of life, without either repenting or amending
themselves of those venial sins, which they are accustomed voluntarily to commit. These sins are the bad
humours that prevent the Eucharistic food from giving
to the soul that nourishment which it ought to give,
and therefore they always commit the same vices and
defects, subject to the same bad habits, slaves to the
same passions as they were before. Then it is necessary to purify the soul well, so that it may be rendered
worthy of becoming the habitation of a God who in
His goodness deigns to visit us ; and be convinced
that you can never use too much diligence.

It is a great thing the receiving of a prince into our
house, and what attention do we not give, what care do
we not take, what diligence do we not use so that
everything may be put in order and properly disposed
for his reception ? And in the holy communion we
receive within us a God, the Prince of princes, and
shall we not give all our attention to the purifying
of our soul and rendering it a worthy habitation for
Him?

When King David thought of building a temple to
the living God, which temple was afterwards built by
Solomon, he prepared an immense quantity of gold,
silver, and other metals, precious stones, marbles, and
valuable timber. When asked why he had made such
preparations, he replied : Because " the work is great,
for a house is prepared not for man, but for God."
Yet that temple was only for the Ark of the Lord, in

which was preserved the manna, a figure of the holy Eucharist. Think, then, what diligence, what preparation ought to be used in making an habitation worthy to receive not the Ark, but God Himself.

So great is the preparation required that, after explaining the dispositions both with regard to the body as well as the soul, which dispositions are remote, I cannot conclude this subject without also explaining to you the proximate dispositions for communion, to the end you may be able to receive it with all the abundance of that fruit, with all the wonderful effects which it is capable of producing in us.

Formerly, when the people were in the Church for communion, the deacon in a loud voice, said: "He who is not prepared let him retire and give place to others." Then he turned to those who were about to receive, and said: "Approach with faith, reverence, and with love." These are the three proximate dispositions with which we ought to prepare ourselves to receive with fruit the Sacrament of the Eucharist. To prepare ourselves well for holy communion we ought, in the first place, to approach it with a lively faith—a faith that firmly believes all the truths of the Catholic religion, all the truths revealed by God, taught by our holy Mother the Church—with a faith that makes us especially believe that under the species of bread, of that consecrated particle, we receive the Body, Blood, Soul, and Divinity of Jesus Christ, that we receive a God of infinite majesty, the King of kings, that omnipotent God Who has created us, Who preserves, rules, and governs the whole world, Who has redeemed us by His passion and death, Who will judge us; that God, immense, wise, and perfect, Who is the glory and the happiness of the angels and saints in heaven; and with a faith that makes us believe this great truth more firmly than if we beheld it with our eyes or touched it with our hands.

Penetrated with a faith so lively and so firm we are led to the second disposition of conceiving sentiments of humility, and approaching holy communion with esteem, respect, and reverence towards a God so great. "And who am I," we ought all of us to say—"who am I to merit to receive within me a God of infinite majesty—a God who is goodness, purity and perfection itself? I am a worm of the earth, a vile creature, a sinner, full of vices and defects; I, who have had the temerity to offend so often a God so great, of injuring and outraging Him under His own eyes—I, who have been so ungrateful to Him, who have always returned evil for good, who have a thousand times merited His eternal punishments, and that I should receive within me a God, enjoy His company, unite myself to His divinity, to His infinite holiness! St. John the Baptist, who was sanctified in his mother's womb, led in the desert a pure and holy life, who was declared by Jesus Christ to be more than a prophet,—that great saint did not deem himself worthy to loose the latchet of the shoes of Jesus Christ; and I, who have been always a sinner full of vices and defects, shall I consider myself worthy to receive the Body, Blood, Soul, and Divinity of Jesus Christ? The Apostle, St. Peter, after having known the holiness of Jesus Christ, knowing himself to be a poor sinner, not daring to stand near Him, cried out: 'Depart from me, for I am a sinful man, O Lord;' the centurion did not consider himself worthy to receive Jesus Christ under his roof; and shall I consider myself worthy, not only to receive Him in my house, but in my breast, and there to become the food of my soul? Ah, no, I am not worthy; we ought to say from our heart when the priest recites those words: 'Lord, I am not worthy that Thou shouldst enter under my roof, say but the word and my soul shall be healed:' no, I am not worthy, O my God, that Thou shouldst come to visit me; no, I am not worthy to receive you, nor your graces, nor your favours, whilst I merit only your chastisements. But because you are a God so good, so merciful, who knows how to compassionate my miseries, my weakness, my defects; because, notwithstanding my demerits, you deign to come to me. Ah! yes, come, O my God, come to visit me—come, that I may enjoy your company—come to defend me from my enemies, to cure me of my infirmities, to enrich me in my poverty, and give me all the lights, assistance, and graces that are necessary for my soul." Ah! if all who receive communion were filled with these sentiments of humility, respect, reverence, and confidence towards God, then the communion would be most fruitful.

Finally, the consideration of the greatness of God, His goodness, His kindness towards us; and, on the other hand, the consideration of our own misery, of our demerit, of our nothingness, ought to excite in us a great love towards God, a great desire to receive Him and to unite ourselves closely with Him, which is the last proximate disposition required for receiving worthily holy communion. Oh! who is there that does not love a God so good, so merciful, who deigns to leave heaven and come here on earth to visit us poor sinners, creatures most miserable, and remain with us, assisting, comforting, and enriching us with His graces, with His gifts, His favours, giving us His Body, Blood, Soul, Divinity, for the spiritual food of our soul, and a pledge of that eternal glory that He has prepared for us in heaven? Ah! who will not desire to be intimately united with a God Who is beauty itself—a God Who is the Fount of every good, of every pleasure, of every consolation? Who will not give willingly his heart, that he may love Him more and serve Him better, and thus render himself more deserving of His graces and favours? Ah! should there be amongst us one without these sentiments towards a God so good, so merciful, it is a sign that one has lost his reason, his religion, his faith; it is a sign that he is worse than the beast of the field; and, consequently, how can he have the temerity to approach that sacred table? Whilst happy shall we be if, presenting ourselves for communion we go with the dispositions I have mentioned, both with regard to the body as well as the soul, especially with a lively faith, a profound humility, respect, confidence, and with an ardent love towards God! Blessed shall we be, because then the communion will infallibly produce in us those fruits, those wonderful effects which it is accustomed to produce in him who receives it worthily, so that we may advance always more in devotion, in virtue, and finally be saved.

Those who can read, with the assistance of a book treating on communion, reading it with attention and recollection of spirit, after having purified the soul, can easily procure all the other dispositions for communicating worthily. Those who cannot read, let them do their best by reflection and consideration. And, if they are unable to do anything else, after having purified the soul, let them exercise themselves in reciting acts of faith, hope, the love of God, and of contrition, as much as they are able from the heart, and in this manner their communion will be also fruitful.

After having received Communion, leave not the Church immediately, as many do; you ought to remain a time proportionate to that you have, adoring the majesty of God within you, thinking of His goodness, mercy, and condescension, thanking Him from your heart for the singular favour bestowed upon you, exciting in yourselves tender affections, promising always to love Him, never again to offend Him, and asking Him to give you His grace to practise your good resolutions, and perseverance to the end.

This is the way you are to receive communion with fruit to the soul; and at the same time the reason why so many derive no fruit from it, is not the fault of the Communion, but of those who receive it without the proper dispositions.

XVI.

ON VISITS TO THE BLESSED SACRAMENT.

MOST useful it is to frequent Holy Communion with the proper dispositions, as it was shown you in the last instruction; it is also of great advantage to visit frequently Jesus Christ in the most Holy Sacrament of the altar. That you may be animated with the desire to perform this act of Christian piety, I undertake to make it the subject of my present instruction.

That great King Solomon, after he had finished the building of the temple of Jerusalem, wondered that God gave a sign, an effect of His omnipotence, by causing fire to come down from heaven and consume the holocausts and the victims; and the majesty of the Lord filled the house. Whence, filled with astonishment, he exclaimed: "Is it credible, then, that God should dwell with men on earth?" But how great ought to be our astonishment, reflecting that Jesus Christ, Son of God, has instituted the Sacrament of the Eucharist, not only to offer Himself daily upon our altar to His Eternal Father for our salvation—not only to give us His Body and Blood for the spiritual nourishment of our soul, but also to dwell continually with us upon our altar, and there remain, not in figure and appearance, but in substance, in reality, as God and Man, with His Divinity, with His Sacred Humanity, and to remain always with us? Oh! who could imagine, who could believe such a thing, unless he had been assured of it by divine revelation, by faith, by an infinite number of miracles, proving the real presence of Jesus Christ in the most Holy Sacrament of the altar? Who could imagine, who could believe that a

God infinitely perfect, should arrive to this sign of goodness and love as not only to remain with us here upon earth, but to find His delight, His consolation to be with us poor miserable children of men ?   When a thing becomes common and familiar, though it be most wonderful, it by degrees causes little or no surprise; thus it is with regard to the real presence of Jesus Christ in the Sacrament of the altar.   Ah ! this is too true.   But let us dwell for a time on this thought.

. In that Sacred Host, enclosed in that tabernacle, or exposed upon our altar, there is really and truly the Son of God, Jesus Christ, King of heaven and earth, with His Divinity, with His Humanity, as God and Man.   Though we do not see Him with the eyes of our body, we see Him with the eye of faith, which is more certain, more infallible than our eyes.   Ah ! let us seriously ponder on this thought, and amidst a thousand affections of wonder and respect, of thanksgiving and love for so much goodness on the part of God, and we will be convinced of the obligation that is incumbent upon us to visit our great God who dwells in the sacrament of the altar, to come and render to Him our homage, our respect, our veneration and our adoration, we will be convinced of the great spiritual advantage to be derived from frequently visiting the Blessed Sacrament, which, as I have said, I will explain to you in this instruction, showing you what we ought to do, how we ought to occupy ourselves when we make our visits to the Blessed Sacrament.

That we be persuaded of not only the fitness but of the obligation incumbent upon us to visit as frequently as we are able the Blessed Sacrament, let us suppose for a moment that we had never heard of the real presence of Jesus Christ in the Sacrament of the altar, and that God were to send an angel from heaven to reveal to us that to-morrow He will be with us in this Church to converse with us, to hear our prayers, and to do all the good He can for us.   Is it not true that such announcement would fill us with admiration and wonder, and, ravished with delight at the goodness of

God, would we not hasten to this Church, prostrate ourselves before Him, venerate and adore Him? Is it not also true that it would seem to us a conduct most base, if we did not come and show Him every mark of our esteem, respect, and veneration? But because for ages past the Son of God has descended from heaven to dwell with us on earth, remaining always with us in the most holy Sacrament of the altar, has He ceased to be that great God that He is? Have we ceased to be under the obligation of coming to reverence and honour Him? Has it ceased to be a base ingratitude to leave Him all day without showing Him our esteem, our respect? Oh! where is our faith? Oh, what a motive we have for humbling ourselves for our ingratitude towards a God so good, so worthy of our love? And here observe if it is not true. If a prince, though he had been for years in the midst of us, though everyone knows him, though he has been seen and known to all, yet all, especially the nobles, consider it an honour, a privilege, and an obligation indispensable to go to him and show him their respect day and night, giving him every proof of their esteem as often as they possibly can, and consider it a great honour to do so. And should this prince leave his palace and come to dwell amongst us, to do all the good he can for us, oh, how all would run to visit and pay him homage! How fortunate would they esteem themselves were they permitted to enjoy his conversation, his favours! And a God of infinite majesty—a God, in comparison with whom all the princes of this world are but worms—a God, the King of heaven and earth, deign to descend from His throne and remain in the Sacrament of the altar, and not only in one church, but in every church in the world, however poor it may be, He honours it with His presence, that all may visit and discourse familiarly with Him; and yet, by Christians little or no account is made of Him, as if He were a person of no importance; few come to visit Him, as if they had never offended Him, or that He were unable to chastise them; few come to weep over their sins and to ask His forgiveness, as if they needed nothing from Him—few come to ask His grace, His assistance! We can compassionate those who are obliged to labour or are burdened with many occupations, but many there are idle and unoccupied, who pass their time in pleasures and amusements, never put their foot inside of the church to make a visit to Jesus Christ in the Sacrament of the Altar; oh, these are wanting in respect! Places of pleasure are thronged with Christians, and the church is empty, where the majesty of the most High resides. Oh! where is faith? What sort of respect is this for God? What ingratitude for so much goodness! Should a person of distinction come amongst us, every one would consider it an obligation to go and see him. Should one have a visit from another, immediately the thought of returning it is entertained, and it would seem to him a want of good behaviour were he not to do so. The Son of God comes from heaven to visit and remain with us in the Holy Eucharist, He comes to us in our houses when we are sick, and we take no trouble to visit Him in the church, or return His visit to us. What incivility! What rudeness! What ingratitude! Yea, I will say more. Many consider it an obligation to visit daily a woman, who in substance is but dust, and remain in her company for hours, conversing with her, showing her every endearing affection, never caring about coming to the church to visit the Son of God, or remaining with Him for a quarter of an hour! Some come to the church, but from their manner you may conclude that they are there not to adore Jesus Christ in the Sacrament; it is seen that He is not in their mind, or that they care not for Him; and if they see Him exposed upon the altar, they do not deign to genuflect in sign of respect; yea, insult Him by their irreverence, turning their backs upon Him, and looking upon all else but Him. And God tolerates these insults, these slights, and continues to remain with us, and honour us by His presence. What an example He gives us of His goodness, of His charity, of His patience, and of His long suffering!

K

The Queen of Saba, having heard of the fame of Solomon, of his great wisdom and riches, came from a great distance to visit and pay him homage; and many Christians living within a distance of a few paces from the church, never come to visit here One infinitely greater than Solomon. The wise men, having received a revelation of the birth of the Son of God, came from the borders of Persia—a long and dangerous journey—to visit and adore the Infant Jesus in the stable at Bethlehem; and Christians, for whom it is not necessary to make a long journey, having Him in this church, close to their homes, where they can, without the least inconvenience, come and adore Him; yet allow weeks to pass by without coming to do so. How can we excuse them of a want of esteem for Him? How can they hope for forgiveness? The Son of God descends from heaven through love for us, and remains in the Sacrament of the Altar, and Christians refuse to take a few paces to come to the Church, and there spend a few moments in adoration. O my good Jesus, You are badly treated by us, and how badly we correspond to Your love! You are love and goodness towards us, and we are without love or esteem for You. Ah! it is well, my God, that You have the angels who descend, adore, and praise You around that altar, otherwise how often would You be alone, abandoned by all as a man most miserable in the world! Oh, what ingratitude! If Jesus Christ appeared in our churches, either under the figure of fire that consumes, or of a cloud, as God appeared in the temple of Solomon—if Jesus Christ appeared in our churches with great power and majesty, we, poor miserable creatures, worms of the earth, would not dare to appear before Him. But our good Jesus, our divine Saviour, to give us, in the first place, an example of humility, then to remove from us all fear, and give us all facility, all confidence to come and speak to Him, humbles Himself, and, as it were, annihilates Himself, remaining, by a continual miracle, in the Blessed Sacrament, concealing His power, His majesty, His divinity,

His humanity, under the appearance of bread, and there remains enclosed in our tabernacle, and thus humiliated He is pleased to remain, and His delight is to receive our visits. Oh, what an excess of love! Oh, goodness indescribable! What excuse can we give for not frequently visiting Him?

Oh, let us revive our faith. It is certain and infallibly true that Jesus Christ our Saviour, the Son of God, is upon that altar, in that tabernacle, true God and true Man. We see Him, not with the eyes of our body, but we see Him with those of faith. Then I say to you in the words of Holy Church: "Come let us adore." Come as often as you can to visit Him, and render to Him the homage He merits. Come, especially when He is exposed upon our altar—come and adore His sacred majesty—come and reverence Him, prostrating yourselves before His throne, declaring to Him your esteem, your respect. Let us fall down before the Lord; come, let us deplore the conduct with which we have hitherto treated Him, and repent of our ingratitude, and ask His forgiveness for our offences, and supplicate Him for His grace and assistance. We may then rest assured that we shall obtain His mercy, and He will be ready and disposed to hear us, providing we present ourselves before Him with modesty, humility, and reverence, and with a heart well disposed towards Him. "Come let us adore and fall down, and weep before the Lord that made us." Yes, come, specially in the time of dangers, and ask Him to forgive you your sins, because this is the only way to appease His justice, move Him to pity, and cause Him to suspend His chastisements; this is what He promised to Solomon, saying, that His eyes shall be open, and his ears attentive to the prayer of him that shall pray in this place. Then will I hear from heaven, and will forgive their sins, and will heal their land. How much more merciful will He be, how much more ready to hear us, and to assist us in this sacred place, where He is truly present as God and Man, if we come with the proper dispositions, and beg of Him to do so?

If it is good and useful to us to come and venerate the image of our Blessed Lady and the saints upon their altars, more excellent and more useful is certainly that of adoring God Himself in person; for there is a great difference between presenting ourselves before a minister of the king and that of presenting ourselves before the king himself, and speaking to him, so, also, is there an infinite difference between presenting ourselves and speaking to the Blessed Virgin and the saints and that of appearing before God in person, and speaking to Him Who is the Fount of all graces, of every good, and upon Whom all else depend. True, the saints can do much before God, but they are only creatures, all that they can do is to pray and supplicate for us. Jesus Christ is by nature the Son of God, equal to the Father, true God and true Man, from Whom alone are derived all graces, all assistance, Who alone can save us. "Come, then, let us adore the God Who made us."

Some there are who say: "We desire to visit the Blessed Sacrament, and adore Jesus Christ therein, but when we are in His presence we neither know what to say or what to do; we remain for a time; then, finding ourselves tired, we go away." This is the great evil produced by ignorance of things belonging to God and to the soul. Listen, then, attentively to what I shall briefly say on the way you ought to employ yourselves in presence of the Blessed Sacrament.

In the Life of Ann of the Cross we read, after the death of her husband, who died whilst she was yet young, in place of thinking of again entering into the married state, resolved to abandon the world, its pleasures and its vanities, retired into a monastery, and became a Franciscan nun. There she had a small cell, with a small window looking into the Church, towards the altar of the Blessed Sacrament. From that window that excellent spouse of Jesus Christ knew not how to withdraw herself, passing her time in adoring the Blessed Sacrament. On being asked how she could remain so long a time before the Blessed Sacrament, and what she said and thought of—she replied: "I could remain for all eternity there. Is there not in the Blessed Sacrament our God, our Lord and Master, King of heaven and earth, our Saviour, our Redeemer? And you ask me what I do before Him? I love Him, and who is there that merits more our love than He? I praise and I bless Him. And who is there that merits more than He to be praised and blessed? Who more than He merits to be honoured and glorified? I thank Him. And how many motives have we to thank Him every moment for the benefits He has conferred upon us, and continues to shower down upon us? I offer myself to Him. And who is there to whom we ought to offer our heart, our will, our affections, our life, our whole self, and all that we possess, unless to that God Who has given us all that we have, even His own self, for the food of our soul? I weep and implore pity and mercy. And before whom ought we to deplore our sins, if not before a God Whom we have so often offended, and Who alone can pardon us? I ask and demand. And to whom can we better direct ourselves than to God for the obtaining the graces and assistance we stand in need of, since He is the only one Who is able and willing to grant our requests? What does a poor man in presence of one rich? He asks an alms for charity, and he asks until he receives. What does a sick man in presence of the physician? Desirous of being cured, he seeks the remedies for his infirmity. What does one that is thirsty when close to a fountain? He procures the satisfying a little his thirst from the water of that fountain." Thus concludes this holy servant of God. And thus ought we to do when we go to make our visits of adoration to the Blessed Sacrament, when we are in the presence of Jesus Christ, true God and true Man. Kneeling before Him as a mark of respect which we profess to have towards Him, making acts of lively faith, of love, and offering our whole being to Him, and all we have; and we ought to be sorry for our sins, and implore of Him forgiveness for our many offences committed against Him, and beg

of Him His grace and assistance necessary for our
wants. And if our heart is cold, and if we feel ourselves
weary, without consolation, without any sentiment of
devotion, without any disposition towards God, then we
ought to be persuaded that we are miserable creatures,
good for nothing, only that of punishment, and with
this idea of ourselves, pray and supplicate God that He
may assist us, that He may give us His grace to love
Him as He merits, that He may give us a true sorrow
for our sins, a love for piety, a good will, and fervour of
spirit. Ah! my God, we ought to say, see how
miserable we are, assist us, then; inflame our hearts
with a great love towards You; if You assist us not we
are lost! And when you visit the Blessed Sacrament,
if you do nothing else but resist your unwillingness,
your repugnance, protesting that you are willing to
remain as a penance for your sins; if you do nothing
else but demand pity and mercy of God; were you only
to continue repeating—my Jesus, mercy!—even then
your visit would be well made, meritorious, and most
useful to your soul. Come, then, as often as you can ;
come, adore and fall down before the Lord that made
us.

XVII.

BEFORE receiving the Body and Blood of Jesus Christ in the Holy Communion, a man ought to prove himself, he ought to penetrate and search all the folds and recesses of his conscience, and should he find himself guilty of mortal sin, he ought to have it quickly cancelled by a good confession, and thus place himself in a state of grace. This is the advice given by the apostle, and this is the advice I give to all of you, so that if you cannot always have the more sublime and excellent dispositions for the receiving all the fruit that can be drawn from Communion, you may, at least, have that necessary disposition for a worthy Communion. Now to the end, that no one may have the temerity to approach Holy Communion without this necessary disposition, having already spoken to you on the advantages of a communion worthily made, to-day I will bring before you the enormity of a Communion unworthily received, by showing you, in the first place, the awful sacrilege committed by one who communicates in a state of mortal sin ; in the second place, the terrible chastisements that await the unworthy receiver.

Is it not true that he who despises the law, transgresses and does not wish to observe it, offends the king, and gives him displeasure. But should such an one advance further, and insult the king himself, maltreat his sovereign, then he commits a crime more enormous; he is guilty of high treason. This is what is done by him who makes a sacrilegious communion—by receiving in mortal sin. Whilst he transgresses the law of God, now in one way, now in another, true he offends God, he dishonours Him, for the apostle says: " By

transgression of the law thou dishonourest God;" but
when one has the boldness to receive Jesus Christ with
mortal sin upon his soul, ah! then he not only offends
God by his sins, but he directly offends, injures, and
maltreats the person of God in a most unworthy manner; consequently, he commits the awful crime of high
treason. That it is so, it is very easy to demonstrate.
When a person receives Communion, it is of faith that
he receives Jesus Christ, the Son of God, Who is
united, incorporated, and made one with Him. What
horror must it, then, be for the heart of Jesus Christ to
find Himself enclosed in a place so unclean, so detestable as that of a soul. stained with mortal sin? Who
is there that could close his eyes were he condemned to
sleep in the same bed with one covered with leprosy?
If the sight of clothes covered with corruption would be
sufficient to cause a loathing, think what it would be
were one obliged to wear them? The Scripture tells
us that that proud king, Antiochus, was struck by God
with an incurable and invisible plague, so that worms
swarmed out of the body of this man, his flesh fell off,
and the filthiness of his smell was noisome to the army,
though at a distance from him. Now reflect upon what
they must have suffered who stood near him. But what
are these worms—this corruption? They are roses in comparison with a soul contaminated with mortal sin. Yet
he who receives unworthily constrains Jesus Christ to
dwell with this soul so horrible, to remain united with
him in Body, Blood, Soul, and Divinity. Tell me is it
possible to show a greater affront, or do an injury more
detestable. Tell me is it possible to maltreat worse
His sacred person.

Furthermore, when Judas, at the Last Supper, which
he made with Jesus Christ and the apostles, communicated unworthily, Jesus Christ told him that he was a
devil. Therefore, whosoever receives Communion unworthily is a devil; he is such if he constrains Jesus
Christ, Who is holiness, to be united, incorporated,
made one with the devil, who is His enemy. What
injury, what affront more enormous could it be possible

to commit? What more sensible disgust could possibly be given? This, at least, is certain, that receiving Jesus Christ with mortal sin upon the soul, you oblige Him to enter and to dwell in the house of the devil, constraining Him to remain in a place where the devil commands, and consequently you oblige Him to remain subjected to every insult and derision. See to what a depth of ingratitude, cruelty, and impiety, the Christian acts towards Jesus Christ—against a God Who has created and redeemed him by His most Precious Blood—against a God who continually maintains and preserves him—against a God who has given him so many marks of His goodness and of His love? Tell me, if one were to take his prince and cast him into a place filled with all that is filthy, could he possibly give a greater affront or inflict a greater injury upon him? Now this, and infinitely more, a Christian does when he receives Jesus Christ unworthily. For whosoever should scourge Jesus Christ, crown Him with thorns, renew all the sorrows of His passion, nail Him to the cross, is it not true that he would have done all that he is able to do to Jesus Christ? And all this is done by him who receives Jesus Christ with mortal sin upon the soul. For, inasmuch as he is able, he renews all the sorrows of that passion, and again puts to death the Son of God. And that no one may suppose that this is an exaggeration, listen to what the apostle St. Paul says: " Whosoever eateth this bread, or drink the chalice of the Lord unworthily, shall be guilty of the Body and of the Blood of the Lord." Now what means this being guilty of the Body and Blood of the Lord? It means that he who receives unworthily contracts a crime such as if he had really crucified Jesus Christ. Whoever has any affection towards Jesus Christ, our most loving Redeemer, cannot think of the calumnies, wrongs, and the barbarous treatment used by the Jews towards Him, without being filled with compassion, without conceiving a great dislike towards those ungrateful Jews, who proceeded so far as to put the Son of God to death. And yet—oh, ingratitude more hateful!

Christians, for the salvation of whom Jesus Christ underwent so many torments.; Christians, communicating unworthily, maltreat Jesus Christ worse than the Jews maltreat Him, and they commit a crime a thousand times more barbarous and more atrocious. And in proof of this, amongst the many reasons that could be given, two will suffice. The Jews maltreated Jesus Christ when He was on this earth in the fashion of man, like unto us, that is to say, He was on this earth, as it were unknown; but Christians receiving unworthily maltreat Jesus Christ now that He reigns glorious and triumphant in heaven; consequently, the crime of such is incomparably greater than that of the Jews; just in the same way that the injury done to a king whilst on his throne, surrounded with all the majesty of the court, is greater than that done to him when travelling unknown. Moreover, if the Jews maltreated Jesus Christ—if they crucified Him, they did it, say the apostles Ss. Peter and Paul, because they knew not that He was the true Messias—the Son of God, looking upon Him as the son of a poor carpenter. But Christians know well, and see with the eye of faith, that under the consecrated species Jesus Christ is there, Body, Blood, Soul, and Divinity; that there is God, Lord of heaven and earth; yet they have the boldness to receive Him unworthily—to receive Him in their breast—to place Him in company with the devil, and renew all the sorrows of His passion, again crucifying the Son of God. Ah! this is a sacrilege that exceeds our imagination.

And if it is thus, whence is it that so many have the temerity to receive Communion with a soul laden with mortal sin? Whence is it that so many, either through malice or shame, conceal sins in confession, and then go to Communion, and, what is worse, continue to do so for years, repeating this enormous crime? Whence is it that so many confess—yes, but without sorrow, without true repentance, without a sincere will to amend, and, after having made a sacrilegious confession, go and commit another in Communion? Ah! is it

ON AN UNWORTHY COMMUNION. 155

possible that they dare to go and receive Jesus Christ
with mortal sin upon the soul? Is it possible that they
have the courage to change into deadly poison that
Eucharistic food that has been instituted to give and
preserve the life of the soul? Is it possible that,
approaching to receive upon their tongue the Lord of
life, they do not feel filled with horror, that they do
not feel their blood chilling in their veins with fear;
that they do not fear the opening of the earth under
their feet and swallowing them alive, as it opened and
swallowed those who murmured against Moses? Is it
possible that they are without fear of being struck dead
at the altar? But because God more frequently does
not punish these sacrilegious sinners by a visible chastisement, can they hope to avoid His most terrible
chastisements? No: it is impossible that a sacrilege
so awful, such as that of receiving Jesus Christ with
mortal sin upon the soul, should go unpunished. If
God does not, by a visible sign, punish there and then,
He will do so by invisible chastisements; if He does
not punish at once in this world, it is because He has
reserved a greater chastisement for them in the world
to come.

Amongst the signs of predestination given by the
Fathers is that of one who knows how to draw good
from evil, and turns to the great advantage of the soul
the sins he has committed, as the bee draws sweetness
from what is bitter: the apostle says: "To them that
love God, all things work together unto good, to such
as, according to his purpose, are called to be saints."
On the contrary, it is a sign of damnation when one
draws evil from good, and converts into a deadly poison
that food which, of its own nature, would give him life.
Such are those who communicate unworthily; because,
in place of drawing a great benefit from this august
sacrament, they draw from it the greatest of all evils;
in place of meriting the grace of God, they bring down
upon themselves His malediction. The expression used
by the apostle is singular and, at the same time, most
terrible when speaking on Communion. After having

said that whosoever shall eat this bread, or drink the chalice of the Lord unworthily, shall be guilty of the Body and Blood of the Lord, he recommends us, before receiving Communion, to prove ourselves, that is, to purify our soul from all mortal sin by the Sacrament of Penance, because, he adds, he that eateth and drinketh unworthily, eateth and drinketh judgment to himself. Now why does the apostle use this expression? Why does he say he who communicates unworthily eateth his own judgment? Listen and tremble. Because what we eat is, little by little, distributed through every part of our body, and so introduced and so changed into the substance of our flesh that afterwards it is impossible to separate it; thus the sentence of damnation of him who receives unworthily is so introduced, and so made one with him that it is a thing most difficult to separate from him; consequently, it is difficult for him to amend, to be converted, and to be saved. See, then, the chastisement with which God punishes those who receive unworthily, a chastisement invisible, indeed, but most terrible.

I have said that those who receive unworthily are guilty of the Body and Blood of Jesus Christ, even and more so than the Jews who crucified Him. If, then, the Jews, besides the temporal chastisements sent by God, besides being deprived of a kingdom—without a temple—without a priesthood—without sacrifice—dispersed here and there, hated and despised by all; more than that, they are chastised by a blindness and hardness of heart, no longer knowing the truth, no longer being converted to God, it is evident that this is also the ordinary chastisement that those who receive unworthily meet with, so that it is seen that they no longer know the truth, and care less about hearing it, despising every thing, as the Holy Ghost says: " The wicked man when he is come into the depth of sins, contemneth." Therefore, their conversion is most difficult—most difficult is also their salvation. King David committed two most grievous sins—adultery and murder—David repents, amends, and is saved.

Baltassar sins by profaning, not the body of Jesus Christ, as unworthy communicants, but only the sacred vessels, and he sees written by an invisible hand, on the walls of the palace, his own sentence—he reads it, has it explained, has time to repent and be converted; but Baltassar dies the same night impenitent, and he is damned. The apostle St. Peter sinned most grievously by his denial of Christ, but he weeps for his sin, is converted, and saved. Judas, after having conceived the idea of betraying Jesus Christ, communicates unworthily, he knows not how to give himself to true repentance, he goes forth, and hangs himself, dies impenitent, and he is damned. Truly it has been said that those who receive unworthily become more obstinate in evil, and their conversion is most difficult.

If God tolerates sacrilegious communicants, if He does not punish them at once by chastisements visible and sensible, it is because He has reserved for them a chastisement more terrible. He is now that meek Lamb, Who dissimulates, enduring the wicked treatment that He receives from them; but, oh! the time will come when He will, in His anger, say to such: "How camest thou in hither, not having on a wedding garment?" How dare you approach the holy altar without a wedding garment, that is to say, without the grace of God? You ought not so much, by reason of your wicked life, to have entered into the church; and you have had the boldness to receive Holy Communion with mortal sin upon your soul, making Me enter into your breast, and there placed Me in company with the devil, My greatest enemy, and there to receive from him every insult. And shall I endure all this? Ah! no: the time has now arrived that I should repay you for your iniquity. "Bind his hands and feet, and cast him into the exterior darkness; there shall be weeping and gnashing of teeth." And O my God! there in that awful prison the most fearful torments are destined for all who leave this world with the sin of a sacrilegious communion upon their souls; for, since it is the greatest of all crimes, so justice requires that it should be punished with the severest torments in hell. Woe to such—better for them had they never been born.

What ought we to do that we may avoid a chastisement so terrible? Are we to absent ourselves from Holy Communion, under the pretext of not making a sacrilegious communion, as many now do? Then we shall be lost? "Except you eat the flesh of the Son of Man, and drink His blood, you shall not have life in you." Then what we ought to do is, that if we are unable to have those sublime and excellent dispositions for the receiving of Holy Communion with great fruit, we ought, at least, to have that disposition absolutely necessary for a worthy communion, which consists in purifying our souls from all mortal sin, placing them in the state of grace by means of a good sacramental confession, as the apostle tells us: to prove ourselves, and so eat of that bread, and drink of the chalice. Then the Eucharistic Bread will be to us a bread of eternal life.

XVIII.

PERHAPS there is not a subject that ought to be more frequently spoken of than that of penance—there is not, perhaps, an obligation upon Christians greater than that of knowing well how to do penance; and yet, perhaps there is not a subject less understood or less observed by Christians than that of doing penance. Therefore, it being my duty to break unto you the bread of the word of God, and explain the obligations of a true Christian, not according to the idea of the world and its followers, but according to the spirit of Jesus Christ, the maxims of the gospel, and the teaching of the Fathers. I will endeavour to do so by giving you a clear and just idea of penance, and then conclude by exhorting you to do penance for your soul's sake.

Penance may be considered under a two-fold aspect—as a virtue and as a sacrament. Of penance as a sacrament, or sacramental confession, I will speak of next Sunday. To-day I will consider it as a virtue.

What, then, is meant by penance? It is a supernatural virtue which inclines the sinner to detest and grieve for his sins, inasmuch as they are offences against God, and to have a purpose of amendment and make satisfaction. The word itself denotes suffering for a past fault, the chastising of ourselves for offences committed. Penance, then, is a just punishment inflicted by one upon himself for offences that he is sorry to have committed.

Now it is a certain and undeniable fact that by sin God is both injured and slighted, for He Himself complains by the mouth of the prophet: "I have brought up children, and exalted them, but they have despised

Me." It is just that an injury be in some way repaired, and compensated, and if it be just, though God be the same justice, He cannot but wish and accept it. Hence the sinner to repair and compensate, in some way, the injury done to God, should punish and chastise himself for his offences; as a judge punishes an offender, that the injury, public or private, he has done, may be repaired. Moreover, by sin the friendship of God is lost, to regain which the sinner must make satisfaction by punishing himself, and thus show his displeasure for the evil he has done. Finally, sin is a great evil, and causes a deep wound in the soul; to repair this evil, and restore health to the soul, it is necessary that the sinner should make use of the remedy left by God, and that remedy is penance. Penance, therefore, is a punishment—a chastisement imposed by the sinner upon himself for his sins, and which he applies to the satisfying of the divine justice, the appeasing of God's wrath, the regaining of His friendship, and for the obtaining of the spiritual life of the soul. We will now see in what properly consists the true virtue of penance.

The followers of Luther say that penance is nothing more than the leading of a new life. Now you who continually relapse into sin, go to confession, fulfil the little enjoined upon you by the confessor, do you think you are doing true penance? Heretics affirm that true penance requires a change of life. But, although it is true that a change of life is necessary, yet it is also true that this is not sufficient for true penance. Because, for true penance it is necessary that the sinner both abhor and detest his past misspent life, conceive a hearty displeasure and sorrow for the evil he has done in offending God, and being touched by this displeasure, this sorrow, he resolve to satisfy the divine justice by punishing in himself the evil he has done, and determine to lead a life entirely different from the past. In fine, true penance is a hatred, a sorrow, and a displeasure for the evil that has been done against God, and a firm will to satisfy the divine justice by penal works, and a change of life. Whence it is this hatred and sorrow for sin ought to be chiefly for the injury done to God: "I am glad," says the apostle, "not because you were made sorrowful; but because you were made sorrowful unto penance; for the sorrow that is according to God worketh penance steadfast unto salvation." In fact, there cannot be true penance without a true conversion to God, that is, without abandoning sin, turning to God, and being in friendship with Him, because wherever Scripture speaks of penance, it speaks also of conversion. "Be penitent, therefore, and be converted. Be converted and do penance. Let the wicked forsake his way, and the unjust man his thoughts, and let him return to the Lord." Now how can a penitent be converted to God unless he repent of his sins, and have a will not to do them again? No: it is not possible for one to be reconciled to a person, and enjoy his friendship, unless he make proper satisfaction for the offence given. True penance, then, consists principally in sorrow for the offence done to God, with a will not only to a change of life, but to satisfy the divine justice by undergoing punishment for sins committed. The prophet Joel, in a few words, gives us a very clear idea of penance. "Be converted to me with all your heart, in fasting, and in weeping, and in mourning, and rend your hearts." True penance wills that the sinner forsake sin, turn to God, never to offend Him again. True penance causes the sinner to weep bitterly, and the heart to become, as it were, broken with sorrow, which leads him to perform penitential works, and thus punish sin in himself. St. Ambrose says: "That it is easier to find one who has preserved his innocence than one who has done suitable penance." And he goes on to say: in vain it is for one to suppose that he has done penance after having sinned, unless he punish, mortify, and deprive himself of those things that give pleasure. To perform true penance he must renounce the allurements and customs of the age, and be filled with sorrow for the offences committed against God, and he ought to pass day and night in sighs,

L

tears, and prayer, and live as if he were dead to the things of this world, denying himself, and being wholly changed from what he was before. Such is the sentiment of St. Ambrose, and such is the sentiment of all the Fathers. Now that cannot be called true penance that promises God more by the mouth than with the heart, going to confession, God knows with what disposition; through custom; without any change of life, suffering, or mortification, that the divine justice may be satisfied. No: this is not true penance; it is but pretending. Read the lives of those sinners who have been truly converted to God and saved, and you will find that they not only sorrowed for their sins, and implored God's pardon for them—not only did they hate and detest their misspent lives, but they renounced the pleasures of this world and passed their days in continual mortification, self-denial, prayer, and other works of penance, thus striving to satisfy, as much as they were able, the injuries done to God by their sins.

From what has been said you will be able to form a right idea of penance, and at the same time you will see that there are two kinds of penance—internal, and external. Internal penance is a sorrow for sin, a hatred and detestation for offences committed, a displeasure and grief for having offended God, joined with a firm and resolute will never to offend Him again, but to love and serve Him. External penance consists in chastising the body, practising penitential works—as fasts, abstinence, almsgiving, and such like; these things the saints practised, and also persons fearing God, and true penitents. Both the one and the other of these two kinds are absolutely necessary for the salvation of those who, after baptism, have fallen into mortal sin. Internal penance is absolutely necessary, because without it God will never forgive sin. External penance is necessary, if we are able to do it, so that we may in some way make reparation for the injuries done to God. Should we be unable to perform it, we ought to have the will and desire to do it. Of the necessity of both

internal and external penance, Holy Scripture clearly
points to it; for God commands us not only to have
sorrow for our sins: " Unless you shall do penance, you
shall all likewise perish," and that if we do it not we
shall be lost. " Be penitent, therefore, and be converted ;" but He expressly tells us: "Do penance . . . .
bring forth fruits worthy of penance." And that we
are to do so " with all our heart, in fasting, and in
weeping, and in mourning." This the Ninivites did
when they knew God was angry with them, and
threatened to exterminate them; not only did they
repent and asked forgiveness for their sins, but they
did the most austere penances, clothing themselves in
sackcloth and ashes, and observed a most rigorous fast
for many days. This is what, says our Blessed Lord,
would have been done in Tyre and Sidon if there had
been wrought the miracles that have been wrought in
you, they had long ago done penance in sackcloth and
ashes. All the saints of the Old and New Law did
thus : they were not satisfied with internal penance, but
practised also external penances. The Fathers of the
Council of Trent, speaking of penance, say : " The
penitence of a Christian, after his fall, is included
therein not only a cessation from sins, and a detestation thereof, or a contrite and humble heart, but also
satisfaction by fasts, alms, prayers, and the other pious
exercises of a spiritual life."

You have now heard what is meant by internal and
external penance, as commanded by our Blessed Lord,
taught by the Church, and practised by the saints of
both the Old and the New Law. But tell me, is this
penance really practised by Christians after their fall?
It will suffice to cast a glance at the customs and
maxims of the present age, and it will be clearly manifest that almost every other thing is thought of but
that of doing penance. To satisfy the passions, to
gratify self-love, to lead an easy, pleasant, and agreeable
life, is studied and thought of; but to the doing of penance little or no thought is given. Customs are becoming
daily more corrupt—maxims more perverse—vices.

increase—detraction, calumny, and licentiousness are everywhere to be found—immodesty openly indulged—liberty of writing, speaking, and doing abounds. And penance—oh! it is becoming more and more in disuse; everything else is done and thought of but that, so much so that the very name of penance, mortification, denying of the will, suffering, and carrying of the cross are looked upon as expressions extravagant, things unknown and not understood. Yet, without penance what will become of us? I will tell you in the words of our Blessed Lord: "Unless you shall do penance, you shall all likewise perish." That we may be animated to do penance, so necessary for our salvation, let us bring before our minds the examples of others, which ordinarily move us more than words. Let us consider the great penances performed by so many saints of noble birth, delicate like ourselves, and perhaps more so. If we read the lives of the saints, we shall find a Pelagia, who, after her conversion, clothed in a coarse garment, shut herself up in a cave that looked over the valley of Josaphat, and there passed her days in fasting, prayer, and great austerities. We shall find a Mary of Egypt, who, after her conversion, passed her life in the desert, exposed to the colds and heats of the seasons, her only food being herbs and water from a spring. We shall find a Margaret of Cortona, who, repenting of the sinful life she had led, gave herself up to the practice of a most austere life; not satisfied by frequently scourging herself, she disfigured her face, that it might not be any more an occasion of sin. We shall find a Mary Magdalene, who, after she had been told by her Lord that her sins had been forgiven, retired to a cave within a mountain, and there for thirty years wept and prayed continually, and did penance. But these we have named were sinners. We shall, however, find a Paula, a noble Roman matron, who had not fallen into mortal sin, but only into certain defects; yet she chastised and punished herself for them with so great a rigour that St. Jerome, her spiritual director, and by no means an indulgent one, counselled her to moderate her penitential life, but she replied, that it was but right her face should be disfigured, which had so often, contrary to the will of God, been painted through vanity. Examples of this kind can we find in our days amongst the daughters of men ? There is no necessity for the confessor to exhort them to mitigate the severity of their penance, since there is little danger of their excess on that point. The confessor, according to the Council of Trent, is obliged to give a penance proportionate to the sins, and the need of the penitent. Should the confessor prescribe to them a penance a little severe, he is immediately considered indiscreet, scrupulous, ignorant. One may be satisfied to go to confession and perform the little penance imposed upon her, but there will be found always the same vanity and ambition—the same idle life amidst pleasures and dangerous conversation. Oh, where is the change of life! Oh, where the penance! We shall find a Saint Teresa, who, during her whole life, committed no other sin except that of having read a book of romance, conceived a thought of vain-glory, an attachment to the vanity of the world, and yet she did so great penance, as the world knows, so that she was accustomed to say— suffer or die. We shall find a St. Catherine of Sienna, who fasted every day in the year on bread and water, slept but for two hours, and that upon a table, passing the rest of the night in prayer, and, not satisfied with wearing a chain of iron that penetrated her flesh, she disciplined herself three times a day. But why did she do so great penances ? For nothing else but for having one day indulged in a vain complacency in her dress. And in our day many hours are lost before the glass by persons seeking to adorn themselves, using every artifice that can contribute to their vanity, and perhaps their end is also bad, and they make no scruple about it. Now if the saints practised such severe penances for venial sins, what penance ought to be done by those who have committed not one only, but many mortal sins, and that for years, without having done condign penance ? What will the end of such be ? Jesus Christ has answered: "Unless you shall do penance, you shall all likewise perish."

Perhaps some of you, hearing of the absolute necessity of sinners doing penance, are filled with a great
fear, and thoughts of diffidence, trouble and grief may
arise in your mind. This or that one may say in his
mind : "Up to the present I have not done that penance that I ought to have done, and now I am unable
to do it by reason of my age, state of life, or indisposition of health ; then how can I be saved ?"

Penance is necessary for salvation, and he who has
not done it to him there is a motive for fear and
trembling: yea, it is well for him to fear, because the
saints had fear. St. Augustine says : "The man that
fears not is not a man ;" because the fear of the divine
justice is useful and salutary. "The fear of the Lord
driveth out sin ; and because God Himself tells us
that we are to work out our salvation with fear and
trembling. Nevertheless, we are not to abandon ourselves to diffidence and desperation. He who has not
done penance, let him do it in future, and if he is
unable to do what the saints did, let him do the little
he is able to do, and thus strive to satisfy the divine
justice. There are a thousand different ways by which
penance may be practised—means and occasions there
are—the will alone is required. Who is not able to
pray ? and prayer is a work of penance. Who is there
that cannot mortify and deny his will, depriving himself
of this or that thing that would give pleasure to the
senses ? and these mortifications of the will are all
penances. The Council of Trent says, that we are able
to do works of penitence not only by the punishments
we inflict upon ourselves for our sins—not only by those
imposed upon us by the confessor, but also by bearing
with patience and resignation those crosses that come
from the hand of God. Now where is the person in
the world without a cross ? Where is the house without a cross ? Here a tempest, a frost, a drought, a
flood, that brings ruin upon the land ; there an epidemic
that carries off the cattle ; death snatches away a husband, wife, or child ; here one brings about an unjust
law-suit, there another oppresses by his power ; one
steals your goods, another persecutes, and calumniates,

and destroys your reputation ; even the son, brother, parent, or neighbour by their bad conduct molest or disturb you. The husband has fallen in with a capricious, vain wife, from whom no good can be obtained ; a wife has taken to husband a spendthrift, passionate, cruel man ; that mother-in-law has a wicked daughter-in-law ; that son, that daughter has a vicious mother-in-law. In fine, every one has his cross, every one has something to suffer—some more, some less. All these evils, these crosses that God sends, if we suffer them with patience and resignation to the divine will ; if we make an offering of them to God for the offences we have committed against Him, are we not doing penance ? Yes, I say, and it is one of the best we can do ; because, by it we are imitating our divine model, Jesus Christ, Who to suffer for us, and to obtain forgiveness from the Eternal Father, desired not His own will, but suffered with great patience all the injuries, calumnies, and ill-treatment imposed upon Him.

Then take courage—be penetrated with a lively sorrow for having so often offended a God of infinite majesty, a God so worthy of your esteem, your love— ask Him to forgive you—have a hatred, an abhorrence for your misspent life ; be resolved to amend and lead a life wholly different for the future—desire to do all the penance you are able, especially during this time of Lent. Suffer something for the love of God and in satisfaction for your sins, and doubt not that doing this and persevering in it till death, the little penance you do, joined with the merits of the passion of Jesus Christ, which are applied to us, the justice of God will be satisfied—you will be saved, and heaven will be yours, since God is merciful, and good, and ever ready to pardon every time we renounce sin and turn to Him with our whole heart, as He Himself has declared : "Let the wicked forsake his way, and the unjust man his thoughts, and let him return to the Lord, and He will have mercy on him, for He is bountiful to forgive."

· XIX.

ON PENANCE AS A SACRAMENT.

ON last Sunday I spoke of Penance as a virtue, to-day I will speak of it as a sacrament.

Jesus Christ has truly instituted the Sacrament of Penance for the remission of sins; this is a truth that needs no proof, because it is of faith, defined by the Council of Trent, and constantly taught by the Church; were anyone to doubt it, he would be guilty of heresy. What is, then, the Sacrament of Penance? "Penance is a sacrament whereby the sins which we have committed after baptism are forgiven." The Council of Trent tells us that Jesus Christ instituted this sacrament after His resurrection, especially when He said to the apostles: "Receive ye the Holy Ghost, whose sins you shall forgive, they are forgiven them, and whose sins you shall retain, they are retained." Whence it is the same Council says: "This Sacrament of Penance is, for those who have fallen after baptism, necessary unto salvation, as baptism itself is for those who have not yet been regenerated." Consequently, as the Sacrament of Baptism is indispensable as a means, so also is the Sacrament of Penance indispensable as a means, so that whosoever is in mortal sin and wishes to be saved, he must absolutely receive the Sacrament of Penance, if he is able, and if he is not, he must have with sorrow, at least, the desire of receiving it.

Hence it is all the Fathers of the Church have said that the Sacrament of Penance is the second plank after shipwreck. For as after shipwreck one only refuge for saving life remains, to seize, if possible, on some plank from the wreck ; so after the loss of baptismal innocence, unless a man cling to the plank of penance, his salvation, without doubt, must be despaired of. The necessary form of the Sacrament of Penance are the words, " I absolve thee." The remote matter of this sacrament are sins committed after baptism—the proximate matter are the three acts of the penitent, that is, contrition, confession, and satisfaction. To instruct you fully upon these three acts time is required, and therefore I shall explain one at a time. To-day I will begin by speaking upon contrition, and I will show you what is its substance, how many kinds there are, and what are the qualities our contrition ought to have, that it may suffice to obtain pardon from God for our sins by means of the Sacrament of Penance.

The Council of Trent has defined "contrition a sorrow of mind, and a detestation for sin committed, with the purpose of sinning no more." From which you will see that contrition, in order to be real, must regard two things—the past, a hatred and detestation of sin; the future, an actual entering on a new sort of life. Contrition may be of two kinds, perfect or imperfect, and this last is also called attrition. Perfect contrition is that which proceeds from perfect charity, an ardent effect, a burning love towards God, by which the sinner, considering that he has offended a God so good and loveable, feels, as it were, heart-broken with sorrow, and therefore he prefers God above all things. This perfect contrition is most difficult to have, which has the power of obtaining pardon from God for sins before they have been confessed, although there remains the obligation of confessing them to the priest, and of receiving the absolution. Imperfect contrition is that which is called attrition, because it is commonly conceived either from the consideration of the turpitude of sin, or from the fear of hell and of punishment, and if with the hope of pardon it excludes the wish to sin, it prepares the way to justice. And although this attrition cannot of itself, without the Sacrament of Penance, conduct the sinner to justification, yet it disposes him to obtain the grace of God in the Sacrament of Penance, and receiving the absolution of the priest, the sins are forgiven. I said, if with the hope of pardon; for this hope is so necessary that without it we cannot make a good confession, nor can we obtain pardon of our sins.

We will now see what are the qualities our contrition ought to have, that so our confession may be good, and that we may receive validly the Sacrament of Penance, and thus obtain pardon of our sins.

Contrition ought to have these four qualities. It must be *internal;* that is to say, it must come from the heart: it must be *supreme*, that is to say, it must cause us to detest sin above every other evil: it must be *universal*, making us abhor all mortal sin whatsoever; it must be *supernatural*, that is to say, it must spring from a motive revealed by faith. Now, it seems to me that there is no better way of giving you a just and clear idea of these four conditions than by bringing before you the example of St. Mary Magdalene. The Church, three times in the year, proposes her to us as a model of that contrition we ought to have, and of the penance we ought to do for our sins; not that the perfect contrition of this saint is necessary, but that we are to strive to imitate her in the conditions required for the obtaining forgiveness of our sins.

It may be, as asserted by some, that Magdalene was a daughter of shame, or, as by others, a worldly-minded woman, filled with pride and vanity, like many in our own day. The truth is that she was, as the Gospel tells us, in the first place, a great sinner, and as such she was known in the city: "A woman that was in the city, a sinner." In the second place, she had committed many sins, for Jesus Christ said so. "Many sins are forgiven her, because she hath loved much." In the third place, the life she led was one of scandal, for the Pharisee murmured that Jesus Christ should have allowed her in His presence, saying within himself: "This man, if he were a prophet, would know surely what manner of woman this is that toucheth Him." In the fourth place, she was possessed of many evil spirits. "Mary, who is called Magdalene, out of whom.

seven spirits were gone forth." But what was her
sorrow, repentance, and contrition? This is what I am
about to show that those who have imitated her by
sin, may be led to imitate her, in as much as they are
able, by penance.

The contrition of Magdalene was, in the first place,
internal, that is to say, it came from the heart. She
had heard of Jesus Christ, and longed to listen to Him.
And oh! the marvellous change that immediately took
place in her? She felt as if a veil had been taken'
from before her eyes: all the enchantments of pleasure
disappeared; the dense cloud of passions that obscured
her mind gave place to a most resplendent light, which
caused her to know the state of her soul, and she
became filled with a fearful horror at the clear and
distinct view it gave her of her sins. Oh, she fervently
exclaimed to herself, I wish to go forth from this state
so abominable, so loathsome. I desire to be converted
to my God, I will seek Him, never more to abandon
Him. "I will rise, and will go about the city; I will seek
Him Whom my soul loveth." Thus she spoke within
herself, and firmly resolved and promised that God,
Who has promised pardon to the sinner to-day, but
has not promised it on the morrow. She resolved to
be converted, and was converted from that moment.
In fact, as soon as she knew that Jesus Christ sat at
meat in the Pharisee's house, without hesitation at that
instant she takes an alabaster box of ointment, and goes
forth to find Him. She enters the house of the proud
Pharisee, and there she prostrates herself at the feet
of Jesus Christ, filled with confusion, and not daring to
look at His face—softened by His goodness in allowing
her to be in His presence—touched by the enormity of
her sins—penetrated with disgust for having so often
offended so good a God, her eyes become two fountains
of tears with which she bathes the feet of Jesus Christ,
and wipes them with the hairs of her head, kisses them
and anoints them with ointment. These are the signs
of a contrition truly *internal*—these are the signs of a
sorrow, a repentance that comes from the heart. These

are the tears desired by the Prophet Jeremias for the offences committed against God. "Who will give water to my head, and a fountain of tears to my eyes? and I will weep day and night."

Some of you may say: "We are unable to shed tears for our sins, we have not a heart tender and sensible like the penitent Magdalene; therefore, we have never had sorrow or true contrition for the obtaining of pardon for our sins, nor for the making of a good confession." Listen—tears, tenderness, and sensibility of heart are good, but they are not necessary for true contrition; for, were it so, those who have a temperament strong and robust, that neither feel tenderness nor shed tears, could never have true contrition; nor are these always infallible signs of contrition, for very often tears do not proceed from a displeasure for having offended God, but rather from an effect of a temperament by nature tender, and then tears are worth nothing. That which is necessary for contrition is to strive to know the great evil sin is, and, knowing it, abhor, hate, and detest it, having a firm will never again to commit it. "I have committed such sins, I have offended God, I have done a great evil, I wish I had never done it, it grieves me that I had not died rather than have committed it; I would rather die than again fall." This, said from the heart, forms true contrition, real internal sorrow. Therefore, sincere sorrow consists not in tenderness, sensibility, tears, or in any other external sign, but properly in the heart, in the will that hates sin as an evil hated and detested by God, that wishes it had not been done, and resolves not to do it again; for, says Jesus Christ: "From the heart comes forth evil thoughts, murders, adulteries, fornications, thefts, false testimonies, blasphemies." So, it is the heart, and it is the will that ought to condemn this evil, hate and detest it, and resolve never to do it again.

But we must not lose sight of the penitent Magdalene. Her sorrow was not only *internal* but it was *supreme*, for she conceived a greater displeasure for her sins than for any other evil in the world, and she resolved to

suffer every possible evil in this world rather than
again return to sin, and she was disposed to submit
herself to every humiliation, insult, and suffering rather
than live another moment in sin. For, as soon as she
knew Jesus Christ was in the house of the Pharisee,
she went directly, cast herself at His feet, nor would
she allow any obstacle or difficulty to stand in her
way.

It must have been a most humiliating and painful
thing for a woman of quality, in the fulness of youth,
and unattended, in the garb of a penitent, to walk
through the streets in a place where she was known only
by the title of a sinner, and to enter into the house of
the Pharisee, in the presence of a large number of guests,
and there, despised and insulted by that proud Pharisee.
No matter, penetrated, as she was, with that supreme
sorrow for her sins, she overcame every difficulty, and
she was willing to suffer every humiliation, every evil,
providing she were made free of sin, the greatest of all
evils. She said within herself: " I had no shame in
being known as a woman in the city, a sinner, much
less ought I to be ashamed of being known as a great
penitent. I did not have fear in committing so many
sins, nor ought I to fear in doing penance for them.
The fear of God did not prevent me from attaching
myself to creatures ; the fear of creatures ought not to
prevent me now from having recourse to God, my
Creator. Whatever evil I may suffer will be nothing
compared to the evil I have done by my sins." Such
was the force of the contrition of Magdalene ; such
ought to be our contrition if we desire pardon of God
for our sins. The evil we do by sin is supreme, therefore our sorrow ought to be supreme. We ought to be
disposed to suffer every kind of evil rather than sin
again. No matter how painful it may be to break off
that habit, that friendship, that pleasure—do it we
must, rather than sin. No matter how painful it may
be to give up unjust gains, usury, and all unlawful
profits—do it we must, rather than sin. No matter
how painful may be penance, mortification, sickness,

affliction, troubles, persecutions, and crosses, we must suffer them and tolerate them rather than sin ; for sin is an evil infinitely greater than every other evil. Now, reflect you who find a difficulty in every thing but that of committing sin—you to whom every thing is painful but sin ; consider your sorrow, your contrition, whether it has been what it ought to be—supreme. And if not, do you suppose God will pardon your sins ? Never : if it is not supreme, what will your confessions be ? Null, or so many sacrileges.

The contrition must be not only *supreme*, but it must be like that of Magdalene, *universal.* "Many sins are forgiven her, because she hath loved much." Some there are who say : "I repent of all my sins, but of that frailty I neither know how to repent or amend ; with that exception I have no other notable defect." You do not know how to repent of that frailty ? Then your sorrow, your repentance is worth nothing; because, if you were sorry for having offended God, you would repent of that sin as well as of every other offence against Him. You have no other notable defect unless that ? And if you do not repent and amend, that alone will ruin your soul, because God has declared : "Whosoever shall keep the whole law, but offend in one point, is become guilty of all." Your contrition, to be good, ought to be universal ; it ought to extend to all mortal sin, not excepting one, so that you ought to repent either of all your sins in particular, one by one, or in general, with the will to amend: Observe the contrition of Magdalene. The Gospel tells us that she had committed many sins, but it also assures us that she repented of many, that is to say, of all. She had committed many sins through her love for creatures, but she repented of them all for the love of her Creator. For, since she had " yielded her members to serve uncleanness and iniquity unto iniquity, so now she yields them to serve justice unto sanctification and penance." The eyes which she had used in darting forth evil looks are now to be employed in weeping for her sins; her hair, that had been an

ornament of vanity, was made to wipe the feet of Jesus
Christ; her feet, that had trodden the path of iniquity,
were now to follow Jesus Christ in the road that leads
to heaven. All her jewellery and ornaments were, in
part trampled under her feet, in part converted to a
good use. No longer filled with pride, vain-glory no
more ruled over her; no longer she felt angry
towards those who spoke evil of her, but left her defence to Him to Whom she respectfully attached herself.
Such was the change made in Magdalene by her repentance, by the sorrow she had for her sins; such ought
to be our repentance, such our sorrow. It ought to be
universal, so that we detest all our past sins not yet
cancelled, and make us resolve to avoid all sin for the
future, according to what God has said by the prophet:
" Be converted and do penance for all your iniquities."
Be converted, not only from some, but from all sin,
" and make to yourselves a new heart and a new
spirit."

Finally, the sorrow and contrition of Magdalene was
supernatural. She did not repent through natural
motives, human and earthly, like many who repent of
the evil they have done, because of the danger there is
of their losing their reputation. No: she did not
repent through any human or earthly motive, otherwise her contrition would have been worth nothing.
Magdalene, touched by the grace of God, repented
through motives divine and supernatural—motives that
sprung from faith. Her mind, enlightened by this
light of faith, was filled with fear at the sight of her
sins. "Ah!" she exclaimed, from the bottom of her
heart, " to what a state have I been brought! To what
excesses of shamefulness have I given myself up!
If I had but lost my peace, my tranquillity, my reputation, but oh! I have lost my soul, grace, heaven, and
by my sins I have deserved hell; I have lost You, my
God, You, Who are the most beautiful, perfect, and
most loveable of all objects. Oh, the evil I have done!
Unhappy me! The majesty of God dishonoured and
despised—heaven lost—hell merited—the soul stripped

of grace. These are the motives of faith and supernatural through which Magdalene repented of her sins, and these are the motives through which we ought to repent of our sins, that our contrition may be supernatural. That these motives of faith may excite in our heart a sincere sorrow and true contrition, so necessary for a good confession and for the obtaining pardon for our sins, we must meditate and reflect seriously upon them; we must consider the great injury done to God by sin; we must reflect on the momentary pleasure and the little that is very often gained by sin; and consider the great evil sin is in itself, its deformity, the ruin it brings upon the soul, and the terrible chastisements with which it is punished by God. We must reflect upon the eternal happiness of heaven, lost by it; we should also think of that inevitable death, the rigorous judgment it draws down upon us. By a serious and profound meditation upon these truths we turn to God and ask Him to give us His assistance, His grace, so that we may repent of our sins, and make a good confession; and then God, Who never denies His grace to those who ask it, will give light to our mind, and soften our heart, so that we may conceive a sorrow sufficient for the obtaining pardon of our sins through the Sacrament of Penance; as He has said: "I will take away the stony heart, and will give them a heart of flesh."

It now remains for me to speak of the last quality of Magdalene's contrition. Not only was it internal, supreme, universal, and supernatural, but it was also a contrition most *efficacious*. She resolved to be converted to God, and to Him she was converted—she resolved to amend, and she did—she resolved to lead a Christian life, a holy life, and she did. Abandoning her house at Magdala, where she had retired to lead a life of independence, she returned to Bethania with Martha, her sister, and Lazarus, her brother—no more was she to be seen in conversation—no more to be seen dressed out with vain ornaments, but in the habit of a penitent she followed Jesus Christ—never again did she abandon Him—she followed Him everywhere, even to Calvary, to death, to the sepulchre. As the follower of Jesus Christ and the sister of Lazarus risen to life by our Lord, the Jews hated her, and sent her into exile. And for thirty-three years she led a life of continual penance, though she had been assured by our Blessed Lord that her sins were forgiven, yet she did penance to expiate more and more the sins she had committed, and for those she had caused in others.

She, then, is the model of contrition and penitence proposed to us by the Church three times in the year. But where are the sinners that strive to imitate her? Where are those true penitents? If they promise to amend, this amendment is never seen—if they promise to break off from sin, those bad habits, evil friendships, they do not—they do nothing else but sin and confess, confess and sin ; how then can we suppose that their sorrow, their contrition, their conversion, is real and good? We can understand how a person may fall through weakness and human frailty ; but when one falls again and again into the same sins, when he leads the same evil and wicked life, when we see no change, then it is not through weakness and human frailty, but malice. Then it is we cannot believe there has been true contrition, for if there had it would have produced some good effect. The sign of true contrition is an amendment of life, and where there is no amendment, there is no true penitence. And what will be the consequence of such penitence? Final impenitence, an evil death : "You shall seek me and you shall die in your sins."

XX.

ON THE EXAMEN.

IF for a good and valid confession it were sufficient to go to the feet of the confessor and tell him those sins -which occur to the mind, without making any examen of conscience, without purpose of amendment, and without sorrow, oh! then I should employ my zeal upon some other subject; but you, yourselves, know that something more is required. I will therefore give a series of instructions on confession, that you may know how to approach the tribunal of penance, and receive the absolution worthily. According to the teaching of theologians five things are necessary for the worthy receiving of this sacrament. 1st, A diligent examen of the conscience; 2ndly, A sincere accusation of all our sins; 3rdly, Sorrow for having committed them; 4thly, Firm purpose of amendment; 5thly, Satisfaction. In all of which very many Christians are wanting. The subject, then, being one of such vast importance, I shall give an instruction upon each one of these conditions, beginning with the examen, explaining how it ought to be done, and in what way faults are committed against this first condition.

What, then, is this examen? It is a particular inquiry into one's own conscience in order to arrive at a self-knowledge of all the thoughts, words, works, and omissions contrary to the Divine law, to the end that a secret self-accusation, before a duly authorised priest, be made with a contrite and humble heart. You have to enter into yourselves and see what use you have made of the powers of your soul, of the inspirations, benefits, and graces received from God, and how you have observed His commands. You are not, however, to suppose that this instruction is directed to those who, by the Divine grace, live in the presence of God, go frequently to confession, make a daily examination of their conscience; for such there is but little difficulty in making this self-examen, and for them but a short time is required to recall to their mind their daily defects. Nor are you to suppose that it is my wish to give an occasion of scruple to certain delicate and timorous consciences, who, after using all possible diligence in trying to find out their faults, are never satisfied; always fearing that their examen has not been sufficiently well made—that something has been forgotten—that some circumstance has been passed over, and thus by their scrupulosity make confession odious and difficult, in place of it giving consolation and peace of heart. To such I say, let them use that diligence that is morally possible, and that will suffice. Every extreme is to be avoided. And since they deserve censure who use little or no diligence in their examen, so likewise do those who, scrupling unnecessarily about the number and circumstances of their sins, are perhaps wanting in that which is most necessary— the detestation of them, and the purpose of amendment. My intention, then, is to direct my discourse to those who have not been to confession for months, a year, or more, and who now desire to approach this sacrament, and to them I say they ought to use great diligence in the examen of their past life.

But here it may be asked what this diligence ought to be? The Council of Trent answers this question, saying that we ought to use the same degree of exactitude that a reasonable and prudent individual would devote to any affair of the very first importance. Suppose a person had to render an account before a tribunal of this world of such importance that upon the success or loss of the case would depend the establishment or the ruin of himself and of his family, such an one would retire to his room, leaving everything else aside—to this alone he would give his whole thought; thinking

and writing upon this subject until he had made everything clear. All this is done for a worldly interest.

Now, were you so disposed you could not condemn
me for severity in asking you to give, at least, the same
diligence in the examen of your conscience, more especially as it is of the soul you have to give an account,
and this account is not to be made to man, who may
err, but to God, Who cannot be deceived. Yes, like
the prodigal son, reflect upon yourself, be ashamed at
having wasted your divine portion by so many offences
against God your heavenly Father, put aside all worldly
affairs, retire to the church, or to your own room, and
there prostrate yourself before the majesty of God, to
Whom all hearts are open, implore His aid that you
may be able to discover the extent of your guilt. Think
also that this may be the last confession of your life,
and that upon it may depend your eternal happiness
or misery, and that by it you have to repair past evils.
Happy you will be if you thus dispose yourself for this
examen by these reflections.

By some of you it may be asked : " What have we to
do, how can we make this examen, we, who have not
been to confession for so long a time ? How can we
lay open so many folds and recesses of our consciences ?
how can we investigate into so many ways, into which
we have wandered ? or how can we recall to our mind
the number of our sins ?" If you give me your attention I will show you how this can be done with the
greatest facility. Supposing, then, as Christians you
know the commandments of God, and of the Church,
the sacraments, the seven capital sins, and these form
the heads of your examen. You know that by the first
commandment that there is but one true and living
God ; and here you examine yourself whether you have
loved Him above all things, served, and adored Him ;
if you have loved and esteemed the goods of this world,
honours, or any created thing more than God, and in
them placed your last end. Whether you have doubted
the mysteries of religion, or divine providence ; despaired
or presumed on the divine mercy ; had any dealings with

the devil, or in superstitious practices. The second commandment—not to take the name of the Lord in vain ; and here make a rigorous examen of the tongue, whether you have by oaths, or by perjury, or by blasphemy, dishonoured the name of God, or of the saints. Examine whether you have sanctified the Lord's Day and other festivals, or employed your time in servile work, neglecting prayer and other spiritual exercises. Examine, children, what has been your obedience and respect towards your parents and superiors. With regard to your neighbour, investigate your consciences whether you have offended him by word or deed ; whether you have any ill-will against him, or injured his good name by detraction or calumny ; whether you have stolen or received things from others that were stolen. Examine whether your conscience accuses you of any thing contrary to the sixth commandment, in thought, word, or action, and with what persons. And thus you will go through the other commandments of God, and those of His Church : whether you have heard Mass on days appointed, and with what devotion ; how you have observed the fasting days; how you have made your confessions and communions, and with what dispositions ; and then upon the capital sins, of which hereafter we will speak in particular. And here it is necessary to observe, with the Council of Trent, that it is not sufficient to confess sin in general, but we must confess the number, kind, and such circumstances as alter the nature of the crime. Every precept has diverse kinds of sin, and these ought to be distinguished and explained in as much as we are able. We have also to mention the number of our sins as far as we are able and capable of determining, without waiting, as most penitents do, till the confessor has himself found out. Nor is it sufficient to confess the number of sins, but also the circumstances that change the nature of sin ; for instance, unlawful intercourse, whether with a single person or one married ; in the latter case it is not only impurity, but likewise adultery. Again, to steal a sacred thing, or in a sacred place is a sacrilege, which would otherwise be a sin only of theft. Not only the kind, number, and circumstances of sin, but also the consequences of them, that is to say, we have to endeavour to discover in how far we have been a stumbling-block to our fellow-men, as in the sins of scandal, which are done either by deeds or words in the presence of the innocent, teaching them evil of which they were ignorant—sins which are so common in our day, and if we have been guilty of them, God alone knows how many souls have been ruined and lost by them! You have to reflect whether you place yourself in such an occasion, in which, ordinarily speaking, you fall into sin, and if the occasion is proximate, you are necessarily bound to manifest it. The same may be said if you find yourself in a position that is sinful, or practise a profession that is the cause of sin to you ; you must abandon it at whatever cost, or whatever gain may accrue to you by it. Also to see whether you have co-operated with others for an evil end. With regard to sins of thought you ought to make a most rigorous examen, of which so many, through an affected shameful ignorance, make no account; and providing they have not done the evil action ; these internal sins they do not confess. But, my God! who is able to comprehend the number of similar sins that are committed by a person who allows the passion of hatred and vindictiveness to rule and govern him, or entertains an unlawful attachment towards a forbidden object ? How many of these bad thoughts pass through the mind ? How many evil desires contaminate the will ? How many sinful complacencies—how many depraved intentions ? The Council of Trent says: that by reason of the facility with which they are committed, and for the number of them, oftentimes they are more pernicious than external sins and give a deeper wound to the soul ; therefore, examine yourself well upon this point.

This is not all. A diligence not less ought to be used in recalling to your mind the sins of omission. The more frequent sins, the more neglected by the greater part of Christians. Look to the duties imposed upon you by your calling, condition, and state of life. Heads of houses and fathers of families, do you pay your just debts, do you satisfy those employed by you, do you watch over the morals of your domestics, do you educate your children according to the will and teaching of the Church? Mothers, do you teach your daughters modesty and retirement? Perhaps you allow them to associate with whomsoever comes or goes. Examine yourselves. Servants and administrators of the goods of others, have you the same care of them as if they were your own; do you look faithfully to their interests? Merchants and shopkeepers, do you adulterate your goods; give short weight and measure; and are your contracts always lawful and just? Persons whose position in life enables them to promote piety and repress scandals, do they do so? Do you assist the poor according to your means? Examine yourselves. Happy you will be if you take the time necessary and use the diligence required for recalling to the memory your sins.

Now let me ask is this diligence used by most Christians in seeking to know their sins? Do they withdraw as much as is necessary from the cares of business, from worldly pleasures and pursuits, in order to prepare with recollection and fervour to a reconciliation with God by penance? Do they give the same time to the examen that they give to some domestic affair of vast importance? Experience says No. Months, and perhaps years have passed by since they made their confession, and on an occurrence of a Jubilee or an Indulgence, the Feast of the Nativity, or that of Easter, and then either through custom or that they may not be pointed at, they go to the feet of a confessor. Wait a while. Let me ask such have you examined your conscience? What time have you spent in your examen? The reply of many is—I have given a glance at my conscience. Then they bring before the priest a confused mass of sins, a general narration of having sworn, blasphemed, detracted, without distinction of circumstances, kind, or number; and thus they expect to make a good

confession with so many sins left out; they deceive themselves if they think God will remit them. True it is,
God remits the sin that does not occur to our memory,
but not when we have given little or no time to the
examen. Others there are, who, when they come to
confession would wish their confession to be made by
the confessor questioning them, as if he ought to be
able to reveal occult things. This class of persons
remind me of the King of Babylon, who had a
dream, and he called together the diviners and the wise
men, and he said to them: "I saw a dream, and, being
troubled in mind, I know not what I saw; tell me the
dream and the interpretation thereof." They said:
"Tell to thy servants thy dream, and we will declare
the interpretation thereof." "Father, question me,"
some will say; "Ask me what I have done." The confessor is there to hear your sins, and not to guess them;
open first your own conscience, and then he will
question you, and apply the remedy. I do not deny
that this disposition of replying to the questions asked
by the confessor may be now and then sufficient for a
good confession. For instance, those who are wanting
in intelligence, and who are incapable of bringing to
their memory their sins, although they give much time
in reflecting upon them; but not for those who have
intelligence and ability for everything else but that of
examining their consciences. These are by no means
excused from the self-examen. You have, I repeat, to
use the same diligence in the examen that a reasonable
and prudent individual would devote to any affair of
the very first importance. Tell me, if you have to
recover or increase some property belonging to you; to
gain some post of honour and emolument, what diligence, what caution do you not use? How much
mental labour do you not give to study and speculation?
And when the soul is to be taken from the hands of the
devil by a good confession, the regaining of the grace
of God, the glory of heaven, there is neither time to be
found for the examen, nor intelligence to make it. Then
if you have any care for your soul and its salvation, take

a little more time, and use a little more diligence in examining yourselves. Think over it again and again.

Others there are who say, " We have thought again and again, and we can scarcely find matter for absolution."

Not find matter for absolution—is this the truth? If you are amongst those who every eight, fifteen days, or once a month go to confession, live in the holy fear of God, observe the Divine law, I am not surprised, since this is the fruit of the sacraments, to preserve souls from mortal sin. But if they who speak thus are of that class who go seldom to confession, say but once a year, live according to the maxims of the world, I fear very much that they are deceived by a false security, and that the reason why they do not find matter for absolution is because they do not seek to find it. Were they to use that diligence which the Council of Trent enjoins of examining and searching all the folds and recesses of the conscience, I know full well they would find sins. But since it would be necessary to reform their life, that reformation they do not wish. They would have to deny themselves of certain pleasures so agreeable to them, and deprive themselves of a certain liberty which they have not the moral courage to do, hence the reason why they find no matter for absolution.

Too true it is that many Christians are lost who fear nothing more than to be enlightened concerning certain sins, for which they have a leaning and an affection, having always some secret within their heart which they have never penetrated, that they may place themselves, so to speak, in security, both from the remorse of conscience and from the reprehensions of their confessor. They choose to be blind to the light of reason by persuading themselves that there is no great evil in those objects in which their heart finds an interest. From this arises those false consciences which now-a-days are so common, that in order not to be troubled about their faults to which they are attached, they neglect to examine and search for them. In fact, if

many tradespeople were to examine themselves, pene-
trating into the secrets of their heart, they would find
injurious lies—frauds and usury—unlawful contracts
and unjust gains; but as they would have to diminish
their profits, restore what has been unlawfully acquired,
for this reason they do not search the depths of their
heart. If that man of pleasure were to examine with
more attention his conscience, he would discover intemperance in those recreations and banquets—filthiness
in those conversations, and a too tender attachment
towards certain persons; but because he knows that
such things would not be approved of by the confessor,
he prefers remaining in ignorance; he searches for
nothing, because he does not wish to amend. If that
woman of the world were to go a little deeper in her
examen, she would find herself wanting in propriety in
her dress, too free in her conversation, having a confidence not altogether holy—thoughts not quite chaste,
and affections, which when stripped of their false idea,
will prove to be wholly sensual; but because it would be
absolutely necessary to dress more modestly, and discontinue certain evening visits and conversations, and other
pleasures, for this reason she allows all remorse to be
lulled to rest, and in them she finds nothing, because
in them she wishes to change nothing. I know full
well that if the examen is made thus, matter for absolution will not be discovered.

Like King Saul, who had received a command from
God to go and smite and destroy everything belonging
to the Amalekites; but Saul spared the king, and the
best of the flocks, and would not destroy them, but
everything that was good for nothing he destroyed.
So you in your examen spare whatsoever is pleasing to
you, and for that reason you have little to confess. But
do not deceive yourselves. Reflect whether the life of
a Christian ought to be one of idleness, diversion, and
pleasure, such as the world offers, and such perhaps as
your life has been. Recall to your mind how the saints
made their examen, and how it is made by so many
holy souls in our own time. They, undeceived by the

world, are filled with the one desire, that of pleasing God. Reflect on the rigorous examen they make of their most minute defects, and in the bitterness of their soul manifest them to their confessor, never ceasing to complain of their ingratitude to God, and their want of attention to the duties of their state of life, fearing lest they may be culpable in those things in which they are not. Were you to reflect in this manner, I am sure you would find matter for confession. Should these holy souls have had the misfortune to spend but one day without thinking of their soul or God—had they been but once to the theatre or to some other place of amusement where every one tries to outstrip others in dress and make an appearance—had they been present at the conversations that you have been present at, where there was so much freedom and where there was a want of that sobriety and modesty that becomes a Christian; oh! then with what rigour, what search, what examen would they not have made, and how much matter would they have discovered for confession? And you that do these things, not for one day, but for months, and perhaps for years, and yet you cannot find matter for confession? Examine yourselves with a little more diligence.

Finally, "What can we confess," some will say; "we do not commit fornication, nor do we steal, blaspheme, or kill." What? Are there not other sins besides these? That young man, perhaps, does not sin by action, frequenting certain places, but does he reflect on the improper conversation spoken in those places, and in hearing it; are there not morbid delectations, unchaste thoughts and desires? That young woman does not steal, but does she make any scruple about robbing God of souls by that want of modesty and sobriety in adorning herself, by the too great freedom she uses towards others; were she to examine herself she would discover that her intentions are not always innocent. Fathers of families, you may not blaspheme, but do you allow those under your charge to dishonour God?

You do not kill, but do you fulfil your obligations in

giving alms to the poor; do you spend in luxury and vanity that which would be the means of saving others from starvation? More exactness, more diligence in your examen. And if you ask me what kind of exactness, I will tell you, if it were possible, that which Jesus Christ will use examining your conscience on the last day. What will that exactness be? He will examine every idle word. Think, then, on what it will be with scandalous and filthy language—with swearing and cursing. He will examine every thought, and even our good works. Oh! then, for this time make the examen well—apply a remedy for your past negligence —use the proper time for making it and the diligence necessary. Allow not a thought, word, work, or omission to pass by unnoticed, so that you may make an accusation of them to the priest, upon which I will speak in my next instruction.

XXI.

WE must confess that Divine Providence is infinitely good for having provided remedies for so many evils, not only for those of the body, but also for those of the soul. The soul is subject to many spiritual infirmities, even after baptism, by which original sin has been taken away; and for these spiritual infirmities Jesus Christ has left an efficacious remedy, forming of His own most precious Blood a salutary bath by which the soul can be healed.

Who could be lost if the loving design of our blessed Lord were never made void? But, oh! even in this the devil has found a means of changing the medicine into poison, and of causing many to be suffocated in that bath, from which they ought to receive holiness and life! This wicked spirit cannot entirely do away with confession, but he does all he can to induce the incautious to abuse it. And oh! how many Christians in our days make bad confessions and are lost! They accuse themselves of their sins to a priest, but not as they ought, and being wanting in this necessary condition, their confessions are invalid or sacrilegious. To prevent, then, or rather to take away so detestable a fault, I give the present instruction, explaining how the accusation of our sins ought to be made to the priest, in order to make a good confession.

This accusation, commonly called confession, is no other than a manifestation of those sins which, according to their kind, number, and circumstances, we have discovered in the examen of our conscience. This accusation is necessary by the divine law, and it is to be made to a priest, who is the judge appointed by God. It is, however, necessary to observe that although this sacrament of confession is administered by way of judgment in which the sinner is the culprit and the priest the judge ; yet there is a great difference between the manner of judging in this divine tribunal and in that of a human tribunal. In the tribunal, in which men give judgment, the culprit who confesses his guilt is condemned to punishment, and he who denies his guilt, when there is no one to prove the contrary, is liberated. But in this tribunal of divine justice, or rather of divine mercy, the culprit, who without any dissimulation confesses his crime, is liberated; but he who refuses to confess, or denies it, is condemned to eternal punishment. From whence arises this difference? Because the priest in the tribunal of penance represents that heavenly Father so loving and so good, and he is also invested with the name of father, and, as a father, the sinner confesses to him. And he who confesses his faults to a father, that he may obtain forgiveness, ought, without any evasion, to accuse himself.

Having then found a father, a confessor, furnished with all those necessary qualifications, confide in him as in one whom you wish to use for the obtaining of your eternal salvation ; as an angel from heaven, or rather as one who holds the place of God on earth. Present, then, yourself to him, show him your wounds, and they will be healed. This is what our Blessed Lord imposed upon the lepers of whom St. Luke speaks. These lepers begged of our Lord to cure them of their leprosy, and he told them to go and show themselves to the priest, and whilst they were on the way found themselves cleansed. But was not Christ able to cure them, as He had done to many others, without their going to the priest? Yes: He could, but He wished to give us to understand what we ought to do in the law of grace, that sinners may obtain the cure of their spiritual infirmities, that is, to go to the priest and manifest what is within their hearts. Then go to the priest if you desire the healing of your wounds and obtain the remission of your sins. Go, this is the com-

mand of Christ. We are not to seek or make excuses
or pretexts to be dispensed from it. Show yourselves
to the priest, and what you are. Let nothing prevent
you from appearing guilty in that tribunal. Manifest
to him your most hidden thoughts, your guilty complacencies, and your wicked desires; open to him those
depraved and hitherto impenetrable inclinations of your
heart; those mysteries of iniquity, and those actions,
which, perhaps, you have up to the present concealed.
No matter how loathsome may be your infirmity, how
deep your wounds, fear not; go and show them to the
priest, he is your spiritual physician, to whom Christ
has given the power to cure all your wounds, and heal
all your diseases. "If your sins be as scarlet they shall
be made as white as snow." Though you may have
committed the most heinous wickedness that it could
be possible to commit in this world, all will be pardoned,
with, however, this indispensable condition, that you
conceal nothing, but manifest everything to the priest.
" Go show thyself to the priest."

Here you must know what ought to be the accusation, and what are the conditions that ought to accompany it to obtain the end? The accusation of our sins
ought to be humble, sincere, simple, and entire. When
we confess our sins to a priest, we are as so many
criminals at the tribunal of our divine King, by us
offended, seeking mercy and pardon from Him. What,
then, can be more seemly; yea, more necessary, than
humility? What would you say of one guilty of high
treason, were he to appear before his sovereign in a
pompous manner, and with a haughty dimension? In
place of moving him to pity it would urge him to punish.
The same may be said of those Christians who present
themselves at the tribunal of penance filled with pride;
the same may be said of those daughters of Eve who go
to confession dressed out as if they were so many idols,
going to a ball or theatre. This sort of demeanour
tends rather to provoke God than move Him to mercy
and pardon.

In the second place, the accusation of our sins must

be sincere. It is one of a confessor's greatest trials to meet with certain penitents, who, in place of honestly making known their faults without a long preface, wish to relate the entire story from the beginning. And very often the whole fault consists in an ill word, in an act of impatience, or a curse, and before confessing it they go through a lengthened and fastidious account, noting most minutely the time, the hour, the persons, and their names, the questions and the answers, which would try the patience of the most phlegmatic person; and if the ill words or the acts of impatience had been ten times, they wish to relate the beginning of each one. Faults are to be confessed, and not things which do not belong to them.

Worse again are those who, in place of accusing themselves with all simplicity, give their mind to the framing of a thousand excuses, blaming others for their own faults. Such persons ought to know that nothing moves God to pardon sins more than a frank and plain confession. Observe the way God dealt with our first parents. Before condemning them He asked them why they had broken His precept, so that they might, by a sincere and humble confession, obtain His forgiveness. But what did they do? In place of confessing their sin, they closed the bowels of divine mercy and forgiveness by excusing themselves; Adam blamed Eve, and Eve the serpent. Ah! too true it is, we have inherited from our first parents not only sin, but also that bad custom of excusing ourselves, and this even in confession. In fact, in the confessional are heard these or similar expressions: "Father, my children are so disobedient and so rude that it is enough to vex a saint;" this is what a mother will say excusing herself for being angry, and using imprecations. "If you were to hear my husband, he would try the patience of Job;" this is the excuse that that proud wife will make, because she cannot bear any suggestion made by her husband. "If you knew my wife—I will not say more, she always wishes to have the last word;" thus the husband excuses himself because his wife reproves him for his vices. One blames this person and another that person. One blames the devil, because he tempted him, whilst another the occasion that led him to do evil. In one word, almost all accuse others, but not themselves, or at least they try in some way to cover or diminish their own faults. Take away these excuses, accuse yourselves, and confess your sins, and not those of others. Say in the bitterness of your soul : "I am guilty, mine is the fault, not that of the husband, not that of the wife, not that of the children ; through malice I have sinned. I knew full well that I was doing evil, and I did it against the remorse of my conscience—against the divine inspirations. It is not the devil who caused me to sin, but my perverse will ; it is not the occasion, but I who have rashly placed myself in it." Thus confessing, you will move the divine mercy to pardon you ; but if you wish to blame others by excusing yourselves, you add sin to sin, and God will not pardon you. King Saul excused himself for not having destroyed, as by God commanded, every thing pertaining to the Amalekites, blaming the people, and God did not forgive him, but deprived him of his kingdom. David, without excusing himself, said : " I have sinned," and God pardoned him. Therefore, God will pardon your sins, and will no more remember them, if you accuse yourselves with all simplicity and sincerity. Yes, the confession must not only be sincere, but entire, without concealing any mortal sin. Whosoever does otherwise his confession is bad ; it is a sacrilege, and adds to the other sins one more enormous. And, oh, my God, how many grave offences are committed under this head ! Nevertheless, I am led to hope that few there are who approach the sacred tribunal of confession with the intention of obstinately refusing to confess the sins of which they are guilty. For this class of persons must have arrived to the greatest excess of wickedness, and have lost all faith. Although the examples of this class of persons are, we hope, few, examples are not so rare of those who seek by artifice to conceal the gravity of certain shameful excesses by passing over

N

them quickly, not giving the confessor time to reflect sufficiently upon them, or by manifesting in a tone so low certain ignominious falls that they are not fully understood, or by using words that do not convey their true and proper sense. How many weak souls there are who, through a certain natural modesty and shame, conceal one or more sins in confession ? To remove the deception from their mind, and to assist them, will form the subject of my zeal.

These souls, having had the misfortune to fall into some unseemly frailty, either in their youth or later in life, against all the inspirations and remorse of conscience, confess every other sin but that. But why do they not unburden their conscience by manifesting also that sin ? O my God, they exclaim, what pain, what shame in being obliged to manifest certain mistakes of the past. If such weak souls are present, let them listen to me. Did you blush with shame when you committed that sin of frailty ? Perhaps in that frailty you had an accomplice, and yet shame did not restrain you, and now you allow it to hinder you ; why do you not with a resolution truly Christian manifest it ? You brought death to your soul without trembling for fear ; you blush at so foul misdeed ; and now you are ashamed to heal the wound, and you carry the bandage by which it is bound. You have stained your soul without shame, and now you are ashamed to wash it by a sincere confession. This is an artifice of the devil to make us ashamed of penance ; on the contrary, God has done otherwise. He has placed shame in sin, that it may serve as a preventative against committing it ; and the facility of doing penance is granted to us, so that we may embrace and practise it when we have the misfortune to fall into sin. When about to commit sin the infernal enemy fills us with temerity and imprudence ; but when we wish to confess our sin he makes us timid and weak. He takes away shame when sin is to be done, he gives it back to us when we wish to apply the remedy to free us from the evil. Impious and cruel, both when he takes away and when he

restores our shame;·like to him who takes the arms
from a soldier when he has to defend himself from his
enemy, and only restores them to him that he may
destroy himself.

You may, perhaps, say that it is impossible not to
feel ashamed and confused in being obliged to confess
certain sins. To this I reply: it is not my intention to
take away from you all shame when you go to confession. Yea, I desire your heart to be filled with shame
and confusion, not such as to cause you to close
your mouth and tie your tongue, so as to prevent you
from accusing yourselves of your sins. Be confused
and filled with shame for having offended God, so merciful and so good. Nevertheless, make yourselves
known to the priest, such as you are to the eyes of
God, show him all your wounds. There are two kinds
of confusion, says the Holy Ghost: "There is a shame
that bringeth sin, and there is a shame that bringeth
glory and grace." Yes, that shame you feel in confessing—that momentary confusion that you may have
will form your happiness and your glory. Undergo it
as a satisfaction and a punishment for your sins.
Sacrifice it to the divine justice in payment of that
shame you had not when you sinned.

That there exists no cause for us to be ashamed,
since it is honourable before God and His representa-
tive to acknowledge the evil done. The confessor is
certainly well aware of the great self-denial required in
order to confess our sins and frailties ; were he an angel
confirmed in grace, of a different nature to yourselves,
not subject to your weaknesses and frailties, then I
should compassionate your shame. But no: he is a
man of the same nature as yourselves, subject to the
same temptations as yourselves, and will fall into the
same sins in which you do, and greater too, unless God
keep His hand over him. And for this reason every
one destined to hear confessions is taken from among
men, who can have compassion on them that err,
because he himself also is compassed with infirmity.

Yes; God has willed to assign this office to man, a sinner, so that he may have compassion on your weakness and misery, for he also has need that others should compassionate him. Then approach this tribunal of mercy without fear of the face of the confessor, or his rebukes. The good physician does not torture his patient with bitter remedies, but rather assists nature when he applies anything, so will the confessor. He will be like the father of the prodigal son; when you appear before him so deformed and so filthy, he will not reproach or reprimand you, but he will feel himself honoured that God has chosen him as an instrument of His mercy to remit your guilt, and by the absolving words to unlock the golden gates of the heavenly Jerusalem.

Again, whatever you confess to the priest he is bound, under the pain of mortal sin, never to disclose, nor is he permitted to mention the sins confessed to the penitent himself out of the confessional. Moreover, it has never been heard that a priest violated the secrecy imposed. In reply to this there are some who will say: "All that is very good, but what will the confessor think of me if I confess such a sin?" You cannot tell the confessor excesses so grave but that he has heard of greater, and in place of losing his esteem, it will only serve to increase it. You are not obliged to accuse yourself to one confessor rather than to another, make use of that liberty God has given you, and choose him whom you please.

Furthermore, let not the thought of your having for years past concealed sins in your confession prevent you from making the accusation of them in the one you are now about to make. No: cast yourself at the feet of your confessor, and tell him that you are a miserable sinner, that you have for years made bad confessions, and that sin of which you feel most ashamed let it be the first you confess, then you will have but little difficulty in accusing yourself of the rest. Happy will you be if you overcome yourself in this which appeared to you so

great an obstacle! How you will feel your heart
enlarged with an internal peace, and sorrow that you
had not before manifested your sins!

After the reflections which I have made, whence is
it, let me ask, this great confusion, this shame to discover your miseries to one man, bound to secrecy,
subject to the same infirmities, and always left to your
own free will to choose that one? Be your confusion,
your shame, as great as they possibly can be, yet you
must overcome them, you must' confess the sin, otherwise there is no salvation for you. You cannot be
saved unless the sin is forgiven, but the sin cannot be
forgiven unless by and through the confession. Every
other thing is useless: you may fast, pray, give alms,
and practise great austerities, all will be of no avail,
the sin is not taken away unless by the sacrament.
Hence it is I reason thus: that sin you have so long
a time had upon your soul, either you have made up
your mind to confess it some time, or you have determined never to accuse yourself of it. If you intend
confessing it some time, why not at once? Do you not
see the longer you defer it, besides the danger of being
suddenly called to your account, the difficulties increase?
In place of having one sin to accuse yourself of, you
will have a hundred, and add to that the number of
times you have concealed it, and the number of sacraments sacrilegiously received. If you are determined
never to confess the sin, then your damnation is
certain, since nothing can supply this defect of the
confession. But do you think you are acting wisely
in concealing this sin, and thus save your good name?
Oh, in that you are deceived! In avoiding a little
confusion so salutary for you, you go forward to meet
one infinitely greater, a despairing and unfruitful one.
Yes, that sin which you now refuse to confess in
secret for your salvation, will be one day known to
the whole world to your shame. Would it not be
better, then, freely to accuse yourself of that sin in
this life, rather than be obliged for all eternity in hell
to suffer shame and confusion? There is no alter-

native—either confess your sins, although they are ignominious and secret, or be eternally lost. Give, then, glory to God, confusion to the devil, and then will follow peace to the soul, grace in this life, eternal glory in the next. "For thy soul be not ashamed to say the truth."

XXII.

IT is, indeed, too true that very many Christians make the validity of their confession to consist in a most rigorous and minute examen of the faults they have committed, and in a sincere accusation of them to a confessor, without taking the least trouble to consider whether they have for their sins the necessary sorrow, which is by far the most important. It is a gross error to suppose that for a good and valid confession there remains nothing else to be done besides a diligent examen of our conscience, and after that a sincere and humble accusation of our sins. He who has not a true sorrow and a sincere repentance for his sins, let him not suppose that he truly receives pardon from God, although the priest pronounce the absolving words over him. How important, how necessary is, then, the subject I now undertake to explain—the sorrow that a Christian ought to have when he confesses his sins.

Saint Teresa, writing to a preacher, amongst the many things she says, tells him to preach frequently on bad confessions, and the reason is, the devil ensnares more souls by this means than by any other. Except in some particular case, there are few but what receive the last sacraments before leaving this world, or, at least that of penance; and yet, so many are lost; for Christ has said: "Many are called, but few are chosen." We must then come to the conclusion that the confessions are badly made. Of what use is it to confess our sins if we are not converted at heart? Ignorance in supposing that sorrow is not necessary, and the defect of it are the reasons why so many persons are lost. And these are the reasons why a confessor, who is a dispenser of the divine mysteries and of the Blood of Jesus Christ, suffers an agony, knowing that he is not doing his whole duty in hearing the sins of the penitent, and then in absolving him. Some penitents there are who present themselves to the confessor with a certain indifference, as if they had no concern, relating their sins as they would a story of little or no importance, and you might read in their faces and tell by their words an almost manifest indisposition for the sacrament. The confessor asks them whether they had made an act of contrition. Some will reply No; but the greater number, however, will say Yes, which consisted in having made an act of contrition that had been committed to memory, or in reading it from some book, without it being accompanied with any internal sentiment of the heart—they have struck their breast two or three times, and with this believe themselves to be more than contrite. The confessor insists, seeking whether there be true sorrow, and the reply is Yes; but such a yes comes forth from their lips, when well considered, he fears there is not sorrow. Here the confessor finds himself filled with a thousand anxieties, whether he ought or ought not to give the absolution. Ah, it is not the number nor the greatness of their sins that troubles and afflicts the confessor, but the little disposition he finds in the penitent, and the little or no sorrow.

The reason and the foundation for these fears and troubles of mind is because of the three parts of penance, contrition, confession, and satisfaction: the most necessary of which is contrition, and this is necessary as a means. It has already been explained that there are two kinds of necessity—one of precept, the other of means. The necessity of precept is when a thing is necessary, because it has been commanded; but, should it so happen that that cannot be done, there is no obligation, and it can be supplied by some other means. Thus, baptism by water is necessary for an adult only by precept, because when it cannot be had, desire will supply its place. But in the case of an infant, which

cannot have the desire, water is necessary as a means
for its salvation. So it is with the two parts of penance—confession and satisfaction. We are bound to
accuse ourselves of all our sins, accept and fulfil the
penance enjoined, but only by necessity of precept, so
that by means of contrition we may be placed in a state
of grace, when a priest cannot be had, or when the
priest is unable to speak the language of the penitent.
The same also may be said of one who, after a diligent
examen, has forgotten some sin. It may also happen
that a sick person is unable to manifest more than one
sin, or none at all, or having lost the use of speech, can
neither confess nor perform any penance; nevertheless,
if he has sorrow for his sins, the priest giving the
absolution, he will be justified and saved, because these
parts of penance are necessary only by precept; but
when you go to confession, not having true contrition,
no matter how exact you have made your examen, or
how sincere and entire you have accused yourself of all
your sins, or how much you thought you had contrition
and received absolution, if you had it not you still
remain in your sins, for contrition is necessary as a
means. And this is what fills the mind of the confessor with fear, and it ought to give greater apprehensions
to the penitent.

If, then, you desire to make a valid confession, before
going to the sacred tribunal strive to have this contrition and sorrow. I said before going to confession;
for although it suffices to have it before receiving
absolution, yet it is dangerous to defer it to those last
moments. And if it is well for all to have it before
confession, how much more so for those who have committed many grievous sins and have contracted many
bad habits. For it is very difficult, not to say almost
impossible, in so short a time, for one to conceive a
sincere detestation, a firm resolution not to offend God
again, and a desire to make satisfaction to Him. It behoveth one, before confession, to dispose himself by acts of
penance, so that he may receive from God that assistance necessary for it. And this is the reason why the

fathers of the Council of Trent have justly called penance a laborious kind of baptism, the sinner not being able to regain lost grace and innocence without much labour, for such the justice of God requires.

Before, then, presenting yourselves at the feet of the confessor, prostrate yourselves before the throne of the divine Majesty, since without the assistance of God you cannot have sorrow; ask it of Him with all humility and sincerity of heart, and strive, with His assistance, to excite yourselves to it. Until you have this internal hatred and abhorrence for sin, so necessary—this displeasure for the injury you have done to God, Whom you ought not to have offended, approach not the tribunal of penance, because it will not be a sacrament, but a sacrilege. Where there is no repentance there is no salvation or life, but damnation and death. "Unless you shall do penance you shall all likewise perish." I do not mean by this that before you go to the confessor to receive the absolution, your sorrow ought to be sensible, and that you have to shed tears for your sins. No: although this sensible sorrow and these tears are desirable and good, especially when they are accompanied with an internal sentiment of the heart; but they are not necessary. It suffices to have an internal displeasure for having offended God by your sins, and although you weep not outwardly you do so inwardly.

Having shown the necessity of contrition and sorrow, you may wish, in the first place, to know what is contrition—how many kinds there are—how are we to know when we have it—lastly, what are the motives that are able to lead us to have it? On a subject of such vast importance I will try to give a reply to each of your questions. "Contrition," according to the Council of Trent, "is a sorrow of mind, and a detestation for sin committed, with the purpose of not sinning for the future." Leaving aside the purpose of not sinning for the future (of which I shall speak in the next Instruction), contrition, then, is a sorrow of mind, and a detestation which the will has for sin above every other evil, because sin is an offence against God. From which it follows sorrow must have two conditions, internal and supernatural. The will must show an extreme dis-pleasure for having committed sin, and it ought to have a greater displeasure for sin than for any other evil in the world—it must be internal. And the reason is, sin having its place in the heart, in the heart ought also the sorrow to be, so that it may be able to destroy sin.

Man sees not as God sees; man sees only what appears outwardly, God beholds the heart. Therefore it is necessary that the heart and the will, which by committing sin are separated from God, loving creatures more than Him, should return to God, that the injury done may be repaired. Yet how many are wanting in this condition so necessary for contrition? Those acts of contrition that are known by the memory or read from some book, if accompanied with an internal sorrow of heart, are good; but if the heart has no part in them, they are nothing more than sorrow of tongue or words. Even tears, fasts, alms-deeds, mortifications, and all other acts of penance are good if they proceed from a contrite and humble heart, if not they are entirely useless. We must not deceive ourselves on this point, for I have known many who fast, weep, beat their breasts, use the discipline in such a way as would lead you to believe they were true penitents, were you to judge from these external signs; but they were not, because the interior did not correspond with them; therefore these external acts were nothing more than the shadow and mask of penance. The second condition is that the sorrow be supernatural; that is to say, that it detests sin, because it is an offence against God, and not for natural or human motives. Antiochus, remembering his sins, sorrowed and wept for them, but it was because he was about to die. Saul detested his disobedience, but it was because he saw himself deprived of his kingdom. Esau wept with a loud cry, but it was because he had lost his birthright. Not one of these had supernatural sorrow, consequently the mercy and pardon of God were not obtained. True sorrow must come from an impulse of divine grace—it must be an operation of the Holy

Ghost leading us to detest sin—a light of faith by which we discover the injury done to God, and the misery into which our soul is plunged.

There are two kinds of supernatural sorrow. Perfect, called contrition, and imperfect, called attrition. Sin being a turning from God to the creature, repentance must be a turning from the creature to God. Man, abandoning sin, may be converted to God for two motives, either for pure love or for fear. In the first case his contrition is perfect; in the second it is imperfect, and is attrition. But here occurs a difficulty; if this imperfect sorrow, *solely* conceived through the turpitude of sin, or through the fear of hell, or of punishment, which fear is called servile—when that attrition excludes the wish to sin with the hope of pardon; if this, *solely* with the sacrament of penance, is sufficient to justify the sinner; or whether for the last and proximate disposition an act of the love of God, at least, an incipient love, be required? This question is of more importance than may be supposed. The Fathers of the Council of Trent, in place of having inserted in its decree the word "sufficient," after mature consideration inserted the word "dispose," a sign that something more than fear is required for the proximate disposition, so that the sinner may be justified through the Sacrament of Penance. Moreover, according to the doctrine of St. Augustine and St. Thomas, the fear *only* of hell or of eternal punishment does not exclude positively the wish to sin, the love of God alone can do that. Whence it is, that frequently the reading of a book, or the hearing of the divine justice condemning sinners to eternal punishments, persons conceive a great fear, which faith alone is sufficient to cause. But then it is much to be feared that this fear is purely human—they fear hell, but not God, having a horror of the punishment, but not of the sin.

The fear of hell is not to be blamed, for Jesus Christ exhorts us to fear it, and when it excludes, at least negatively, the wish to sin, is is most useful in preparing the heart for the love of God, this being the ordinary way by which God conducts sinful souls to His love. "Unless the soul begins to serve God by fear, it will never attain to a love of Him." This fear is most useful to the just in preserving them in the grace of God, and in repelling temptations. This fear, however, may not positively exclude the wish to sin, or be positively opposed to it, that can only be obtained through charity and the love of God. For what is sin but a disordinate love for the creature? Then penitence ought to be a turning to God and a holy love towards Him. In fact, the Council of Trent, speaking of the dispositions adults ought to have for the Sacrament of Baptism, places as one of them the beginning to love God as the fountain of all justice. Now, for a greater reason is the love of God required in the Sacrament of Penance, since it is a laborious baptism. Besides, the distinguishing mark of the followers of the law of grace from those of the written law is the spirit of adoption. "You have received the spirit of adoption of sons, whereby we cry: Abba, Father." And, "he who loveth not abideth in death." And St. Paul says, "If any man love not our Lord Jesus Christ, let him be anathema." How can we then be restored to the grace of God without the obligation of loving Him above all things? How can we suppose that we shall be saved without loving God with our whole heart, which is the first and greatest commandment? This truth may be made clear by example—suppose one had done a great injury to his neighbour, casts himself at the feet of his confessor, detests and promises to amend, but at the same time he does not wish to have towards his neighbour any effect of benevolence or love: would such an one be well disposed for the absolution? Certainly not. Much less will that Christian who, detesting the injury done to God, does not desire to love Him. A child has grievously offended his parent, he is sorry for it, but only for this motive, that of escaping the merited punishment of being deprived of some property: would this be a good disposition for obtaining forgiveness? Certainly not. And will it be for a sinner who does not wish to do more for his heavenly Father? You may say that you have been told that fear alone, with the sacrament, is sufficient; but of what use is that when you are not certain? It would not be prudent to follow it.

I have dwelt rather long upon this subject because it is of such great importance. I will now speak of perfect sorrow, that is, the contrition by which the sinner has the greatest displeasure for having offended a God so loveable and so good, and detests sin as the greatest and only evil. Then the soul is troubled and afflicted for having sinned, but moved only by the love of God. Not because it has lost heaven and deserved hell, but purely reflecting that by sin it has displeased God. Although there were no hell to fear or heaven to lose, the soul grieves because it has injured God. In the same manner that a son having grieved his father, repents not through fear of being expelled from his father's house, or deprived of the property, but through the love he bears towards him. Happy shall we be if we have this sorrow so perfect, so noble! Then the soul will be justified, and its sins remitted before approaching the tribunal of penance, with the obligation, however, of doing so afterwards. Before, then, going to confession, or receiving the absolution, if you are not able to have this perfect contrition, strive to have attrition in the manner already explained.

But how are we to know whether we have the necessary sorrow? To explain to you the rules and signs given by the Fathers fill me with fear. I will, therefore give you their own words. St. Augustine says: "We are to have as great a sorrow of mind as we had pleasure in the sin." St. Gregory says: "This sorrow has to conceive so great a hatred for the sin, until it loves virtue." "This sorrow of mind is to be such as to bring the sinner to hate sin as much as he had loved it, and not only hate sin as an evil, but as the greatest of all evils;" thus writes St. Bernard. And St. Ambrose, speaking of this sorrow of mind, says: "Your heart ought to be so deeply wounded, and give such signs of it, as a delicate plant would give when pierced through with-a knife, and soon loses its flowers, leaves, or fruit; as the hammer beats a hard substance that it may be broken into pieces, so has the heart of the sinner morally to be broken by this sorrow of mind." These are the rules and signs given by the Fathers, and by which we are to discern true sorrow.

If, then, it be thus, tell me, can you discover from these rules and signs the sorrow in your past confessions? When you went to the feet of your confessor, did your repentance of having offended God produce in your mind as great a grief as you experienced pleasure in the sin? Did you have as great a hatred towards the sin as you had love for it? Was your heart morally broken? Did you consider sin the greatest evil in the world?—as a serpent that seeks to poison you? Were a serpent to attack you, with what horror would you look upon it; how quickly you would try to remove it from you. Now did you look upon sin, that has poisoned and killed your soul, with the same horror? Have you fled from it with the same fear, or rather did you not caress it? Oh, how much I fear that the sorrow of very many has been only in appearance, approaching the confessional with so little disposition! How much I fear that there has not been a real hatred for sin, or a sincere will to be healed! If your heart were touched with sorrow, if, indeed, you hated sin, and wished to be cleansed from it, other dispositions would be discovered in you—you would present yourselves to the priest with other sentiments and words, you would show your wounds, and you would ask for remedies for them. Oh, then, before presenting yourselves at the tribunal of penance, examine and give more serious reflection upon the reality of your sorrow.

" We wish to have this true sorrow and repair our past errors, but how are we to excite ourselves to it?" I answer, in the first place, that all the means you may make use of will be useless unless you have the divine assistance. The sorrow necessary, as you have been told, ought to be supernatural, consequently it is a gift of God and an impulse of the Holy Ghost. Therefore

you must ask it from the Father of light, without whose
assistance you cannot have a good thought. · The
assistance of God, then, being supposed, which He will
give if you ask it with humble prayer.   If you ask me ·
how you are to excite yourselves to sorrow, I reply—
being sinners, how can you live without this sorrow ?
You have offended a God so good—a God who deserves
all your love, and how can you live a moment without
being sorry for it ?   " Knowest thou not that the
benignity of God leadeth thee to penance ?"   When
you sinned you offended a God who could have cast you
into hell.   He has not done so.   He has deferred His
chastisement that you might do penance.   He has
waited for you, and still waits and invites ; yea, I will
say He begs you to abandon sin, and return to Him.
This thought of having offended a God so good, ought
it not to fill you with sorrow ?   Again, you have
outraged a God from Whom you have received every
good.   Without any merit on your part, from all eternity He has loved you, creating you from nothing, and
that you might serve Him, for you He has formed all
other creatures, and loaded you with so many benefits,
leaving you nothing to desire.   Furthermore, this good
God descended from heaven, became Man, suffered
and died, that you might not be eternally lost.   The
thought of so much love, can it be possible that you
will continue to offend Him or remain without sorrow.
By the testimony of the apostle you know that by sin
you have again crucified the Son of God, and made
Him a mockery.   If, after these considerations, your
heart still remains unmoved, make use of others ; open
your mental eyes, and behold that heaven, filled with
every delight, prepared for you; then look below into
that abyss of torments, destined for everyone who rebels
against God.   Oh, God, for so little heaven has been
lost—for so little drawn down to hell !   It will be
necessary either to repent or to be lost, and, what is
most deplorable, to be lost for all eternity ?   And
you—would you not rather repent than be eternally
damned ?

 If, after all these reflections, you still remain unmoved,

and your heart hard, with all humility and confidence cast yourselves at the foot of the cross, and supplicate Jesus Christ, that by His infinite mercy, and by the merits of His passion and death, by that blood shed for you, that He would soften the hardness of your heart. Implore the assistance of Mary Immaculate, the angels and saints, your guardian angel, that God may grant that sorrow so necessary. Persevere in prayer, say with the Church to our Lord: "That Thou wouldst vouchsafe to bring us to true penance." Repentance and sorrow, accompanied with those conditions, will obtain for you forgiveness and grace. And then, when you feel yourselves penetrated with this sorrow, go to the tribunal of penance. You ought also to examine whether this sorrow be accompanied with a firm and efficacious purpose of changing your life and of sinning no more, which is the fourth condition required for a good confession, and of which in the next Instruction I shall speak.

XXIII.

ON THE PURPOSE OF AMENDMENT.

THAT the repentance of the sinner be available, and dispose him for a good confession and for the obtaining of forgiveness in the Sacrament of Penance, it must regard two things: the one relating to the past, the other to the future. With regard to the past, for sin committed, there must be a true sorrow and a sincere detestation, as you have already heard. With regard to the future, an absolute purpose of committing no more that sin into which you had fallen, or any other sin. Of this purpose, which is the fourth condition necessary for a good confession, we will treat in this present Instruction.

There are some who may say in a certain case—very rare—that a virtual promise is sufficient; and that would be when the sinner had conceived a great sorrow, and a vehement contrition for having offended God, never thought of the purpose, but which he would have made had he thought of it. Nevertheless, the purpose necessary for a good and valid confession ought to be formal and explicit. This is clearly deduced from the Council of Trent, which, in the contrition and repentance, not only does it require sorrow for having offended God, but it also requires this stable purpose and firm resolution to change of life, to practise in future piety and virtue, and to sin no more. This purpose of change of life, to abandon sin, and to practise virtue, God requires, as it manifestly appears in the book of Ezechiel, where He declares that He wills not only the sinner to repent of his iniquities, detach himself from them, but that he also observe with exactness the law, practise piety and justice, and cast away from him all his transgressions, by which he had transgressed, and make to himself a new heart and a new spirit. Again, God says by the prophet Isaias: " Let the wicked forsake his way, and the unjust man his thoughts, and let him return to the Lord, and He will have mercy on him." This purpose our divine Lord prescribed to the woman taken in adultery : " Go, and now sin no more." The same He imposed upon the paralytic whom He had healed : " Behold thou art made whole ; sin no more." And reason itself tells us that these two conditions are necessarily required, that is to say, besides sorrow for sin, also a purpose and a promise to sin no more. Were you to offend seriously a very dear friend—were you, both by words and deeds, to outrage a person of distinction, and then wish at any cost to be reconciled with the one or the other, it would not be sufficient to show your displeasure and sorrow for the offences you had committed, but it would be necessary that at the same time you assure him of your determined will of never again offending him. Otherwise what sorrow would yours be, unless you were determined not to offend again ? Who will be reconciled to an offender when he knows that there is neither the thought nor the will of ceasing to offend him ? Now, if it is not only becoming but of necessity that one should act thus when he wishes to be reconciled with his fellow-men, how much more ought it to be necessary for a miserable sinner, desiring to be reconciled to his God ? Whoever, then, repent for having offended God, and seek forgiveness and wish to be restored to friendship, it is indispensably necessary that the sorrow for having offended God be united with the purpose of never offending Him again.

This, then, being undeniable, it now remains for us to see what this purpose is, and what it ought to be. According to the doctrine of St. Thomas : " Purpose is a deliberate act of the will." Such ought to be the purpose, accompanied with sorrow, that it be profitable to the sinner for the remission of his sins, and restore him

to the grace and friendship of God in the sacrament.
Three are the conditions it ought to have. It must be
firm, universal, and *efficacious.* First, it must be *firm.*
Thus the penitent must be resolved to bid a perpetual
adieu to sin. Whatever allurements the world may present
to him—whatever pleasures the flesh may offer—whatever suggestions may come from the devil—however
much the bad habit may urge us to sin, we are no more to
return to it. Like a valiant general to whom his sovereign
has commanded to defend a fortress, the enemy attacks
him on all sides, and he does all that he can to defend it,
and he is ready to give his life rather than deliver up the
fortress to the enemy. Such ought to be the firmness
of the penitent's purpose. Secondly, the purpose must
be *universal.* It must be a purpose to avoid all
mortal sin without any exception. God hates all sin,
so also ought the true penitent. When David wished
to give a sign of true repentance, he did not content
himself to purpose avoiding adultery, or murder, into
which he had fallen, but he swore an eternal hatred
against every sin, saying: "I have hated every way of
iniquity." Lastly, this purpose must be *efficacious.*
The true penitent says not: "If God will assist me, I
wish to see an amendment. Certainly I should wish
to amend, and I hope I will do so." No—not if I am
able—I hope—I should wish to amend—these are all
useless desires. It is necessary to say absolutely, I will,
without any condition, and by deeds confirm this
will, and make use of those means which will be of
avail for the future. Like a sick or wounded man, who
submits to the prescribed remedies, and at the will of
the physician allows himself to be cut or burnt, providing
he regains his health. Thus the penitent ought to be
resolute, so that in no time, under no circumstances, on
no occasion, or for any gain, or to avoid an evil, will he
commit a mortal sin and lose the grace of God. Be
not deceived—if your purpose is not firm, universal, and
efficacious, approach not the sacred tribunal of penance.
Should your heart be hesitating, or should you be
thinking that after a time you will again take to sinning

—should you retain an affection to one mortal sin alone —should you not wish to make use of the means necessary for an amendment, you are wanting in what is essential, and I say what I have before said, you go to make a sacrilege. If ever there was a motive for desiring with the prophet a fountain of water to the eyes that the shortcomings of Christians be deplored, it is certainly that of which we speak, the purpose.

Ah! how much I fear that the purpose of many Christians is neither firm, universal, or efficacious. And in the first place what firmness can I suppose there is in certain persons who, as soon as they leave the confessional, like dogs return to their vomit, who present themselves many times to their confessor, more or less with the same number of mortal sins, and who commit them with the same facility, with the same satisfaction, and with the same negligence as before. It is easily seen that they are not converted at heart, but only by halves, that is to say, they rend their garments, and not their hearts—their purpose has been only in appearance, having no firmness, no resolution. In your past confessions you have promised to sin no more, and yet is it not true that almost immediately afterwards you took to sin again? You knew those sins killed your soul, and put to death Jesus Christ, Who dwelt in you by His grace; and with this knowledge you promised to fly from sin, and with all that, so soon after you entered into a close alliance with it. How can I from that judge that your resolutions, your promises were firm? They were promises only of the tongue, false and deceitful—signs not of a true, but of a counterfeit repentance, or, as St. John Chrysostom calls it, a repentance theatrical. Nor could the saint have used a word to express more truly the nature of such repentance, accompanied with a purpose so weak, so faint, and of so short duration. A repentance that may deceive and lead the simple-minded to believe real, but not those of sound mind and good judgment.

You may, perhaps, have seen in representations at the theatre persons who, with swords in hand, as it were

214 FAMILIAR INSTRUCTIONS ON THE SACRAMENTS.

declared enemies, aiming at each other, and after a few strokes one of them falls down upon the stage, apparently mortally wounded, and gives no sign of life. Simple-minded people and children, who have never seen such representations before, believe it is all real, and that he is really dead, but others know that it is only feigned. And why? Because they see that as soon as the scene is over, the one that appeared dead rises, returns to his house, eats and drinks as before. The same thing happens every day with many Christians. Were you to judge from appearances and what you see, you would believe them truly penitent for their sins, penetrated with a true sorrow, accompanied with a holy resolution to amend their lives. Why? Because they externally do all that true penitents do—they enter the church, cast themselves at the feet of their confessor, accuse themselves of their sins, strike their breasts and promise to sin no more. Those who do not penetrate into the hearts of such penitents believe them to be thoroughly converted and dead to sin. But those who see things as they really are, remain persuaded that such are only the shadow of repentance, and that their promises of change of life are counterfeit. And what are the proofs of this? Scarcely have a few days elapsed when they are seen leading the same life they did before, frequenting the same profane representations—with the same disorderly companions—speaking the same unseemly language, and detracting their neighbour. And are these firm purposes, true penitents? No; they are feigned purposes—repentance theatrical.

I do not say, nor do I mean, that relapses into the same sins are always evident signs of a want of a true purpose. No; I know that human frailty is great. But I know also by the testimony of the apostle that the purpose which accompanies true repentance ought to be a steadfast and immoveable perseverance in the good begun—this is the sign of a true reconciliation with God. For the sorrow that is according to God worketh penance steadfast unto salvation. The Fathers

of the Church speak the same language—they say that
we are so to weep for our past sins that we may not
commit others for which we should have again to weep.
For he who weeps for his sin, and then returns to commit it again, is like the fool who washes an undried
brick, for the more he washes it the more filthy it becomes. St. Augustine says : " He is a mocker and not
a true penitent who stains his soul with the same sins
for which a little before he had repented—for repentance implies the deploring of sins in such manner that
one no more relapses into them." This is the idea
Sacred Scripture and the Fathers give of true repentance—To be steadfast and firm in our purpose—persevering in good, and amend of the evil committed.
Now, think what judgment ought to be formed of those
purposes that have not for their character these signs.
What judgment is to be formed of those penitents whose
whole life is a constant passing from sin to repentance,
and from repentance to sin.

I know full well that you always ascribe your relapses
to your frailty, and to that you attribute the reason.
But although I believe this frailty has its share, yet I
fear very much that to the heart, not being touched
with true repentance, and not being entirely changed
by a firm and resolute purpose not to sin again, may be
ascribed your relapses; and if sin is abandoned sometimes for a time, that may be through fear or human
respect. St. Augustine explains that by a familiar comparison : "The wolf," he says, "filled with the desire of
devouring the sheep, goes towards the flock. It happens
sometimes the dogs, perceiving the wolf is coming, commence to bark; the shepherd is awakened from his
sleep, and with assistance drives the wolf back to the
forest before any evil has been done." Now, do you
suppose the wolf has changed his nature because he
returned to the forest before doing any harm? No,
replies the saint, he did no harm because he was not
able, the fear of being killed caused him to return to
the wood—he remains still a wolf whether he devours
or whether he trembles for fear. Thus it happens with

216 FAMILIAR INSTRUCTIONS ON THE SACRAMENTS.

many Christians, and this is the cause of their relapses. They are always the same, for their hearts are not changed. True, on beholding a sudden death, or hearing from the pulpit one of the eternal truths, they may tremble and fear damnation, and run to the feet of a confessor. Here it is fear that moves them—the Feast of the Nativity or Easter is near at hand—a Jubilee is announced, they go to confession through fear of being pointed at. Here is human respect; but they are the same wolves as before, and their returning so soon to sin again is a clear and manifest proof of it. This, however, does not happen after a firm purpose has been made; the object of which is to preserve a frail life. One resolves no more to taste what from experience he knows to be injurious, and he does not; the very sight of it fills him with horror, and the smell of it causes disgust. But you are not horrified at the sight of those sinful objects—yea, you look upon them as before and entertain them. What conclusion, then, must I come to? It must be this one, that the tongue says one thing and it determines another in its heart. The tongue protests that it will avoid sin, and it promises the same to the confessor and God; but the bottom of the heart does not expect anything but that when the Feast of the Nativity, Easter, or the Jubilee shall have passed to follow the same life of sin as heretofore. Our purpose of amendment is not to be such; it ought to be resolute and firm, like to that of the apostle; we ought to protest that neither death, nor life, nor things present, nor things to come, nor might of the world, nor hell, nor any creature shall be able to separate us from the love of God, and lead us again to sin. This is the true idea of a firm purpose of amendment.

Moreover, this purpose, besides being firm, ought to be also *universal*, avoiding all sin, not excepting one. Now, if we have had motives of fear regarding the firmness of the purpose of many Christians, how much more so with regard to the purpose being universal, seeing that certain persons do not ever break off from certain sins. They are willing to renounce all the rest when

they may be allowed to satisfy that passion, that particular sin.   With this they know not how to break off—
this they wish to keep alive in their own hearts, yet
they ought to know that this alone brings death.   They
imitate the policy of King David.   That prince knew
that only the death of his son Absalom could give
security to his kingdom, and yet he gave a command
to his captains to save the life of his son, although so
wicked : " Save me the boy Absalom."

Oh, how many there are who cannot be induced to
sacrifice some passion, some sin, which they keep as a
sort of reserve ;   and   either because they have no
difficulty in overcoming others, and purposing to avoid
them, or because they are not guilty of certain sin,
believe themselves to be, as it were, innocent !   Be it
that one is not avaricious of what use is it, if he be as
haughty and proud as Lucifer?—Is he therefore innocent ?   What does it avail another if he is not proud,
if, at the same time he is invidious and malicious?
What does it avail that other who is neither invidious
or malicious, if, by usury and fraud, he wastes the substance of the poor ?   It is true that everyone is not
guilty of all kinds of sins.   The drunkard may not be
either avaricious or impure.   One may say, I neither
defraud, rob, or do any injury to anyone ;   I have but
one sin, and that of human frailty, if it were not for that
I should be a saint.   Since, then, you do not keep from
that one sin, you are not a saint, and your repentance
is not real, because your purpose is not universal.   It
is absolutely necessary to purpose avoiding all sin,
otherwise you can neither hope for pardon or grace.

You present yourselves at the tribunal of penance
with a soul sick unto death that you may regain health,
life, and grace.   The priest will give them to you, upon
this condition, that you destroy all those idols you have,
up to then, kept in your heart to the injury of God.
It is necessary that you make a resolute purpose never
to commit sin again, and have all sin in abhorence.   If
you maintain an affection for only one, no matter how
much you detest the others, you can never be cured, nor

receive spiritual life, you will always remain infirm and dead to grace, because your purpose is not universal.

The third condition that ought to accompany the purpose of amendment is that it be *efficacious*. We have seen that this purpose of many Christians is neither firm nor universal, and, ordinarily speaking, it is not efficacious. What efficacy is there in the purpose of that slothful penitent, who does not rise as he ought, and make the effort required for an amendment of life? He does not will the end who refuses to make use of the means for it. What means have you used to unloosen the chain that binds you to sin? What fasts, what penances have you done in order to put down that rebellion of the flesh against the spirit? What spiritual exercises have you practised—what devotion to the Mother of God and the saints, that for you they may obtain the divine assistance not to fall again? Nothing —absolutely nothing. And, with this, how can you pretend to call efficacious your purpose? Were a poor man to purpose to become rich, but at the same time take to no profession, no office, no employment: were a sick person to wish his recovery, and then not wish to follow the orders given by the physician, what would you say of such purposes? You would say these are the purposes of fools. The poor man neither wishes to become rich nor the sick person his recovery. The same may be said of those who do nothing towards the amendment of their lives, and yet wish, by the means of the sacramental confession, to enrich themselves with divine grace and be cured of their spiritual infirmities. Deeds and not words are wanted, that our purpose may be efficacious.

Then, before you approach the tribunal of confession, examine a little more yourselves and see whether your repentance is accompanied not only with sorrow for past sin, but also with a firm, universal, and efficacious purpose never to commit sin in the future, since for the want of it very many Christians are lost. The Fathers and theologians ascribe the want of this purpose as the cause of the small number of the elect and the damna-

tion of the many.   In fact, according to the account
given by Pope Innocent the Fourth, of a vision seen by
a holy man, souls descended into hell like flakes of
snow in the winter.   This, perhaps, happened because
they did not go to confession.   No : for we said before,
very few Catholics die without making, at least, their
confession ; but because their confessions were not well
made, concealing some sin through malice, or through
shame, or by not repenting sincerely for sins committed,
or not resolving with firmness to avoid sin.   There are
certain sins, such as hatred, love of revenge, attachment
to the substance of others, and particularly attachment
to the pleasures of sense, that are difficult, and cannot
be rooted out of the heart without great difficulty.   No
matter how great may be your desire to reconcile yourselves to God by means of holy confession, upon which
depends your eternal salvation, do not trust, however,.
to those confessions, which, for want of purpose of
amendment, relapses into mortal sin, followed so soon
after, for there are very grave reasons for judging them
false.   Say with the Royal prophet: " I have sworn,
and am determined to keep the judgments of Thy
justice " during the remainder of my life.   If you have
these holy dispositions you may be certain that you will
obtain the divine grace here on earth and eternal glory
ib heaven.

XXIV.

ON SATISFACTION.

AFTER having treated of two of the conditions required on the part of the penitent for the forgiveness of sins, viz.: sorrow of heart and confession of one's own sins, there now remains for me to speak, on the third part, that is, satisfaction, which is the acceptance and voluntary fulfilment of the penance enjoined by the confessor, in order to compensate for the injury done to God by sin. Of this part of the Sacrament of Penance, we may say, little is understood by Christians, having but a poor idea of it, and in no way corresponding to that given us by Holy Scripture, by the Fathers, or to the nature of the reparation required from us by God after having made a most merciful exchange through the Sacrament of Penance of an eternal punishment that we had merited, into a temporal satisfaction. This satisfaction, then, being so little known, it is by no means a subject of surprise that it is so badly complied with. To what is this satisfaction reduced? To a few and easy practices for grave excesses, to a few moments of prayer for years consumed in every kind of sin. You yourselves will be convinced of this after the explanation I am about to give on this subject.

The Catechism of the Council of Trent says : "Satisfaction is that compensation by which a man makes some reparation to God for the sins he has committed." Every Christian is bound to make this reparation, even after having received in the Sacrament of Penance the remission of his sins, since, as the same Council declares, "The temporal punishment is not always wholly remitted." Again : "If any one saith that God always remits the whole punishment, together with the guilt, let him be anathema." The Sacred Scripture furnishes us with many examples of this truth. In fact, Adam sinned by disobedience, and obtained from God forgiveness of the sin and eternal punishment, but was the temporal punishment remitted? No: driven out of the terrestrial paradise, he had to do a most rigorous penance for nine hundred years. The Jews sinned by idolatry, Moses prayed to God and obtained forgiveness for them, but the temporal punishment was not remitted, for God immediately threatened them with severe punishments, and Moses himself gave them to understand that for the sin the people had committed God would punish unto the third and fourth generation. Moses sinned by diffidence in the power of God—he was forgiven, but in punishment for his sin he was not allowed to enter into the promised land. King David sinned, and the prophet Nathan assured him that the Lord had taken away his sin; nevertheless, he wept day and night for his sin, did penance for it, eating his bread with ashes, and continually imploring God to wash him yet more from his sin, that is, as the Cate-chism says: "He besought the Lord not only to pardon the crime, but also the punishment due to the crime, and to restore him, cleansed from the remains of sin, to his former state of purity and integrity. And although this was the object of his most earnest supplications, yet did the Lord punish him with the death of the child of his adultery, with the death of his dearly beloved son Absalom, and with the other punishments and calam-ities with which He had already threatened him." If, then, God did not remit to many saints, not even to King David, the temporal punishment, notwithstanding the many tears they shed day and night for their sins, can we expect God to remit the temporal punishment due to our sins, we who are so cold and have so little sorrow for them? It is a great mercy on the part of God towards us in forgiving the sins and the eternal punishment, but the temporal punishment due to them He wishes us to satisfy either in this or in the other

world. And woe to us if we have to undergo this temporal punishment in the other world! The sufferings
of this world cannot equal the least of the pains of purgatory. Therefore, it is clear that we must do penance
in reparation for the injury we have done to God by our
sins. It is also clear that it is to our advantage to do
penance here, that we may be liberated from the
greater temporal punishment which the divine justice
will cause us to undergo either in this or in the other
world. But in what manner are we able to satisfy the
divine justice by penance? Many are the ways, and
the Roman Catechism reduces them to three principal
heads—prayer, fasting, and alms.

Under the name of prayer is understood vocal and
mental prayer, assisting at the holy sacrifice of the
Mass, frequenting the Sacrament of Penance and the
Holy Eucharist, the reciting of the Acts of Faith, Hope,
Charity, and Contrition ; acts of virtue, such as humility,
patience, meekness, and resignation to the will of God.
All these come under the head of prayer, and when
these are practised with devotion, attention, and a right
end, they serve to satisfy the divine justice. For instance, meditation made for a quarter of an hour daily
for one month, having confessed and received holy communion, a person gains a plenary indulgence, that is, a
full remission of all temporal punishment due to his
sins. Spiritual reading, from which we may learn how
to avoid sin and do good—assisting at Mass with devotion, at which is continually offered to the Eternal
Father His only-begotten Son, serves in an especial
manner to satisfy God for our sins—confession, by which
a proud spirit feels shame and confusion in manifesting
its sins and miseries, serves to lessen the temporal
punishment due to them. Holy Communion, according
to the dispositions and fervour with which we receive
it—the reciting of the Penitential Psalms, when one
recites them with sorrow and with compunction—the
Acts of Faith, Hope, and Charity, to all of which there
are annexed indulgences. The acts of virtue serve in
a wonderful manner to lessen the temporal punishment;

for instance, when one feels himself governed by pride, he practises humility—by impatience, and he practises meekness; above all that he resigns himself to the divine will in the midst of trials and afflictions, making an offering of them to God in satisfaction for sin.

The second way of doing penance and of making satisfaction to God is by fasting. Under the name of, fasting is understood not only the abstinence from certain kinds of food, commanded by the Church during Lent and at other times, but also every kind of corporal penance—every kind of mortification of the body and of the spirit, as remaining on our knees in prayer—abstaining from that food and drink that pleases us most, depriving one's self of that conversation, that pleasure, though lawful and permitted, and such like, as the saints practised, though delicate and perhaps more so than ourselves. But some may say these penances are for the religious and not for the laity. Do not believe it. Have the laity the privilege of sinning without the obligation of doing penance? If they commit more sins than the religious, then they have to do more penance. And if they do it not they will have to undergo a greater punishment in the other world, and perhaps such as will have no end.

A third way of doing penance and making satisfaction to God is that of giving alms. By alms is meant the corporal works of mercy which consist in assisting our neighbour in his necessities, both of body and soul. Prayer, fasting, and alms deeds are the three principal means we ought to make use of in reparation for the injury done to God by our sins, and in freeing ourselves from the temporal punishment due to them. By these three means we can give satisfaction to God for whatever sin we may have committed, for all our sins may be reduced to these three heads—offences against God, or against ourselves, or against our neighbour. Now, by prayer we appease God, by fasting we mortify ourselves, and by alms deeds we do good to our neighbour. Therefore, by these three means we can satisfy God for every kind of sin. We must, however, observe to the end that these means may serve to satisfy the justice of God they must be performed in a state of grace, for works done without faith and charity cannot by any means be acceptable to God.

The satisfaction we make to God by voluntary penance belongs to penance as a virtue. The satisfation belonging to penance as a sacrament, and which is a part of it, consists in doing that penance enjoined by the confessor upon the penitent, after the manifestation of his sins, with sorrow, and with the will to do penance. This penance the confessor is bound to impose upon the penitent, and in doing so he is to be guided by justice, prudence, and piety, and the penitent is bound to accept the penance imposed, unless it should be one that he is unable to comply with; in that case the penitent should represent his inability to perform it, and then the confessor will change it, giving him another. After the penance has been accepted, the penitent ought to fulfil it in the manner prescribed, for if he neglect or defer it for a very long time, it is always a sin; and should the penance be a grave one, then it would be a grievous sin to neglect it. And yet how many there are who neglect to fulfil the penance given by the confessor, and thus the sacrament is deprived of its integrity! How many make a difficulty about accepting the penance, because it seems to them too much, and sometimes they consider the confessor indiscreet! How little do such understand their obligations and the indispensable necessity of doing penance to satisfy the divine justice for the injuries done to Him by their sins! Listen to the penances formerly prescribed by the Church. For the sake of brevity I will only refer to a few, regarding the Commandments of God and the Church. The denying of the faith or doubting an article of it, seven years of penance. The taking of God's name in vain, seven days on bread and water. The uttering of an oath against God, the blessed Virgin, or the saints, to remain seven weeks on the knees at the door of the church during the celebration of High Mass, and the last week barefooted with a rope around the neck, and then to fast seven Fridays on bread and water. The doing of servile work on Sunday, ten days on bread and water. A want of respect to a father or mother, three years' penance. A disregard for the advice and correction of the parish priest, forty days on bread and water—for a sin against the sixth commandment, three years penance—for hatred towards a neighbour, a fast of forty days on bread and water—for theft, one year's penance—for detraction, three years of penance. But this is not all, for formerly there were two kinds of penances, public and private. Public faults were expiated by public penance, and the guilty persons were not admitted to the participation of holy Communion before they had expiated their misdeeds with fasts, macerations of the body, and other works of satisfaction. The order and duration of the penances were fixed for every kind of sin. "The whole period of penance was then divided into four parts, which constituted so many degrees or stations. The first degree was that of the sorrowers, the second of the listeners. the third of the prostrate, the fourth of the assistants." Of which I will give an explanation; for example, suppose a person had been guilty of voluntary homicide, if he wished to be absolved from his sin, it was necessary that he should remain four years among the sorrowers, whose station was in a court or dwelling-place close to the church, or in the portico outside the church, at the threshold of which he would have to remain, like the poor who stand there asking alms. After that time he would then have to remain five years with the listeners, whose station was at the portico just inside the door, where he would have to stand as far up as the place of the catechumens, and he would have to go out with them, after having heard the holy Scripture and Christian Doctrine, and held unworthy to join in the prayers or to assist at the celebration of the Divine Mysteries. Then after that he would have to remain seven years with the prostrate, whose station was in the portion of the church between the listeners and the rest of the faithful. During this time the penitent on his knees

P

would receive the imposition of the hands of the priest, which ceremony, with certain prayers, was performed after the mass of the catechumens, before the oblation of the Unbloody Sacrifice, at which he would not have been allowed to assist. Finally, it would be necessary for him to remain four more years among the assistants, whose station was with the rest of the faithful in the church. And then after a public penance of twenty years the penitent might be absolved and admitted to holy Communion.

You have now heard what were the penances in bygone times imposed upon penitents, and you, who are always relapsing into the same sins, feel so much difficulty in doing that little imposed upon you by the confessor—you, who abhor so much mortification and penance, would wish to go to heaven without putting yourselves to any inconvenience. Sins that are committed now, are they different from those that were committed then? Certainly not; they are the same and more numerous. The offences committed against God are perhaps different from those that were done then? No, they are the same, and perhaps more injurious. If, then, they did so much penance in those days, ought not you to do it in these days? If then so much satisfaction was given to the divine justice, why ought it not to be given at the present time? Perhaps you think that God is not the same now that He was then. Perhaps you think Christians of our day have a privilege which they had not in those days. No; God is the same, His law is always the same, and the obligations of Christians are the same as they were then. True it is the Church does not now impose those severe penances, and that the canonical penances are no longer in use; but it is also true that the obligation of sinners doing penance in proportion to their offences to satisfy the divine justice has not nor will it cease. "Bring forth, therefore, fruit worthy of penance: unless you do penance, you shall likewise perish." Such has always been the sentiment of holy Church, of the Fathers, and such has been the practice of all who have been truly

converted to God. Penance, says St. Ambrose, ought
not to be less than the offence; if the sin has been grave,
grave ought to be the penance. Do you wish to be
penitents according to the fashion? I know not what
to say to you beyond what I have already said, but bear
in mind that you may be, according to the fashion, lost.

That so great a misfortune may not befall you, take
the firm resolution of doing as much penance as you can
to satisfy the divine justice—accept the penance imposed upon you by the confessor—perform it with exactness, and since ordinarily speaking this penance is very
light, do something on your own part, remembering
always the words of the Apostle: " That the sufferings
of this time are not worthy to be compared with the
glory to come, that shall be revealed in us."

XXV.

ON THE PROXIMATE OCCASIONS.

To complete the instructions on the Sacrament of Penance there remains one most essential subject yet to be spoken of, viz.: the indispensable obligation we are all under of avoiding not only sin, but also the occasion of sin. This Instruction is useful to those who, with a contrite and humble heart, have been converted to God; for, if they do not avoid the occasion of sin, they will not be able to keep their good resolutions, nor persevere in the grace of God. It is also useful to those who are not yet converted to God; for, without this firm resolution to abandon not only sin, but also the occasion of it, they will never make a good confession or gain the grace of God.

That this subject may be well understood and made intelligible to all, before treating of it, it will be necessary for me to explain what is meant by an occasion of sin, how many kinds there are, and what are those occasions we are bound to avoid and abandon.

An occasion of sin is everything that induces or draws us into sin; everything that may place us in the danger of committing sin. For example: familiarity with certain persons, going to taverns, balls, and theatres, may be an occasion of inducing us to sin, and place us in the danger of offending God grievously; then this conversation, this ball, this theatre, are for me evil occasions. When the danger is slight, the occasion is called *remote*; if the danger is grave, then it is *proximate*. So that the proximate occasion is that which places us in the proximate and probable danger of grievously offending God, and this proximate and probable danger is easily known, either from the frailty common to all, or from the particular frailty of each individual, and by the frequently falling into sin through that occasion. If the proximate occasion is *voluntarily* sought, or can be easily avoided, as, for example, the abandoning a certain house, a theatre, or dismissing a person, then the proximate occasion is called voluntary. But if the occasion is one of those that we do not seek, or that we can in no way avoid without incurring great inconvenience, such as the loss of our good name, or that of a son who cannot leave his father's house, for he is not free to do so, then the occasion is *involuntarily* proximate, *morally* or *physically* necessary. If we speak of *remote* occasions of sin they are such as occur every day, and it may be said every moment, to every one living in this world—so full of dangers—and are necessarily annexed to our life on earth. These oblige us to be always cautious, but not always to avoid them ; " otherwise," says the Apostle, " you must needs go out of the world." So that with regard to these *remote* occasions, it is sufficient to be attentive to ourselves, implore the divine assistance, that God would give us His grace to overcome them, so that we may not fall into sin.

But if we speak of *proximate* occasions, which expose us to the proximate and probable danger of grievously offending God, whenever these are *voluntary*, and in that case it is certain that we are bound to entirely abandon them. The penitent, who is in the proximate *voluntary* occasion, if he desires to make a good and valid confession, and place himself in the grace of God, it is necessary that he should not only repent of his sins, having a resolution of never committing them again, but that he also should have a will most firm of absolutely abandoning the proximate occasion of sin ; without this firm will no confessor in the world can absolve him, for to give the absolution to one who has not this will would be a sacrilege, both on the part of the confessor as well as on him who receives it, and thus bring damnation on confessor and penitent. And

the reason is evident, for whosoever refuses to abandon
the occasion of sin, in spite of all his promises not to
commit sin again, it is a sign that he is not truly penitent, and that he has also the will to sin ; were it otherwise he would have the will to avoid the occasion, in
the same manner that one wishes to avoid the cause
who wills not the effect.   Moreover, to expose one's self
to the proximate occasion of offending God is of itself
most sinful, so that those who can, and do not wish to
avoid the proximate occasion, do actually sin by the
bad will that dominates in them ; consequently, you
see, that such can never be disposed to receive the
absolution, or find a confessor that can give it.   No, a
penitent cannot be absolved unless he firmly promise
to abandon the voluntary proximate occasion, nor can
the confessor give it, though the penitent may give
excuses and reasons, adduce difficulties, and make protests, because these excuses, reasons, difficulties, and
protests, though they may have the appearance of
truth, when well examined are frivolous, and, ordinarily speaking, can be overcome by one who has
real sorrow for his sin and a firm will to be converted
to God.   The great reason is that the soul ought to
occupy the first place, and the salvation of that is to
be preferred to everything else.   Hence, it is necessary
to deny ourselves, to mortify our own will ; we must do
violence, and overcome every obstacle, every difficulty.
Without using this violence, so much recommended by
Jesus Christ, it is impossible to be saved.   "The kingdom of heaven suffereth violence, and the violent bear
it away."   It would occupy too much time to adduce
all the excuses, reasons, difficulties, and pretexts given
by some penitents, that they may be exempted from
the obligation of avoiding the occasion.   But an experienced confessor will know how to examine them
and show their inconsistency, and if the penitent does not
resolve and promise to abandon the occasion he can never
absolve him.   Yea, if the occasion is such that it is
always before the penitent's eyes without his going and
seeking for it, as, for instance, keeping a person in the

house with whom he frequently sins, no matter how
much he promises to avoid the occasion, the confessor
ought not to give him the absolution, but deny it until
he has really abandoned it, because the confessor is a
spiritual physician, and cannot cure a wounded man
until the ball is removed that caused the wound; so,
the penitent can never make a sacrifice pleasing to
God as long as there remains an abomination in the
temple.

Those who have made good confessions, having been
truly repentant, and made a firm resolution not only to
avoid sin, but also the proximate occasion of it, ought to
carry out the good resolutions they have made, maintain-
ing their promises, avoiding the proximate occasions, and
removing themselves far from them, otherwise they
can never retain the grace of God or persevere in
good.

Methinks I hear some of you present saying: "Is it
not sufficient to keep from sinning? What evil is
there in going now and then into that company, ball,
or theatre; to that public-house, or to speak with this
or that person? I will go there, but absolutely I have
no wish to sin; I will speak with great reserve, I know
how to take care of myself." This is sufficient—I
know all that you would wish to say. These are the
usual excuses, pretexts, and reasons, given by those who
desire to follow their own perverse will. What you
wish to say is that you can place yourself in the occasion without committing sin. Give me now your
attention.

In placing yourself in the occasion of sin without
sinning, tell me upon what do you rely? It is either
upon your own strength, or upon the assistance of God.
If upon your own strength only, you hope, without
God's grace, to expose yourself to the proximate occasion without committing any sin, you, in the first place,
are guilty of heresy, it being of faith that of ourselves, and
by our own strength, we can do absolutely nothing, not
even conceive a good thought. But where is this great
strength you believe you have, in putting yourselves in

the occasion without sinning? That absolution given you by the confessor, when you were resolved to be converted to God, did it make you become as a piece of bronze, indifferent to all the stings of the flesh, to temptations, to dangers, and to the attractions of certain objects? No; you are what you were before, flesh and blood—you are what you were before, weak, subject to the same passions and to the same inclinations. Therefore, with all your good will never to sin again, what strength will you be able to have to keep you from sinning when placed willingly in the occasion? If, in the same occasion, you had not strength to keep from sin in past times, how will you be able in the future? Do you wish to know what your strength is? It is that which God, by the prophet Isaias, has said: "Your strength is like that of one enveloped with tow, having a spark of fire within—the tow commences to smoke, and then to burn." Do you rely on the assistance of God? Do you go into the occasion, saying within your heart, God will assist me, I shall not fall into sin. But how can you place yourself in the proximate occasion and in the danger of committing sin, presuming that God will give you His grace, so that you may not fall? Ah! no, you can never hope for that, because it is a presumptuous and diabolical hope; it is tempting God, and an attempt to oblige Him to work a miracle. You may hope for His assistance and grace should you be accidentally, or by reason of duty, placed in the proximate occasion of sin, not wished or sought for by you; but to put yourself voluntarily in the danger and in the proximate occasion, and then to hope for the assistance of God, ah! it is entirely useless. God will abandon you to your temptations, your passions, your corrupt desires; He will permit you to fall into sin worse than before, and then die impenitent; for so God has declared in Holy Scripture, by representing the danger, and the proximate occasion, and final impenitence, as united and, as it were, inseparable from each other: "A hard heart shall fear evil at the last; and he that loveth danger shall perish in it." St. Thomas,

as if you had never known them.   Do you not wish to
do this ?   Do you not wish to abandon the proximate
occasion ?   Well I tell you, with that frankness that
my office imposes upon me, that with all your good will,
you will never be able to live a life of grace, nor will
you persevere in good, but you will again fall into sin,
and your sins will be greater than before.

The reply that some will give to what has been said
is, that they have gone into the proximate occasion, have
entered into that house, spoken and conversed with that
person without committing any sin.

To which I say it does not follow that you will not
sin if you continue to go into the occasion.   Experience
has always shown that, without any exception, all those
who have continued in the proximate occasion, sooner
or later have fallen into sin, and in a manner worse than
before.   If, then, all have fallen who have gone into the
proximate occasion, you also will fall into sin.   If, then,
this be most certain, you are bound to abandon it.   The
proximate occasion has more force in drawing us into
sin than we can possibly imagine.   But if you suppose
for a moment that you can return, and place yourself in
the proximate occasion, without falling into those sins
which you were in the habit of committing, and believe
that you can live in the grace of God without sinning,
you are greatly deceived.   Though you no longer commit those sins you were in the habit of committing,
going into the occasion is sufficient to make you guilty
of sin, and as often as you voluntarily place yourself in
the proximate occasion, so often do you sin.   This is
an undeniable truth admitted by all theologians ; for
God not only prohibits sin, but also the exposing ourselves to the danger of committing it.   God commanded
our first parents not to eat of the fruit, and, at the same
time, forbade them to touch it, lest perhaps they die.
But why did God forbid them to touch it ?   Because
the touching of that fruit would have been a proximate
occasion to them.   In fact, Eve, having exposed herself
by looking and touching that fruit, she finally took of
the fruit thereof, and did eat, and gave to her husband,

who did eat. Therefore in whatever way we view the proximate occasion, we must come to the conclusion that there is no other way of avoiding sin than by absolutely abandoning it.

What has been hitherto said regards those voluntary proximate occasions which are in our power to avoid. But those who are in the proximate occasions necessary and which cannot be avoided, what course must they pursue so that they may not sin?

The Holy Ghost does not say, he that is in danger shall fall therein, but only those who love and will the danger. Thus, the first thing to be done by those who are placed in this necessary proximate occasion is to conceive a lively and ardent displeasure in being in this unfortunate position, of not being able to abandon it. In the second place, since they cannot abandon the occasion, they must at least remove themselves from it as far as they possibly can. They must also pray incessantly, frequent the sacraments, and perform other works of piety, of penance, and mortification. Finally, they ought to place themselves entirely under the direction of their confessor, and put in practice the means, and use the remedies that he suggests, so that the proximate occasion may become remote, and thus will cease the proximate and probable danger of offending God.

I will end this Instruction with the words of the Holy Ghost: "He that is aware of the snares shall be secure." That is to say, do you wish to secure your salvation? Then keep from the proximate occasion of sin. Unless you do that you are lost, and being lost, the fault is your own, either because you willingly closed your eyes and would not see the precipice, or you wished to cast yourself into it with your eyes open.

XXVI.

BY means of the Sacrament of Penance the sinner, truly repentant, obtains undoubtedly from God a remission of the guilt and the eternal punishment due to his sins ; but ordinarily, as it has been defined by the Council of Trent, he does not obtain also a full remission of the temporal punishment to be undergone, either in this world or in that to come, in satisfaction to the divine justice. This temporal punishment we can and ought to satisfy by penance, by willingly performing penal and afflictive works, by supporting patiently the crosses, afflictions, tribulations, and adversities which come to us from the hand of God. But since we are so weak, so delicate, and so miserable that we can neither suffer nor do sufficient penance for the paying of all the temporal punishment due to our sins, and fully satisfying the justice of God, holy Church, using that authority which she has received from Jesus Christ, furnishes us with a means most easy of paying the debt, and of making to God that satisfaction required, by indulgences.

But what is an indulgence ? What is meant by it ? how many kinds are there ? What virtue, what efficacy has it ? What effects does it produce ? What dispositions are required in us for the gaining of an indulgence ? This is what I now propose to explain.

The word indulgence, in the sense we now take it, denotes the yielding up of some debt or right of action to which one has a claim in respect of another. So that in the Catholic Church an indulgence means a remission of the temporal punishment due to sins committed after baptism, by applying to us the superabundant merits of Jesus Christ, of His blessed Mother, and of the saints, outside of the sacrament. These words being rightly understood we are able to form a just idea of an indulgence. For thus considered it is a remission, granted by the Church, of the temporal punishment, not of the sin, nor of the eternal guilt, which has been remitted through the Sacrament of Penance, but of that temporal punishment which remains to be undergone either in this world or in purgatory, for the satisfying of the divine justice. Secondly, an indulgence is a remission of the temporal punishment due to sins committed after baptism, because with regard to the punishment due to sins committed before baptism, that is forgiven through the same sacrament, so that should any one die immediately after baptism, he would go direct to heaven without suffering the fire of purgatory. Thirdly, an indulgence is a remission granted by the Church to its pastors, who are the Pope and the bishops, with, however, this difference, that the Pope can grant a plenary indulgence, which is a full remission of all the temporal punishment due to sin, and the bishops can only grant a remission of a part of the temporal punishment, that is to say, an indulgence of forty days, or at the most one year. Fourthly, an indulgence is a remission of temporal punishment granted by the Church by applying the superabundant merits of Jesus Christ, of the Blessed Virgin, and the saints To understand these words it is necessary to know that all good works are of themselves both meritorious and satisfactory ; that is, they serve for two things ; as meritorious they obtain from God some spiritual good and as satisfactory they satisfy the divine justice for the injury done to Him by sin. The merit of good works belongs to him who performs them, and it cannot be applied to another ; but the satisfaction made to God by good works can be applied to another ; just as if I were to pay the debt of a friend, and by this satisfy for him his creditor, and release him from the obligation of paying it at another time. Now, every one will agree with me that the satisfactions given by Jesus Christ to

His Eternal Father were superabundant, and of an infinite value, as St. Paul clearly says, writing to the Romans: "Where sin abounded, grace did more abound." It is also certain that the satisfactions given to God by the Blessed Virgin by her sorrows and sufferings, by her heroic virtues, were superabundant, because she was conceived without original sin, and because during the whole course of her life she never committed the smallest sin: whence it is she had nothing with regard to herself to satisfy the justice of God. The same might be said of the satisfactions given to God by the other saints without having contracted the obligation, as St. John the Baptist, who, after being sanctified in his mother's womb, passed his life in great austerity, and ended it with the crown of martydom. Nor can we pass over in silence the many glorious martyrs who, no sooner were they baptised, contended to the death, at the cost of their own blood, against diabolical wickedness, consequently without any sin upon their conscience, without any debt of temporal punishment to pay to God. Now, is it credible that all these superabundant satisfactions of Jesus Christ, the Blessed Virgin, and of the saints should remain idle and without effect, they not having need of them, may they not serve for so many others who have need of them? No, it is not credible, because God gives to every good work its reward; and although the good works of the Blessed Virgin and of the saints, as meritorious, have been rewarded with the glory of heaven, yet as satisfactory they have not had their effect; hence, that they might have, what has Jesus Christ done? He has formed a spiritual treasure of His superabundant satisfactions, and of those of the Blessed Virgin and the saints; this treasure He has confided to the Church, with an authority to dispense it to the faithful, outside of the Sacrament of Penance, so that by the application of these superabundant satisfactions, they may be able to satisfy the divine justice, and thus in whole or in part free themselves from the temporal punishment due to their sins. This is the true idea of an indulgence.

And is it true that Jesus Christ has composed this spiritual treasure, and that He has confided it to the Church with the power of remitting the temporal punishment due to sin, by the application of His superabundant satisfactions, of the Blessed Virgin, and of the saints? Yes, it is true. It is an article of our faith, which no one can deny without becoming a heretic. In fact, Jesus Christ said to His apostles: "As the Father hath sent me, I also send you. Behold I send you with the same authority with which My Eternal Father has sent me." Then to explain better the fulness of that authority given to them, He says: "Whatsoever you shall bind upon earth, shall be bound also in heaven; and whatsoever you shall loose upon earth, shall be loosed also in heaven." It is, then, clear from these words that as the Church has had from Jesus Christ the authority to impose upon the faithful temporal penalty, so she has also authority to remit it by granting indulgences; it is also clear that as the Church has received authority to forgive, together with the sin, the eternal punishment of it, so she has authority to remit the temporal punishment, for the reason that he who can do the greater can also do the lesser. St. Paul, after having separated from the communion of the faithful the incestuous Corinthian, and subjected him to salutary penance, made use of that authority, remitting to him the debt of satisfaction which yet remained to him to pay.

After the Apostle St. Paul, our mother, the Church, has made use of this authority up to our own time, in granting indulgences to the faithful as often as she has considered it becoming to do so; and the Council of Trent has defined that " the power of granting indulgences having been given to the Church by Jesus Christ, and the Church having made use of this power from the earliest times, the Sacred Council teaches that the use of indulgences is especially wholesome to Christian people, and it fulminates its anathemas against all those who assert that indulgences are useless, or that there exists in the Church no power to grant them.

We will now see how many kinds of indulgences there are. There are those that have the power of remitting to those who gain them all the temporal punishment due to their sins, and these are called *plenary* indulgences. There are those that have the power of remitting not all, but only a part of the temporal punishment, and these are called *partial* indulgences. Such are the indulgences of forty days, of seven years, and such like. A *partial* indulgence has reference to the penitential satisfaction to be performed according to the ancient discipline of the Church, in this respect, that as the canonical penance of seven years or forty days, or other similar penance, were enjoined in order to expiate the penalties which were due to certain sins, so, by indulgences issued in these forms, the penitential satisfaction of such a number of days or years is remitted; and by consequence, so much temporal penalty cancelled as would be remitted were the canonical satisfaction fulfilled in its integrity.

There are also indulgences *perpetual* and *temporary*. Perpetual indulgences are those intended to last for ever. Temporary are given for a definite time—as for three, five, or seven years, &c.; after that time the indulgence ceases. This time is computed from the day when the rescript or brief is dated, and not from the day of publication.

Moreover, indulgences are divided into *local, personal,* and *real*. *Local* indulgences are inherent to places for the use of persons frequenting those places, as to a church, to an altar, so that to gain them it is necessary to visit that church, that altar; real indulgences are granted in favour of certain moveable objects—as, for instance, chaplets, crosses, &c., by means of which indulgences are gained. These indulgences, as it has been decided by the Sacred Congregation, can be gained only by those for whom the beads, cross, or medal, has been annexed the indulgence. *Personal* indulgence is granted as a favour or grace, and clothes a man, accompanying him wherever he goes, being attached to his person directly. Such is, for example, the plenary indulgence of the papal blessing which is given to the dying.

Q

Lastly, some indulgences are granted only for the living, and some only for the dead. The indulgences for the living are of use only to the living, who desire to gain them; the indulgences for the dead are those granted by the Pope, with the express leave to him who gains them to apply them to the souls in Purgatory, not by way of absolution, because the Pope has no jurisdiction over the souls in Purgatory; therefore, he cannot absolve them from any punishment, but apply them only by way of suffrage, that is, to offer to heaven those indulgences for that soul, to the end that God, accepting them, may deign to remit in whole or in part the temporal punishment which remains for that soul to undergo. But that these indulgences may be applied to the souls in purgatory, that they may really assist them, it is necessary that they be granted by the Pope, with the express leave that they may be applicable to the souls in purgatory, otherwise they will not be of any avail to them, because the dispensation of the treasure of the merits of Jesus Christ, of the Blessed Virgin, and of the saints, does not belong to a private individual, but only to the Church.

Amongst the indulgences for the dead those especially are named that are applied to the souls in purgatory through Masses being celebrated at a privileged altar, each of which can obtain for a soul the full remission of all temporal punishment, and thus free it from purgatory. And here I will give an objection made by those who ridicule everything sacred, and which perhaps you have often heard; they say: "If a Mass celebrated at a privileged altar be sufficient to free a soul from purgatory, then it is useless to celebrate many Masses for a soul, since one is sufficient. Moreover, in the world there are many privileged altars, many priests celebrating Masses thereon, so that in a short time purgatory will be empty of souls; and if this takes place it is quite useless to celebrate so many Masses for the souls in purgatory, or to make suffrages in other ways." To this objection I will briefly reply, though it does not merit a reply; since it is made by those whose object is to contemn the Church and put forth maxims prejudicial to the souls in purgatory; but I reply that you may give a reason for the faith that is in you. In the first place, then : " The privilege of an altar consists in this, that when the unbloody sacrifice of the Mass is celebrated there by a priest for a soul departed, the soul of that person (supposing it to have been united with God in charity when it passed out of this life) is thereby aided by the suffrage of a plenary indulgence." These words mean: "By the indulgence annexed to the privileged altar as far as regards the mind of the granter and the use of the power of the keys, a plenary indulgence, which forthwith liberates the soul from all the pains of purgatory. As regards, however, the effect of the application, such an indulgence is meant to correspond in its extent with the good pleasure and acceptation of the divine mercy." There-fore, it is not certain that a Mass celebrated at a privileged altar infallibly liberates that soul from purgatory for whom it has been applied, because it does not appear that God is ever bound to accept this application; consequently it is not known whether He will accept it. Hence, Pope Gregory has said : "A Mass celebrated at a privileged altar can free a soul from purgatory, should it please God." Secondly, if the Mass or any other suffrage does not assist that soul for whom it has been applied, either because it has no need of it, or because God has not accepted its applica-tion, in that case, says St. Thomas, that Mass, that suffrage God will distribute, and will cause other souls more in need or more deserving to benefit by it. Finally, I say that the indulgences applied to the souls departed can assist and obtain for them the remission of the temporal punishment, but they cannot assist in obtaining for them the forgiveness of venial sins which they had committed, and which had not been cancelled by true repentance; consequently, those souls, being obliged to remain in purgatory until they have can-celled all the stains of venial sins, because nothing defiled can enter heaven, it is evident that by Masses and suffrages that we apply to them, purgatory will not be empty of souls. Therefore, for every reason it will be always good to apply Masses, alms, pray, perform works of piety and penance in suffrage for the souls in purgatory, that they may be speedily delivered from the pains they suffer; for, as St. Augustine says: it is better that suffrages should abound for those that have no need of them, than that they should be wanting for those who have need of them.

We will now consider the dispositions required for the gaining of an indulgence. We observe, then, in the first place, "that every Christian who is a member of the Catholic Church, and who, accordingly, is subject to her jurisdiction and authority, is capable of gaining indulgences; it follows, then, that no one is capable who is separated from the communion of the faithful by the greater excommunication, or who is a catechumen, because such an one has not yet been made a member of the Church by holy baptism." Secondly, it is absolutely necessary, in order that a man may reap the fruit of an indulgence, that he be in a state of grace, by means of a good confession, having obtained forgiveness from God for all the mortal sins he may have committed. To enjoy the full fruit of a plenary indulgence, is also necessary the entire remission of venial sin, and an efficacious determination of avoiding them. Without this it is impossible to gain the indulgence. Finally, to gain an indulgence it is necessary to perform the works enjoined. For example, when the indulgence is granted to such as shall go to confession and communion, visit such a church or altar, pray for the extirpation of heresy, the exaltation of the Church, for peace amongst Christian princes, and such like. All these things are called works enjoined; all of which ought to be exactly performed, and that a person should be restored to a state of grace during the time within which the indulgence was to be gained.

These are the dispositions required for gaining an indulgence, and it is also the reason why so many do not gain an indulgence, for there are so few who have

the necessary dispositions for gaining it, especially that
of a plenary indulgence.

After what has been said, it will be well to observe
that among Christians there are two prejudices. The
first is that of not caring about indulgences. Some there
are who do not care about them, because they esteem them
useless and superfluous, and say: "That an indulgence
is nothing more than a remission of that punishment
which the Church in bygone times imposed upon sinners, and at the present time this canonical penance,
having grown out of use, therefore it is useless to have
a remission of it." This is false. An indulgence is not
only a remission of the canonical penance imposed by
the Church, but it is also a remission of that temporal
punishment that may remain for us to undergo in purgatory; for if it were not so the Church, by her indulgences, would do us more harm than good, inasmuch
as by freeing us from the punishment in this world, she
would submit us to undergo greater pains in purgatory.
Is it credible that the Church, having the spirit of
truth, being infallible in her teaching, could deceive
herself and her children in an affair of so great
importance? Is it credible that the Church, a mother
so kind, should, in place of assisting us by indulgences,
act so cruelly towards us by freeing us from the punishment she could impose upon us in satisfaction to the
divine justice, make us suffer the more severe pains of
purgatory? No one could suppose that, unless he be
blinded by his passions or an enemy to the Church.

Others there are who have no care for indulgences,
because it is tedious to them to perform with exactness
the works enjoined for the gaining of them. To such
I will content myself by applying the reproof given
to Naaman by his servants. This general, covered
with leprosy, went to the prophet Eliseus to be cured
of his disease. The prophet told him to go and wash
seven times in the Jordan, assuring him that he would
infallibly recover health and be made clean. But he,
hearing prescribed to him a remedy so easy, was angry,
and went away without doing anything. Then his

servants, desirous for their master's recovery, said to him: "Father, if the prophet had bid thee do some great thing, surely thou shouldst have done it: how much rather what he now hath said to thee: Wash, and thou shalt be clean?" The same I say to all who neglect this most precious treasure of indulgences. By repenting, by amending yourselves of your sins, by doing the works enjoined by the Church, by this little you will be able to free yourselves from the temporal punishment which remains for you to undergo to satisfy the divine justice, and thus deliver yourselves from the more severe pains of purgatory. If the Church prescribed things arduous and difficult, so that you might be freed from those most awful pains, prudence would dictate to you to do them. Then what negligence more shameful, what foolishness more deplorable than that of not willingly performing things so easy, and willingly profiting of a remedy so good as that proposed by the Church of indulgences? If you do not wish to know it in time, you will know it to your cost in eternity, if nothing else worse happen to you—to suffer those pains so terrible, so severe, which in activity are not less than those endured in hell; for one alone of those pains is greater than all the pains of this world united together.

The other prejudice is that of those who have too great a reliance upon indulgences. They consider themselves, by indulgences, to be exempted from all else, and that they can fly to heaven. If there is an indulgence to be gained, they are at once on the move to gain it—if there is an order or society to be enrolled in, they wish to join it. All these things are good and excellent in themselves, but then observe their behaviour. With all this eagerness for gaining indulgences, all the devotion they have for this or that order, you find they take no care or trouble in amending themselves of their vices, their defects—never striving to observe with exactness the maxims of the Gospel, nor imitating Jesus Christ in His virtues, in His example—never giving themselves to the practice of penance and mortification, being always the same vicious, proud, bad-tempered, unmortified. And very often they carry their prejudice to the order so far that in order to fulfil the duties of it they neglect those of their state of life, the care of their families—neglect the functions of their own church, the instructions given by their own pastor, and to say all, in one word, they neglect what is of obligation to do that which is only of counsel and of supererogation. Devotion badly regulated! These are prejudices often carried so far as to lead them to believe that the indulgences annexed to this or that order are better than any others, and can bring them to heaven before anything else. Every confraternity or order is good, but unless you amend yourselves of your vices and defects—unless you observe the Gospel—unless you practise virtue—unless you are in the company of Jesus, that is to say, unless you imitate Him in His virtues and example—unless you fulfil the duties of your state of life and those of a good Christian, of what use will it be to you to belong to a confraternity or order? Absolutely none. Indulgences are good and useful, and you do well to try and gain them; but unless you, on your part, do penance in as much as you are able, chastising your own body, mortifying it by works of penance, of what use will indulgences be to you? Absolutely none: because neither God nor His Church grants an indulgence that you may remain slothful and exempted from doing the penance that you ought to do for the satisfying of the divine justice; but the indulgence is granted to assist you in your insufficiency—to help you in your misery, so that after having done what you on your part were able to do, should that not be sufficient for the satisfying of the divine justice for your sins, you may be able to do so by indulgences taken from the treasure of the superabundant merits of Jesus Christ, of the Blessed Virgin, and of the saints, and thus be freed from the temporal punishment due to your sins. An indulgence is a spiritual alms which the Church gives to the faithful standing in need. Since, therefore, one who is healthy and strong, able to work and will not, is undeserving of an alms, so one, who is able to satisfy the justice of God by his own works, is undeserving of this spiritual alms.

We will therefore conclude. Indulgences are a great benefit granted to us by God and His Church, and we ought by every means in our power to profit by them; at the same time we ought to attend to the performance of good works, to mortification, to penance in as much as we are able, because then only the indulgences of the Church will be to us useful and advantageous.

XXVII

CONTINUING the explanation of the Sacraments, that of Extreme Unction comes next in order. What means the words Extreme Unction? They do not mean, as some suppose, an anointing just as the soul of the Christian is about to leave its body. No; it is called Extreme Unction because it is the last anointing made by the Church to the Christian. The first is made at baptism, the second at confirmation, and the last is this. What then is Extreme Unction? It is of faith that it is a sacrament instituted by Jesus Christ, which, by means of certain anointings with the oil blessed by the bishop, and by means of certain prayers of the priest, the soul is wonderfully assisted, and also the body, should it be expedient to him who receives it.

The *remote* matter of this sacrament is the oil blessed by the bishop—the *proximate* matter is the anointing made with that oil on the different parts of the body. The *form* are the prayers used by the sacred minister; finally, the minister of this sacrament is no other than a priest, with, however, this observation, that the ministration of this sacrament belongs to the parish priest, so that other priests cannot lawfully administer it without his permission. But is there any necessity, any obligation of receiving this Sacrament of Extreme Unction? Yes, in danger of death by sickness we are commanded to receive it; so much so that being able, and not doing so, we are guilty of a grave sin, because when we are in danger of death we are bound to receive the blessed Eucharist, so also we are bound to receive Extreme Unction. In fact, God, by the Apostle St. James, has said: "Is any man sick among you? Let him bring in the priests of the church, and let them pray over him, anointing him with oil in the name of the Lord." Therefore, says the Council of Trent, God not only exhorts us, but He has expressly commanded us to receive this Sacrament of Extreme Unction. If He has commanded us, then he, who is able to receive it, and does not receive it, sins, and not only does he sin, but he shows a contempt of so great a sacrament, despising the benefits of God, Who, after having instituted so many other sacraments for our benefit whilst in life, has willed to institute this to assist us also at death.

And if it is thus, who can sufficiently deplore the blindness and negligence of those who, being dangerously ill, take no care to receive this Sacrament of Extreme Unction—who can not even bear the mention of it—hence it ordinarily happens to them that either they do not receive this sacrament, or they receive it in their last moments, when deprived of their senses, consequently they receive it with little or no disposition, with little or no fruit. What a deception of the devil is this! As if this sacrament would injure them, or hasten their death. On the contrary, the Sacrament of Extreme Unction, as we shall show, besides the virtue of doing good to the soul, has also that of benefiting the body, restoring it to health, when God sees it expedient.

Then why is it neglected? If they do not neglect the use of remedies, of medicines, &c., why do they neglect this sacrament which is called by the Fathers the medicine of the soul and of the body? Either they will or will not die of that sickness. If they are to die, it is certain they die without a sacrament which was able to comfort and strengthen the soul, giving a particular grace, so that they may make a happy death. If they are to recover from their sickness, true that will come to pass, and receiving the Sacrament of Extreme Unction they will recover quicker or more easily. Therefore, looking upon it in whichever way they choose, if they reflect well on it, they will find that it is better to receive this sacrament than neglect to do so. For they who neglect Extreme Unction are not earnest Christians, having but little of the fear of God, without resignation to the divine will, wishing to do their own and not the will of God. To receive Extreme Unction means there is danger of death; but as they do not wish to die, they would wish to live, were it in their power, in spite of God; for this reason they cannot make up their minds to receive this sacrament. But willing or not willing when the hour comes, depart from hence they must. Consequently, whatever may happen it is always better for them to dispose themselves for a good death. Not less deplorable is the folly of friends and relations, who, for fear of alarming the sick person, dare not advise or exhort him to receive the Sacrament of Extreme Unction; neither do they wish others to advise or exhort him to receive it, their only study consists in flattering and giving hopes to the sick man of his recovery. But this is a charity, a compassion wrongly directed—this is a compassion for the body and not for the soul—this is a placing the poor sick man in danger of losing eternal life, for fear of his losing his temporal life—it is exposing him to the danger of dying without the sacraments, of being alarmed at the moment of death and for all eternity, rather than have given him a little fear, when he was alive, when that little fear might have been most useful to him, causing him to enter into himself, leading him to settle the affairs of his conscience, and thus dispose himself for a happy death and be saved. Oh, what compassion, what charity is that! When a person is in danger of death, and gives no thought to the affairs of his soul, he ought to be advised to do so with charity, because silence at that time for fear of alarming him is no longer charity, but cruelty. And as soon as he has been admonished of his dangerous state, he ought to give his mind to receive not only the Sacraments of Penance and Eucharist, but also that of Extreme Unction, without waiting until the last moments of his life, exposing himself to the danger of not receiving it, or of receiving it without the proper sentiments, without

252 FEMILIAR INSTRUCTIONS ON THE SACRAMENTS.

being sensible of its administration, with little or no disposition, consequently with little fruit. Listen to what the Church says on this subject: "Those sin very grievously who defer the holy unction until all hope of recovery now lost, life begins to ebb, and the sick person to sink into insensibility, and also those who ought to advise and do not."

Before speaking of the wonderful effects of this Sacrament of Extreme Unction, we will say a few words regarding those who are capable of receiving this sacrament; that is to say, those who can and ought to receive it. It is necessary, in the first place, that the person be baptised. Secondly, to no one who is not visited by heavy sickness is it lawful to give the Sacrament of Extreme Unction. Therefore all persons in sound health are excepted, even though they should incur risk of life by undertaking a perilous voyage, or engaging in battle from which certain death may impend over them, or even though, condemned to capital punishment, they should be hurried off to execution; besides all who are deprived of the use of reason; nor are children, who have committed no sins, from the remains of which they would have no occasion to be healed by the remedial efficacy of this sacrament, nor fools or madmen, unless they have lucid intervals, and then give sign of piety, and ask to be anointed with the sacred oil, for a person insane from his very birth is not to be anointed; but if a sick person, whilst yet in full possession of his faculties, had expressed a wish to be made partaker of this sacrament, and subsequently becomes insane, he is to be anointed.

One of the effects of this sacrament is that it remits sins. The Apostle says: "Is any man sick among you? let him bring in the priests of the church, and let them pray over him, anointing him with oil in the name of the Lord; and the prayer of faith shall save the sick man, and the Lord shall raise him up; and if he be in sins, they shall be forgiven him." Then the first effect of this sacrament produced in the sick person is to cancel the remains of sin, that is, it liberates the soul

from the languor and infirmity which it contracted through
sins, giving it vigour and fervour and a good inclination
to virtue, piety, devotion, and the love of God. And if
the sick person has venial sins that have not been cancelled, or mortal sins which he had not recalled to
his memory, being sorry in general for all his offences
committed against God, the Sacrament of Extreme
Unction obtains for him their forgiveness, and not only
increases in him grace, but confers upon him a right to
the divine grace.

The second effect produced in the sick person by this
sacrament is that it conduces to banish sadness, and disposes him to await with a joyous mind the coming of our
Lord, freeing him from that excessive fear and anxiety of
mind, filling him with hope in the mercy of God, animating and comforting him. Animated and comforted in
this way the sick person suffers willingly for the love of
God in punishment of his sins the pains and inconveniences of his sickness, gains strength, and a particular
assistance to resist more easily the temptations of the
devil. For although the enemy of the human race
never ceases whilst we live to meditate our ruin and
destruction, yet at no time does he more violently strain
every nerve to destroy us, and if possible deprive us of
all hope of the divine mercy, than when he sees the
last day of life approaching. Therefore, arms are supplied to the sick person in this sacrament, to enable
him to break the violence and impetuosity of the adversary, and to fight bravely against him.

The third effect is to assist the sick person in his
recovery, and restore him to his former health, that is,
should it be expedient for his soul; this is a condition
that should always accompany our prayers whenever
we ask of God things spiritual or temporal. But that
this sacrament may procure for the sick person all these
good effects, it is necessary that he should receive it
with the best dispositions he is able.

The first disposition is to be in the grace of God,
because this is one of the living sacraments, principally
instituted to increase in us the grace of God, conse-

quently to be augmented it is necessary that it be in the soul already, otherwise receiving this sacrament in sin, a sacrilege would be committed. When, therefore, a sick person is about to receive Extreme Unction it is his duty to purify the soul by a good confession of all his sins ; and should he have lost the use of his speech, and therefore be unable to confess, he ought at least to be sorry for all his offences against God, to implore of Him forgiveness, and have a firm will to amend, giving, if he can, a sign of his repentance—doing this, through the sacerdotal ministrations, he will obtain from God forgiveness, and receive with fruit this sacrament.

The second disposition is to have a lively faith, believing firmly all the truths of our holy religion, and especially the virtue and power of the Sacrament of Extreme Unction to produce all the good effects which I have explained above. In fact the apostle says, prayer, accompanied with faith, will save the sick man.

The third disposition consists in receiving this sacrament with sentiments of piety, of devotion, and of the love of God, of resignation to the divine will, of detachment from the world and its vanities, even that of ourselves, being willing to make a sacrifice of our life, and of accepting death, should it please God to demand it of us.

The last disposition is to accompany with the heart the prayers recited by the priest during the ministration of this sacrament in the anointing of the eyes, ears, nose, hands, and feet of the sick person. The priest, anointing the eyes of the sick person, says this prayer : "Through this holy unction, and through His most tender mercy, may the Lord pardon thee whatever sins thou hast committed by seeing. Amen." And the sick person ought to say in his heart : "Ah ! too true, O my God, I have offended Thee often by my eyes, by unlawful looks, by dangerous and improper curiosity— too true these eyes have been the door by which sin entered into my soul. Ah ! my God, pardon me !" Anointing the ears, the priest says : "Through this holy unction, and through His most tender mercy, may the

Lord pardon thee whatever sins thou hast committed by hearing. Amen." The sick person ought to say from his heart: "Ah! my good God, too true, often have I offended Thee by listening to wicked and danger-ous discourse, contrary to charity. Pardon me, O my God." Anointing the nostrils, the priest says: "Through this holy unction, and through His most tender mercy, may the Lord pardon thee whatever sins thou hast committed by smelling. Amen." And the sick person ought in his heart to say the same. The priest, anointing the lips, says: "Through this holy unction, and through His most tender mercy, may the Lord pardon thee whatever sins thou hast commit-ted by taste and speech. Amen." And who can number the sins committed by the sense of taste and of speech? By excess in eating and drinking, by bad conversation, by detraction and bad counsel, by having spoken when you ought to have been silent—silent when you ought to have spoken? "Ah! my God," the sick person ought to say, "have mercy on me, and by the blood Thou didst shed for me pardon me!" The priest then anointing the hands and the feet, says: "Through this holy unction, and through His most tender mercy, may the Lord pardon thee whatever sins thou hast committed by touch, by walking. Amen." And the sick person, filled with confusion for the many injuries done to God by these senses, and at the same time filled with confidence in the divine mercy, ought to say from his heart: "The sins I have committed by these senses are innumerable, but do Thou, O my God, pardon them!"

These are the dispositions with which the sick person ought to receive the Sacrament of Extreme Unction, if he desire to receive it with fruit and advantage to the soul. But if he neglect this sacrament until he is more dead than alive—when he shall have lost his senses how can he have these good dispositions? How can he draw from it fruit? We will, therefore, conclude, and having understood all that is necessary to know regarding this Sacrament of Extreme Unction, let us bear in mind that we must most certainly die; let us remember that death may overtake us at any moment, and sooner than we expect. Let us recall to our minds that God has provided us with all that is necessary for our salvation—the sacraments to assist us during life, and also a sacrament to assist us at death. Let us profit by these gifts of God, receiving them frequently and worthily during life, if we desire of God the grace to receive them with profit at the hour of death, and thus procure for us the salvation of our souls, which we ought to have most at heart.

XXVIII

THE Sacrament of Holy Order follows that of Extreme Unction in the course of our Instructions on the Sacraments. It may seem useless to speak on this sacrament, since women are incapable of receiving it, and married persons have no thought of doing so. Yet, it is well that an explanation of this sacrament should be given, because it is necessary that parents should know what the Sacrament of Holy Order is, and what are the dispositions required for receiving it, so that they may know how to regulate themselves with regard to their children, should they be inclined to embrace the ecclesiastical state, or when they show themselves adverse to it, or when they have not the necessary qualifications for that state. That what I am about to say may be understood, you must recall to your mind what I have said on former occasions, that religion is a virtue which consists in rendering to God a fit and proper worship, that is to say, in showing Him that esteem, that respect, that veneration—in giving Him that honour and glory which is due to Him, practising those things that He has commanded, observing those rites, those ceremonies, and all that He has taught us, or that He has made known to us by holy Church. But this proper worship, who ought to direct and regulate it, so that it may be such that God requires from us? Can each one regulate it according to his own caprice or idea? Certainly not; for religion in that case, in place of giving that honour pleasing to God, would be a confusion. In every affair, if things are to go on well, there must be some one to direct and regulate them. Thus, in a family, if things are to go in order, it is

R

necessary that there be a head who rules every thing. In an army, in the time of war, there must be a general at the head to direct the military operations; in a kingdom there are superiors—the sovereign, ministers, magistrates—who administer those things belonging to the state. Thus also in religion there ought to be persons destined to things pertaining to God. And these persons consecrated to the divine worship, destined to regulate and administer sacred things, are called sacred ministers of God—priests.

That there ought to be these sacred persons, ministers of God, priests, is a truth not only of faith, but nature itself declares it, and it is therefore known and exercised by every nation in the world. Every country upon the earth has its religion to render to God—a worship, and wherever there is a religion there are also sacred persons to regulate and minister things pertaining to worship. In the law of nature, from the beginning of the world—in the law of Moses there were, and there are, at present amongst pagans and heretics, ministers to regulate the worship, and these were and are maintained by the people, were and are respected and reverenced by all, perhaps more so than they are by Christians of our own time.

Then, for a greater reason the Catholic religion ought to have its ministers, this being the only true and holy religion that gives to God that worship pleasing to Him; if it were not, it could never have existed. And for this religion Jesus Christ has instituted the Sacrament of Holy Order, by means of which there might be always in His Church persons wholly consecrated to Him, to His worship, to His honour and glory, destined especially to the exclusion of all others, to regulate and minister things sacred and divine.

What, then, is this Sacrament of Holy Order? "It is a sacrament by which bishops, priests, and other ministers of the Church are ordained, and receive power and grace to perform their sacred duties." It is called Order, because amongst those who have power over

sacred things, there ought to be various orders of persons: of superiors, of inferiors, of those who have the
fulness of power, and of those who have only a part,
nor can they have its fulness until they have passed
through several grades, which are like so many steps
by which they ascend to it. Under the name of Order
there consists seven degrees, each distinct the one from
the other ; four of them are called *minor*, the remainder
are called *sacred* or greater orders, all of which, because
they are directed to one principal order—the priesthood,
form but one Sacrament of Order.

The first of the four *minor* orders is the Porter, whose
office it is to guard the door of the Church, to prevent
the entrance of infidels, excommunicated persons, and
such as may interrupt the divine offices of the Church,
and also to call the faithful by the ringing of the bell.
The second is the Reader, whose office it is to read the
Holy Scripture in the Church and to instruct the people
in what regards faith. The third is the Exorcist, whose
office it is, with the permission of the Bishop, to exorcise possessed persons, that they may be liberated from
the wicked spirit. The fourth is the Acolyte, whose
office is to serve the sub-deacon at solemn mass by
giving him the water and wine, and holding a lighted
candle at the gospel. Before one is admitted to minor
orders he has to receive the tonsure; this is not an order
but only a preparation for the receiving of it, a sacred
ceremony instituted by the Church, by which a person
is enrolled and dedicated to the ecclesiastical state, and
for that reason he is called a cleric. The crown of the
head is shaved to remind him that he is to imitate
Jesus Christ bearing a crown of thorns.

The sacred or *greater* orders are the Sub-diaconate,
Diaconate, and the Priesthood. To the sub-deacon is
given the power of serving the deacon at a solemn
Mass, handing to him the paten, with the host, the
chalice, and wine, and of reading the epistle. To the
office of sub-diaconate is annexed the vow of perpetual
chastity, and the obligation of reciting the divine office.
To the deacon is conceded the power of assisting the

priest at a solemn mass, and of singing the gospel. Moreover, his office is to receive from the sub-deacon the paten with the host, the chalice with wine, and present them to the priest, and he can also be the extraordinary minister of Baptism and of the Eucharist. Finally, the priesthood receives the power of consecrating the bread and wine, changing them into the body and blood of Jesus Christ, celebrating the holy sacrifice of the Mass, absolving from sins, of being appointed to rule and govern the faithful, as also of preaching the word of God, and of administering the sacraments, always, however, depending upon his own parish priest, with the exception of the Sacraments of Confirmation and Holy Order, the ministration of which belong to the Bishop. To these Holy Orders is to be added that of the Episcopacy, which is the highest, and gives to the Bishop power to administer the Sacraments of Confirmation and Holy Order, to rule and govern the diocese confided to his care and jurisdiction.

But are these orders lesser or greater so many sacraments? That the lesser and sub-diaconate are is uncertain. The diaconate may be said certain. The priesthood is a sacrament, and it is an article of faith also that there is, by divine institution, a hierarchy in the Church, over which the Pope is the visible head, having jurisdiction over all other bishops; and these are superior in jurisdiction over all priests, and these again are superior in order to deacons, sub-deacons, and simple clerics.

Holy Order, then, is a sacrament by which a simple Christian is made a person wholly consecrated to God, to His worship, to His service; therefore, separated from all worldly care and solicitude, the apostle says: "Let a man so account of us as of the ministers of Christ, and the dispensers of the mysteries of God. For Christ, therefore, we are ambassadors." It makes him as an angel, and more than an angel by the special power given him by God of changing the bread and wine into the body and blood of Jesus Christ, and of forgiving sins. What great dignity is that of the priesthood!

What purity of life, what holiness is required for a dignity so high! Who is able to comprehend it?

But shall it be permitted to every Christian to aspire to this dignity—to this office of minister of God, even as one aspires to a worldly office or dignity? Oh, that would be a grave error even to think so! If, before entering into any state of life, it is necessary to consult the will of God, so as not to err in the choice, how much more so before embracing an ecclesiastical state, which requires a special vocation and a certainty that God has called us to that state? In fact, who would have the boldness to take upon himself the office of minister of a king, without having been selected by him, and were he to do so would it not be an insult to the sovereign? Thus he would offer a great insult to God who should take upon himself to be His minister without having been called. Our blessed Lord says: "He that entereth not by the door into the sheepfold, but climbeth up another way, the same is a thief and a robber." Whosoever enter into the ecclesiastical state, not by the door of a true vocation, he is not a true ecclesiastic, a true pastor, but a thief, a robber, who dishonours himself, his dignity, and holy Church. God, by the mouth of the apostle, says: "Neither doth any man take the honour to himself, but he that is called by God, as Aaron was." For this reason Jesus Christ said to His apostles: "I have chosen you." And the apostles, after the death of Judas, prayed thus to God: "Thou, Lord, Who knowest the hearts of all men, shew whether of these two Thou hast chosen to take the place of this ministry and apostleship."

And if it is thus, it does not belong to the parents to determine the ecclesiastical state for their children. No, it belongs to God to call, choose, and destine them to be His ministers, His ambassadors, dispensers of His graces, of His mysteries, teachers of His law, His doctrine, pastors, guides of souls redeemed by His most precious blood. And if God does not choose them, do you not see that your wishing them, destining them, and placing them in the sacred ministry against the will of God is the greatest insult you can make to heaven—the most enormous crime you can commit? Do you not see that you render yourselves culpable of all the evil consequences that follow from it?

That son whom you have forced to enter into the ecclesiastical state without a divine vocation, should he become idle, vicious, a scandal, dishonour himself, the character, the dignity of the priesthood, laden with sins and sacrileges, who is the cause of all these evil consequences? That parent who willed his son to be an ecclesiastic, without having been called by Jesus Christ. On the contrary, when God honours you by calling your son to the dignity of the sacred ministry, is it possible that you have the courage to refuse, by giving him to the world? Do you not see the great injury done to God, to His Church, and to souls, by depriving them of a good ecclesiastic, of his learning, piety, devotion, and zeal? Do you not see that it is, as it were, to take him from the hands of God and give him to the devil? Woe to those who do not follow the call of God! Woe to those also who intrude themselves or force others into the ecclesiastical state against the divine will! Only those who are called by God ought to ascend to the honour of the priesthood. "Neither doth any man take the honour to himself, but he that is called by God, as Aaron was."

If, then, it is true that before receiving Holy Order it is necessary to be certain that God has called us, how are we to know that we have this true vocation, now that Jesus Christ does not call us one by one, as He did the apostles? St. Bernard says: "When God requires anything of us, He knows how to make us feel and know His will." There are means by which we may know a divine vocation, and we have only to make use of them.

The first means is that of prayer. We ought to place ourselves in the hands of God, to be indifferent whether we are in this or that state, providing it be that which will be pleasing to Him, and then say to Him, with the prophet Samuel: "Speak, Lord, for Thy

servant heareth;" and with David: "Make the way
known to me wherein I should walk. Teach me to do
Thy will, for Thou art my God." And, continuing to
pray in this manner, God, without doubt, will make
known to you His will.

The second means is to examine the end, the intention we have of aspiring to the priesthood. What is
an ecclesiastic? He is a person who, renouncing every
worldly office, consecrates himself wholly to the service
of God, to the salvation of souls, and attends only to
things sacred. "Every high priest taken from among
men, is ordained for men in the things that appertain
to God." If, then, the end one has in view in becoming
a priest is that of renouncing all to give himself
entirely to the service of God and the salvation of souls,
then it is good and just, and consequently it is a manifest sign that he has a true and real vocation from God.
But if the end is self-love, that he may lead a life of
ease and pleasure; if for interest or ambition, that he
may reach a place of honour or of advantage to his
family, oh! then an end so vile, so base, and so unworthy, comes not from God, hence it is a sign that he
has not a vocation to that state.

That we may be assured that the good end is firm
and permanent, and not a passing desire, we ought to
examine ourselves to see if we possess the necessary
qualities for the ecclesiastical state; if we have learned
to curb our passions and overcome temptations, particularly those against purity; to see if we have piety
and devotion and the virtues of humility and mortification; if we possess that purity of conscience, for which
so many saints did not permit themselves to be ordained
priests, or, if ordained, did not venture to celebrate
Mass through fear of not having that purity of conscience required. Also we ought to see if we have a
true ecclesiastical spirit, that is, an inclination for study,
so that we may acquire the necessary knowledge in
proportion to our ability; if we are animated with an
inclination for prayer, spiritual reading, and for sacred
things; because, if in place of this ecclesiastical spirit,

264 FAMILIAR INSTRUCTIONS ON THE SACRAMENTS.

we are governed by a spirit worldly in our speech and actions, showing ourselves lovers of this world by our dress and conversation; oh, then this would be anything but a sign of a vocation from God.

The fourth means is to observe if there be any of those defects of mind or body which the Church makes an impediment to the ecclesiastical state; because those whom the Church rejects are neither called nor chosen.

The fifth means is to take counsel of a wise, pious, and discreet person, sincerely manifesting to him the end we have in view, the passions to which we are subject, our inclinations, and all our internal and external dispositions. And if this person, after examining our case well, forms a judgment that we may enter into the ecclesiastical state, we may conclude that our vocation is a true one, otherwise it is necessary that we should embrace another state.

The best means, however, for knowing if we have a vocation from God is, says the Roman Catechism: "When one believes himself unworthy of Holy Order, neither seeking or desiring it; nevertheless, his ecclesiastical superiors consider him worthy, because the voice of our superiors is the voice of God; and, feeling himself called by his superiors, he goes to the sacred ordination with fear, and more through obedience than desire for it." Yes, this is a sign of a true vocation. In fine, this is the rule laid down by St. Gregory. For such is the office of a priest, that were one a great saint, he ought not to presume to seek it, but to be called by God, either by obedience to his superior, or by the counsel of one whom he ought to believe, and with all that he ought to tremble, because the office is such that would make an angel tremble.

These are the means to assure ourselves of a true and necessary vocation for the ecclesiastical state. Happy the Church, happy the people, if all those who aspire to the Sacrament of Holy Order were worthy, and truly called by God to a dignity so great!

And you who are not called to receive this sacrament, what ought you to do? You ought to pray to God, especially at the time of the sacred ordinations, that He would deign to give you good priests, good pastors, because upon their worthiness depends your own good; upon their holiness depends, in a great measure, the holiness of your souls and your eternal salvation.

XXIX.

ON THE RESPECT DUE TO PRIESTS.

On last Sunday I explained to you all that is necessary to be known regarding the Sacrament of Holy Order. I did not judge it necessary to explain more fully the functions of the different grades that belong to Holy Order, but I cannot dispense myself from making known to you something of the dignity, the greatness, and the excellency of the priesthood, to which all the other grades are referred ; and I do this with the view of inspiring you with horror of that contempt and scorn shown by so many Christians of our day towards sacred ministers. It is an evil greater than it is generally supposed to be—an evil such that either supposes the loss of faith or certainly leads to the loss of it; for religion, without worship, cannot exist, neither can worship without ministers ; ministers without honour and respect cannot serve the object for which they have been destined. Therefore, the most wise God willed to preserve us from so great an evil by placing a rule that does not separate His honour from that of His ministers. "Honour God with all thy soul, and give honour to the priests . . . . With all thy soul fear the Lord, and reverence His priests." The subject is one that would be rather long, but I will endeavour to restrict it to a few reflections that will suffice for your instruction.

I do not know of anything that could impress us with a greater idea of the priesthood than the words of our blessed Lord to the apostles, in the act of investing them with that character : "As the living Father hath sent Me, I also send you." Weigh and ponder well

the meaning and force of those words. The Eternal
Father sent His only Son into the world to save it, and
for that object He gave Him all power : "All power is
given Me in heaven and on earth." This divine Son,
having completed the work given Him to do by His
divine Father, and being about to ascend into heaven,
appointed in His place priests to continue perpetually
His functions ; hence He appointed His vicars here on
earth, co-operators with Him in the salvation of the
world, interpreters of the will of God, advocates of His
mercy, and mediators between God and man, dispensers
of His grace, depositaries of His mysteries ; so that He
communicated to them in many ways that divine power
which properly belonged only to Himself. "As the
living Father hath sent Me, I also send you." What
more can be said in praise of the priesthood, when it is
one in dignity and power with the priesthood of Christ,
delegated and committed to us, and, as it were, trans-
fused in the sacred ordination ?

    That I may not be too long I will confine myself
only to the thought of two powers, truly divine, that
priests have—the one over the mystical body of Christ,
that is, the Church ; the other over the real Body of
Jesus Christ, which is the most holy Eucharist. With
regard to the first, Jesus Christ says : "Whatsoever you
shall bind upon earth, shall be bound also in heaven."
By these words we are given to understand that tremendous power given to priests of remitting the sins
of others, though they themselves are also men, weak,
mortal, and sinful. And how great is that power ?
You make no account of it, because you see it frequently used, because you see it common to many.
Besides, looking upon a priest raising his hand to
absolve the sinner, you should also cry out with astonishment : "Who can forgive sins but God only ?"
Much more so, if with your eyes you were able to
penetrate and behold the prodigious change wrought
in the soul of the absolved sinner. For when the priest
pronounces the absolving words, these words have such
a power and efficacy that the chains, by which the devil

held the soul in bondage, are loosened, that soul becomes whiter than snow, from being what it was, a slave of the devil, it becomes the child of God, the gates of hell that were open under its feet are now closed, and the gates of heaven opened to receive it. Oh, what a power is this! Out of God there is not another like unto it in heaven or on earth!

To have a more sensible idea of this power, represent to yourselves a man mortally wounded. He is at the point of death; recalling to his mind the state of his soul, he is filled with anguish, and trembles at the mental sight of what awaits him. Who is able to give him assistance? The kings of this earth have no power to release his soul from the chains that bind it; the angels and the saints can pray, but they cannot loosen the chains; the Blessed Virgin can intercede for him before God, but she also is unable to remit his sins. Should, however, a priest draw near unto him, and he being disposed and repentant, the absolving words pronounced by the priest would immediately restore to that poor soul the grace of God, deliver him from the jaws of eternal death, and entitle him to eternal happiness. Thus it is, in those moments when the world is unable to help us, our only hope rests in the sacerdotal hand of removing the fear of death. For as nothing can be more terrible at the moment of death than a conscience laden with sins, so nothing can free us from that terror, except the hand that can remit them, and this is that hand to whom it was said: "Whatsoever you shall loose upon earth, shall be loosed also in heaven."

In fine, by this power the priest is constituted plenipotentiary of God, to conclude peace between Him offended and man the offender; made arbitrator of the mercy of God, without reversion of the cause, without appellation, obliging God to ratify in heaven the sentence pronounced by the priest on earth.

But this is nothing in comparison with that other power conferred by Jesus Christ on every priest, in regard not of his mystical, but real Body. By which

that Body which is inseparably united to the person of
the Divine Word—that Body which was formed by the
power of the Holy Ghost, for which formation the
Blessed Virgin furnished the matter from her pure
blood—that Body which was once on this earth mortal
and passible, and now impassible, glorious, immortal in
heaven: that is the Body over which priests extend
their dominion, their power—yea, over Jesus Christ;
whilst to that Body is indivisibly united His soul, His
divinity. And this by that power which they have received
from Jesus Christ Himself to consecrate—" Do this in
commemoration of me." What do you believe the
priest does at the time of Mass when he adores most
profoundly the sacred species? He calls God Himself
before him by those tremendous words; he commands
God to descend from heaven, and, at the sound of those
few words, God—that God to Whom all are subject, and
upon Whom all depend—comes and places Himself in
his hands, and to him He gives Himself to be offered,
carried, and given to others, as it may please him. What
a prodigious power is this! If it was a great prodigy
that Mary, by the words, " Behold the handmaid of the
Lord; be it done unto me according to Thy word," drew
down from heaven the Eternal Word, to be incarnate in
her womb, is it not also a prodigious thing that the
priest, by these few words, "This is My Body: this is
My Blood," the same Divine Word, not once, but every
day, descends, and becomes, as it were, again incarnate?
" O venerable dignity of priests," exclaims St. Cyprian,
" in whose hands the Son of God is incarnate!"

Behold the greatness of the sacerdotal dignity, as far
as our weak understanding can comprehend it. Behold
this two-fold Divine power which raises the priest above
angels and saints—power, not extrinsic, of which he
can be deprived, but intrinsic and inherent in him,
through a particular consecration, by an illustrious and
noble character indelibly impressed upon the soul,
which makes the sacerdotal dignity eternal. What
conclusion ought we to draw from what has been said?
The conclusion that I and every priest ought to draw

and apply to ourselves is, that, as representatives of Jesus Christ, we ought to copy the character of Him in ourselves, by a life pure and immaculate, and approaching that of angels. But the consequence to be deduced for your own instruction is, that there is nothing that merits greater respect than the sacerdotal character. In fact, if, to the eye of faith, there is no work more venerable than that which Jesus Christ exercised here on earth; if this work is transferred and perpetuated by priests; if, finally, Jesus Christ has made them participators of the same Divine power and authority—it follows, as a necessary consequence, that you should regard them in the same light with which you would have regarded Jesus Christ, were He visibly to converse amongst you; for the honour you give to them is given to the Divine Institutor of the priesthood, and the respect you refuse to them is an injury done to Jesus Christ. Truly, I have not deduced this consequence, but Jesus Christ, speaking to the apostles, says—"He that heareth you, heareth Me; he that despiseth you, despiseth Me." In this manner He makes known the honour due to Himself, and that to the priest, declaring the one to be inseparable from the other.

The saints, penetrated with a lively faith, have left us an example of the esteem in which they regarded the priestly character. Read the lives of a St. Anthony, a St. Francis of Assisi, and a St. Catherine of Sienna.

But, in our day, how much despised is the sacerdotal character, even amongst those who boast of their reverence for the faith, religion, and the Church. That unbelievers and libertines should have an aversion and contempt for priests, creates no surprise. How could it possibly be otherwise? That which induces them to hate religion, leads them, as a necessary consequence, to hate its ministers, who preach, advance, and defend it. And it is no little triumph to religion and its ministers to see that class of persons, when their last moments are drawing to a close, seeking most anxiously the assistance of a priest, and recommending themselves most fervently to him, whom but a short time before they hated—a most evident sign that their former aversion did not proceed from a firm persuasion of priciples, but only from a corruption of heart and will.

But what is worse, that this contempt, scorn, and disdain for priests is so widely disseminated amongst so many persons who are not entirely unbelievers and irreligious—many of whom do net give that proper respect due to priests, judge them maliciously, and speak evil of them, and they do so more willingly of them than of any one else, making them the object of their derision, jeers, and satire. Many are the causes that concur to produce this evil, and are wholly independent of us; neither does it regard me to mention them now. I will only have in view the usual reason given by which they pretend to justify themselves—namely, that the conduct of some gives but little edification, and that they do not live in conformity to their character. But this reason, let me ask, is it sufficient to excuse you ? To me it seems not.

First of all,, there is an injustice in denying respect and esteem to all, because some are defective and wanting. If your excuse were worth anything, there is not a society, a profession, or grade that might not be oppressed and derided, since in every profession and grade of society there are degenerated and bad persons. In fact, tell me are all merchants just and honest ? Are all judges untainted ? Are all married persons faithful ? If daily reports are worthy of any credit, certainly not. Then, by defaming all, and inflicting upon them censure for the wickedness of some, be they many or few, does it seem to you that this is according to justice ? Should this seem to you unjust in regard to other conditions of life, ought it to cease to be unjust in regard to ourselves ?

There is no state or condition of life without some fault. The angels sinned in heaven—Adam and Eve in a state of innocence—Peter and Judas in the school of our Lord. And God permitted that to the end, that we may know that in every state and profession there is danger of prevarication ; but we are not, on that

account, to despise such a state and profession, and
although the bad conduct of some may beget contempt,
you cannot extend that without grave injustice to the
whole sacerdotal order ; for if you find some unworthy
of the vocation to which they have been called, there
are very many others, by the mercy of God, exemplary,
labouring unceasingly in their own and in the salvation
of others, and who are like what the gospel wishes them
to be, burning lights of zeal and holiness.

But I go further, and I say, that you ought not to
despise those priests who live not according to their
vocation. There are two things to be considered in
them—the person and the dignity. If really no respect
is due to the person, the dignity merits every respect,
for sin can never destroy the divine character of the
priesthood, which always exists, and that suffices to
oblige you always to respect them. However defective
and wanting they may be, they never cease to be priests,
ministers of God, and ambassadors of Jesus Christ, and
exercise to your advantage all the most important
functions of their ministry. But upon what foundation
rests your obligation of holding them in the highest
esteem ? Upon their dignity, which is from God,
intrinsic, inherent, and inalienable from them. Upon
this reason God Himself has said, when He spoke in
general : "Touch ye not My anointed." He intended
by this command not only to defend from your scorn
and insults the good and holy, but also those priests
who show themselves not to be so, all without any
exception, because all are consecrated to be His
ministers.

With all that, I do not say but that the faults of
priests are very great in him who commits them, and
very deformed in the eyes of Him who sees them, but
on that account you are not to lose esteem and respect
for the priesthood. The more so, since from disrespect
for priests, it is very easy to pass to a disrespect for
things sacred and for religion itself. And experience
proves that those who began by showing disrespect for
priests have, for the most part, ended in a loss of faith.

In the meantime excite your faith, and acknowledge in priests a marvel of the divine power, and another, not less, the divine goodness towards you, look upon them with an eye of religious veneration. The instructions and admonitions given by the Holy Ghost to children on the respect they owe to their fathers, ought to serve you as the rule you should follow towards priests, who merit the name of Fathers, since they have regenerated you to grace by means of the sacraments, so that you may be born to a life of immortality.

Finally, think that at death you will consider yourselves fortunate to have present in those your last moments one of them to hear your confession and absolve you from your sins, and comfort you in your last mortal agony. Have, then, at the present time for them a just esteem and respect, so that you may not in punishment of the little respect you have for them, be deprived of their assistance. May God grant that you may not be deprived of their assistance in the moments of your great need.

XXX.

ON THE RESPECT DUE TO PRIESTS—*continued.*

FROM the teaching of the Church you know the power and office of those who receive the Sacrament of Holy Orders—that they become sacred persons, wholly consecrated to the honour, glory, and worship of God—that they are the dispensers of His mysteries, sacraments, and graces—that they are the ambassadors and ministers of Jesus Christ Himself—the teachers and interpreters of His law, doctrine, and gospel—the guides, conductors, and shepherds of souls redeemed by His most Precious Blood. All this, I say, you fully understand, as also the exalted dignity and excellence of the priesthood, and the respect due to those who discharge its functions. But there are many persons who cannot understand some things unless they be made self-evident. Treating, then, of a subject of such vast importance as that of the dignity of the priesthood, I feel that I should be wanting in my duty were I to omit making it a special subject of instruction. I know that there will always be persons malignant, or ignorant, who will say—"Ah, see how the priests sound forth from the pulpit their own praises, and plead their own cause!" That is false, most false. The priests are the followers of Jesus Christ, and, as such, seek not the esteem of men, which they do not value. And when they speak of the respect due to the sacerdotal dignity, it is certainly not for themselves, but for God; it is to instruct Christians in a truth revealed and taught by God Himself—and, therefore, the cause is that of God and your own souls. We treat of the cause of God: for if the ambassadors and ministers of an earthly prince are respected because they represent the person of their sovereign, much more does God wish and command that respect be given to His ministers, for they are the ambassadors of His Divine Son, the "King of kings." It is a precept made for all, for the Holy Ghost says—"With all thy soul fear the Lord, and reverence His priests." The cause is also that of your own soul: for in explaining to you the respect due to the ministers of God, we do so that you may not, by despising them, commit sin, and do injury to your own souls and religion. For when a priest is despised, disbelieved, and defamed, what good can he do? He may preach, exhort, advise, correct, and even work miracles, but he will no longer be believed, heard, or obeyed, and thus, to the injury of souls, he is prevented from doing that good which he otherwise would do. It is not, therefore, to plead my own cause, which God forbid, that I speak to you on the dignity of the priesthood and the respect due to priests, but solely that of God and your own souls, and, in doing so, I will, as far as I am able, show you that the dignity of the priesthood surpasses every earthly dignity, and that it emulates with that of God Himself.

From history we know that there has never been a nation without a religion, nor a religion without its priests, and that they have always been respected and venerated, even by uncivilized barbarians. The priests of Pagan Rome had an authority so great, that they were able to change the existing laws, and every word falling from their lips was regarded as an oracle. For the natural instinct of men led them to acknowledge that God ought to be worshipped, and that persons set over the Divine worship ought to be respected. In the Mosaic law disrespect to a priest, by not submitting to his authority and judgment, was to be punished by death, according to the command of God: "He that will be proud, and refuse to obey the command of the priest, who ministereth at the time to the Lord thy God, that man shall die, and thou shalt take away the evil from Israel." If, then, the priests of Pagan Rome, although false priests, and those of the Mosaic law, who were but a figure of the priests of the new law, were so much respected and esteemed, what ought to be the respect for the ministers of Jesus Christ, who are not in figure, but in substance, the true priests of God? And yet, in these evil days, we see a sacrilegious disrespect shown them, whilst a worship almost divine is given to those invested with the power of this world, and the dignity of the priesthood is treated as if it were inferior to every other. Let us now see if it is. Place on the one hand all the power and splendour that this world can lend to royalty, the sight of which might dazzle our eyes and cause our hearts to beat quickly, and then let us confront this power and splendour with the dignity of a simple priest, considered with the eye of faith, the grandeur of the former would pale before the latter, even as the morning star pales before the glory of the sun. True it is that God has said of the kings of this world—"By Me kings reign:" "By Me princes rule;" and to them we owe obedience and respect, for the apostle says—"Let every soul be subject to higher powers, for there is no power but from God. . . . Be obedient to them that are your lords." Nevertheless, the Emperor Constantine, at the Council of Nice, took a place below the clergy, and behind them; also King Bolaslaus would not sit, but stood in the presence of the ministers of God. And why did these princes show such great respect for the priesthood? Because they knew that the honour given it was by every title merited, and that it would be an usurpation to arrogate to themselves a preference. These princes knew that they had been raised above other men, but they also knew that the sacerdotal dignity was as far above theirs as is heaven above earth. In fact, we have only to compare the one dignity with the other, and we shall see, as St. Ambrose says, that that of the priesthood surpasses every other. For the royal power extends only to this earth—nor can it pass its own dominion; but the power of the priesthood stretches itself forth to the ends of the earth, and ascends to heaven. Princes have the right to make laws for the good of their subjects; the sacerdotal power, for the spiritual welfare of the people. One has authority over the body, the other over souls, and wages war against the spirits of darkness. One possesses the treasures of this world, and may make the plebeian a noble; the other possesses and distributes the treasures of Divine Grace, making him a friend who was the enemy of God—a slave of hell, an heir of heaven. Finally, one is extrinsic and temporal, and may be lost —certainly, it ceases at death; the other is intrinsic and eternal, because there is impressed on it a character indelible. Moreover, what shall I say of that more than human power, which, at the bidding of the priest, in the consecration of the adorable Sacrament, the Son of God obeys? Of that power which not only forgives sin, but takes away the punishment merited by those who have lived for years rebels to God? It is a heavenly power, that not only makes priests superior to the kings of this earth, but even to the angels in heaven. And with regard to the power of forgiving and retaining sin, who has ever possessed it except the priesthood? To that, and that alone, has God given the keys of the kingdom of heaven—"Whose sins you shall forgive, they are forgiven." But because this power is common to many, it is not esteemed, as a gem ceases to be precious when it is no longer rare. If, however, we could see the change wrought in the soul of a sinner, well-disposed, after the words, "I absolve thee," have been pronounced—oh! then, we should be enchanted with delight, and impressed by the greatness of that power! Let us suppose, for a moment, that we saw a man of colour, with his hands and feet bound in chains, his body covered with wounds, and a stranger passing by were to say to him, " I absolve thee," and the chains were to fall from his hands and feet, and his body to become immediately white and healed—at such a sight we should exclaim, "This stranger is more than human." Yet, infinitely more than that is wrought in the soul of the sinner when the priest pronounces the absolution, for he heals that soul of its wounds, caused by sin, taking away the deformity, making it like unto an angel, breaking asunder the chains that bound it, and, from a slave of the devil, it becomes the spouse of Jesus Christ. We are, therefore, forced to acknowledge that the sacerdotal power is more than human, and greater than that of an angel. For example, a man has been mortally wounded; his body is stretched out upon the ground, bathed in its own blood; life is despaired of—oh! how much the loss of his life afflicts him. The presence of Jesus Christ, his Judge, frightens him; but that which terrifies him most is the thought of the eternal torments of the abyss over which he finds himself. In this deplorable state, who is able to deliver him from eternal damnation? The kings of this world can do nothing for him. The saints and angels in heaven can pray and recommend him to God, but they have not the power of breaking the chains that bind his soul to the slavery of Satan. Who, then, can assist him? Is he to be eternally lost? Oh, no! The minister of God coming to him, disposes him to repentance, animating him with confidence in God, and then, raising his hand over him, pronounces the words of absolution, which free him from the bonds of sin, and close for him the gates of hell! The devils are put to flight with confusion, and the gates of heaven are opened to him. This is a power truly divine, for "Who can forgive sins but God alone?"

We may, indeed, say, with St. John Chrysostom, that the sacerdotal dignity is above that of the angels, for there is a power in it not given by God to an archangel. Hence it is that we can now understand why the angel mentioned in the Apocalypse forbade the Apostle St. John to adore him, for he, being a priest, was superior to the angel in dignity. St. Gregory says, "that angels venerate the priesthood." And St. Dionysius exclaims, "Oh, dignity of priests, truly great and divine!" And St. Clement says, "that after God, a priest is a God on earth."

Great, indeed, must have been the power of Josue, at whose command the "sun stood still till the people avenged themselves of their enemies, "but what comparison is there between that and what is done daily by the priest, when at his command, not the material, but the Eternal Sun of Justice descends upon our altars? The Lord, obeying the voice of man, who not only obliges him to come down from heaven into his hands, but commands the earthly substances of bread and wine, to be changed into His Most Precious Body and Blood, so that if Jesus Christ had not been born into this world, the power of his voice would immediately cause Him to descend. Oh, the voice of power and magnificence! A voice like the voice of God, when, in creating the heavens and earth, "He spoke and they were made." No, there is not to be found a power on earth or amongst the angels in heaven equal to that of the priests of the New Law. For they offer not in sacrifice, as the priests of the Mosaic Law, the blood of goats and oxen, but they offer to God the sacred Body of Jesus Christ. No angel or archangel has power like unto it. It is true the Blessed Virgin offered to God the same sacrifice, Jesus Christ, at the foot of the cross, but she offered Him mortal and passible—the priest offers Him immortal and impassible—she offered Him but once, the priest daily—she carried Him in her womb for the space of nine months—the priest in his hands whenever he pleases. This thought made St. Bernardine (a most devout servant of our Blessed Lady) say that the power of priests exceeded that of the Blessed Virgin. If, then, the dignity of the priesthood is greater than any on earth or in heaven, nothing remains but to assimilate it to that of God Himself. And if, indeed, the priesthood of Melchisedech—for having offered to the Most High bread and wine—a figure of our sacrifice, was by the Apostle St. Paul likened to the Son of God, can it be surprising that the dignity of the priesthood of the New Law should be likened to the dignity of God Himself. For its function is such that none greater can be conceived, and its ministers are justly called not only "angels," but also in Scripture by the name of "gods," for they hold the power and authority of the Immortal God. And for this reason the Emperor Constantine gave precedence to priests, and he was grieved when accusations were brought before him against them, refusing at the same time to interfere in such matters, for he said that he was unworthy to judge persons having a dignity almost divine, and that were it in his power he would cover with the imperial mantle all their shortcomings, so that they might not be known to anyone. What a lesson is this for malignant, prattling persons, who rejoice at hearing something, true or false, against ecclesiastics. Such will see at God's tribunal the injury done to religion! St. Anthony, esteemed by princes, and whose virtue was so great as to put to flight the wicked spirits, would, at meeting a priest, fall on his knees and ask a blessing, nor would he depart until it was given. St. Francis used to say: that "were he to meet a priest and an angel together, he would first do reverence to the priest;" and St. Catherine had so great a reverence for priests that she kissed the print of their footsteps.

And now let me ask, how is it that in this so-called "enlightened nineteenth century," so little respect is shown to the ministers of God? How is it in these days the words of the Prophet Isaias seem verified: "And it shall be as with the people, so with the priest." How is it, for the most part, persons possessing a little of this world's goods, treat the priesthood with contempt? How is it that even women assume an authority of judging in matters belonging to those of whom Our Lord has said: "He that heareth you, heareth Me." This is the pride of Lucifer. Again, let me ask, how is it that so many criticise and speak evil of the ministers of God, the ambassadors of Jesus Christ, superior to the angels in dignity? Oh! where is the faith?

We shall now see what are their reasons for speaking all manner of evil, and for treating the minister of God with disrespect. It is, in the first place, because they neither fear nor respect God, for in those who love God you will always find a great respect for His ministers; but in those who speak evil and treat with disrespect

the priesthood, generally speaking, you will find they
are persons morally bad, and given to particular passions. And, for this reason, they speak evil against
priests, and wish others to believe it, hoping thereby to
cover their own faults or excuse themselves. This will
explain the reason why so many of that class are
enemies to the faith, and, if it were possible, they would
banish religion out of the world; but, seeing that
religion cannot exist without its priesthood, which sus-
tains, rules, and governs it, they would destroy that if
they could. It being, however, out of their power, what
do they do? They hate, persecute, and say all manner
of evil, particularly against those who labour with zeal
for the salvation of souls, so that their words may be
disbelieved, rejected, and despised, that by this means
religion may be lost, or that others may be led to think
and act as themselves. Another reason also may be
given for this disrespect and evil speaking, and it is,
that priests are frequently obliged to reprove and correct, both publicly and privately, the vices of individuals,
and these, finding themselves thwarted in their nefarious
designs, seek to gratify their wounded pride by calumny
and detraction. And these are the particular kind of
enemies to which we are now exposed, whose calumnies
and censures we must endure with patience and resignation, bearing in mind that we are "set up a wall for
the house of Israel." And St. Ambrose says: "That
nothing is so dangerous before God, and contemptible
before men, as silence when it is our duty to denounce
sin;" and we must look for help and comfort to Him
only who comforteth us in all our tribulations. These
are, then, the reasons why evil is spoken, and disrespect
is shown to priests, and sometimes, if we hear persons,
otherwise good, speaking disrespectfully of them, it is
because they have been misled by the jests and calumnies of the enemies of religion. And hence we see the
necessity of guarding ourselves against associating and
conversing with such persons, for it is very easy to be
deceived and led astray. But what shall be the end of

these malignant despisers of the priesthood? Ah! it is impossible for them to end well. The Holy Ghost tells us that "the malignant shall be destroyed." How much more so those who malign the ministers of God, against the express command—"Touch ye not My anointed, and do no evil to My prophets." It is to be feared that God will not vouchsafe to such persons, in their mortal agony, the grace of having the assistance of those whom, during their lifetime, they had despised and calumniated, or of having the absolving words pronounced over them, or of receiving the Bread of Heaven. For if it be a great crime to dishonour a father or mother, who gave us nought but this mortal life, how great indeed must that be to dishonour those who are our spiritual fathers, and who have so often re-generated the soul by means of the sacraments. Ah! this is an outrage that Jesus Christ regards as done to Him-self, even as a prince considers an insult offered to his minister as done to his own person, and our Lord has said: "He that despiseth you despiseth Me." It is an outrage that "toucheth the apple of His eye."

When the Israelites murmured against Moses and Aaron, God complained of their disrespect as done to Himself, for He says: "How long will this people detract Me;" and here it may be observed, that the people had had an occasion of murmuring against Aaron, for it was he who had made the golden calf, and had led them into the sin of idolatry. Nevertheless, God was so angry that He declared He "would strike them with pestilence;" but at the prayer of His servant, Moses, He forgave them, at the same time saying, that all from twenty years old and upwards should die in the wilderness except Caleb and Josue, who had been respectful to His ministers. See, then, the terrible chastisement of those who dishonour and despise the ministers of God. In speaking, therefore, to you on the dignity of the priesthood, and the respect due to priests, I am not pleading my own cause, but that of faith and religion. That you ought to honour them is the command of God, because their character and dignity merit every respect, for they are the ambassadors and ministers of Jesus Christ. You ought, for your own interest, to respect them, so that you may avoid the severe chastisements pronounced against those who dishonour the representatives of God here on earth. " He that despiseth you despiseth Me."

XXXI.

MARRIAGE AS A CONTRACT AND AS A SACRAMENT.

THE Sacrament of Matrimony is called by the apostle "a great sacrament in Christ and in the Church," because it is expressive of other mysteries. Speaking, then, to you upon this sacrament, there is opened out before you a subject of the greatest importance, for the married state is the more common one in the world, and it is the foundation and basis of all happiness and unhappiness, both in time and in eternity. In fact, a marriage well associated results in connubial peace and concord; in connubial peace and concord prospers the good education of the children; upon the good education of the children springs up a wise and regular conduct in them, whatever may be the state, condition, and business in life which Providence may call upon them to fulfil.

The contrary to all this takes place when a marriage is badly concluded—strifes, contentions, and quarrels between the married couple: the children indevout, giving bad example, and growing up in every kind of immorality, which they carry with them into the various conditions of life they may hereafter be placed. It is, therefore, an evident truth, that marriage is, so to speak, that pivot upon which turns all the good both of private and public life, temporal and eternal.

The subject, then, I propose to speak of, is marriage considered in itself, which is a divinely appointed and most intimate union between man and woman for the propagation of the human race, to live together during the whole course of their life, and to educate their children for God and society. This union was not always and in all times a sacrament, but it was always and in all times a contract, instituted and blessed by God—a dignity certainly unknown to those who see nothing in this union beyond a carnal tendency, not differing from that of irrational beings. In the beginning God instituted marriage when He gave Eve to Adam for a companion. The Sacred Scripture tells us, after having described the creation of the world, that the Lord God said—" It is not good for man to be alone ; let us make him a help like unto himself. Then the Lord God cast a deep sleep upon Adam : and when he was fast asleep, He took one of the ribs, and filled up flesh for it. And the Lord God built the rib which He took from Adam into a woman, and brought her to Adam. And Adam said, This now is bone of my bones, and flesh of my flesh : she shall be called woman, because she was taken out of man. Wherefore, a man shall leave father and mother, and shall cleave to his wife, and they shall be two in one flesh. And God blessed them, saying, Increase and multiply." From this simple, but divine history, you may gather not only the primitive institution of matrimony, but also the productive cause of it, the principal properties, and the primary end for which it was instituted. God Himself declares the natural convenience of giving to man, by Him created, a companion and the help of a woman—" It is not good for man to be alone : let us make him a help like unto himself." God having decreed that Adam should be the natural father of all men, destined to occupy the places lost by the rebel angels, who had been cast out of heaven, consequently for this end it was necessary there should be a woman, at least, supposing that God had pre-ordained such a means for the human generation. Up to this we have the formation of both sexes, but not as yet matrimony. The institution of matrimony took place when God, after the creation of Eve, presented her to Adam—" And He brought her to Adam." The offering made by God of this woman to Adam, and the offering Eve, by an impulse of the Creator, made of herself to Adam, asking him, by this act, his consent to take her to wife, as she was willing to take him to be her husband, was a true marriage, of which God was the only Author, and He willed also to be the Minister. God, without doubt, could have created Eve, and then have withdrawn Himself; but He did not do so—He willed to bring her to Adam. And why did He do so? He did so not only to declare the holiness of marriage, to which He Himself deigned to assist as the Father of the betrothed, but principally to manifest the freedom of marriage, and the necessity of a mutual and free consent. The nuptials were not contracted until Adam and Eve had seen and known each other, and given their free consent. From this you see that the mutual consent of the parties is the efficient cause of marriage, and the union that follows from that consent between the man and the woman forms the essence of marriage. But what union is this? It is a union by which the woman belongs privately and exclusively to the man, and the man to the woman—a union of affection and will—a union by which two persons form themselves into one person, both according to the spirit and according to the flesh—in fine, a union permanent and perpetual. These are the two principal properties of marriage, clearly known by Adam himself, and are expressly declared in the answer, divinely inspired and given by him—that is, the indissolubility and the unity of marriage. The indissolubility is shown from these words—"Wherefore a man shall leave father and mother, and shall cleave to his wife"—words declaring the perpetuity of the bond, which is indissoluble till death. It is true that in the progress of time there was introduced divorce, by which the man and woman were allowed and made free to marry again. But this custom, either permitted or perhaps only tolerated, was certainly abolished by Jesus Christ, Who declared the bond of marriage to be indissoluble from the beginning, saying—"Moses, by reason of the hardness of your hearts, permitted you to put away your wives, but from the beginning it was not so." Whatever may be thought by some in our day regarding a real and formal divorce, bringing about a dissolution of the marriage bond, this by the Evangelical law is absolutely interdicted; and, moreover, it would be most injurious to the public peace and the good of families. If permission be given to the married to separate, and to enter into other nuptial contracts, how many inconveniences must necessarily follow from it? Their union would be precarious, for there might arise in persons eager after pleasure desires for other objects, and thus seek to withdraw themselves from the one already possessed. Married persons would no longer be united together with a true affection, being unable to give the heart to what is not secure and stable. What affection can there be for children, or what interest in their education, when there is a danger of their passing into the hands of others? See, then, how the good harmony of both parents and children would be disturbed. These and other inconveniences cannot weigh sufficiently in favour of a contrary system. The martyrdom that some undergo by reason of their being badly associated together, would not be so frequent had they entered into the married state in a Christian manner and according to the dictates of religion; for the most part have to accuse themselves and not the indissolubility of the marriage bond for the miseries they have to suffer. Moreover, the Church has made a provision sufficient to secure their peace, by allowing them in certain cases to separate, always, however, with this proviso, that they are not to pass to a second marriage. Balancing, then, the good and the evil on the one and the other side, the law regarding the indissolubility of marriage is to be preferred, and the sentence of Jesus Christ ought to be firmly held— "What God hath joined together let no man put asunder."

The other property of marriage is unity, expressed by Adam in these words—"And they shall be two in one flesh;" that is to say, marriage by its nature is of one man with one woman. It was never allowed a woman to have more than one husband, for such would be a disordination terrible in its nature. On the other hand, it was permitted for men to have more than one wife, as the history of the patriarchs clearly demonstrates. But since this custom was contrary to the first institution of marriage, and subject to many inconveniences, and only tolerated for a temporary necessity, that the earth might be populated, Jesus Christ revoked that custom, and abolished the having of many wives, restored marriage to its primitive unity, as it was instituted in the terrestrial paradise. Finally, the words "Increase and multiply" demonstrate the primary end of marriage, blessed by God, so that it should serve for the propagation of the human race—a blessing, says the Church, that remains upon men even after original sin : nor was it revoked after the universal deluge. From these two words, "Increase and multiply," some have said that an express command is given by God to all to marry, and that the command is given in such a way, that it is better to marry. This is the reasoning of fools. For when was it God said to our first parents, "Increase and multiply ?" It was after they had been joined in matrimony. Consequently, by those words God wished to teach them and us the end for which marriage was instituted. Again, those words do not, properly speaking, express a precept, but only the power of multiplying, and the force of efficaciously doing so, communicated by God to nature. Moreover, should these words be taken as a real precept, it does not regard every individual of the human race, but the whole of mankind to whose preservation and propagation sufficient provision has been made by the marriage of the many, which, considering the diversity of inclinations, will never be wanting : though others, using that liberty given by God, do not wish to enter into the matrimonial state. Therefore, the state of virginity is not to be condemned ; yea, Holy Scripture declares that it is a better and more perfect state, because it is a state of greater purity, and approaches nearer to that of the angels and of God Himself. Besides, it is a state that has more means of union with God. Hence the apostle says—" He that is without a wife is solicitous for the things that belong to the Lord, how he may please God: but he that is with a wife is solicitous for the things of the world, how he may please his wife, and he is divided." I will, however, tell you what kind of celibacy is prohibited by God, contrary to the public good, and prejudicial to population. Not religious celibacy, nor that practised by many persons living in the world, who have not taken the vow of celibacy: but that of the wicked libertine, who refuses to marry in order that he may follow a life of sinful indulgence. This kind of celibacy is most ruinous to society, because it enkindles the fire of discord amongst families, spreads the poison of jealousy, and decreases the marriage state—because it is the cause of many poor, unfortunate creatures leading a life of dishonour and misery, or makes uncertain the legitimacy of children. This kind of celibacy ought to be persecuted, and not that of religion, which, to please God, and a desire for greater perfection, and for the good of others, embraces evangelical celibacy.

But to return to the subject, although the state of virginity is to be preferred to that of marriage, nevertheless the married state is a holy state, having been instituted by God. And if, in the history of the Church, we find examples of illustrious persons leading a holy life in a state of virginity, we find also in Scripture examples of many who led a holy life in the married state. It would, therefore, be an error, and it is condemned by the Church, to regard marriage as a state to be despised, since it has God for its Author.

Marriage, since the coming of Jesus Christ, has acquired a greater strength, veneration, and holiness. Before His coming marriage was a natural contract, but it was raised by Him to a sacrament of the New Law. He was not content in bringing it back to what it was in the beginning—a state of union and indissolubility—but He made it an efficacious sign of holiness and grace, and this is believed to have taken place when He assisted at the marriage feast in Cana, so memorable for the wonderful miracle wrought there by the changing of the water into wine.

T

Hence, in the Church of Jesus Christ, after the institution of Christian marriage, there is not a true and lawful nuptial contract between Catholics that is not a sacrament, and this contract ought by every Catholic to be celebrated according to the rites of the Church, the contracting parties expressing outwardly their consent in the presence of the parish priest and two witnesses, and receiving the nuptial blessing. That moment for them is a moment of special sanctification, as was for us ministers the moment when in the sanctuary we received the episcopal imposition of hands— a moment that places them in a state called by the Apostle "honourable in all," that is to say, a state holy in its substance, in its end, in its effects, and in its representation. It is holy in its substance, because it is no longer what it was, a simple contract, but a sacrament that sanctifies and consecrates the parties in the act of being joined in matrimony. It is holy in its end, being a remedy against concupiscence, sanctifying the union of two different persons, giving not only population to the earth but saints to heaven. It is holy in its effects, because it increases sanctifying grace in the soul, imparts many spiritual helps for the well-being of a married life, gives grace to bear with the difficulties of that state of life, charity to love each other, the grace of temperance and sobriety, so that they may not go beyond the limits prescribed, the grace of prudence, so that they may govern their children. It is holy in its representation, for it represents and signifies the hypostatic union of the divine with the human nature in Jesus Christ, and the moral union of Jesus Christ with His spouse, the Church. Therefore St. Paul says: "It is a great sacrament in Christ and in the Church."

Then I wish you, who may be thinking of entering into the married state, to reflect seriously upon these things. Consider its first institution in the terrestrial paradise, and of it being raised by Jesus Christ to a sacrament of the New Law. From this consideration you will see that this state is not to be embraced unless with a holy end in view, using holy means, and having holy dispositions becoming the holiness of that state. Consult God with regard to your vocation to that state and the choice of the person whom you desire to have as a perpetual and indivisible companion. The custom of the world is to look upon marriage as a worldly affair, over which religion and eternal salvation have no part. For that reason there are so many unhappy marriages, and the spiritual and temporal ruin of so many persons unequally associated. Having now given you my first advice, if you wish to know all that is necessary to know, in order that your marriage may be blessed by God, listen to the Instructions that are to follow.

XXXII.

ON THE DISPOSITIONS FOR MARRIAGE.

THE matrimonial state of which I have undertaken to speak to you is a state into which all who enter do so with their own free will, but after having done so, before a long time has elapsed, the most part of them find themselves disappointed and dissatisfied ; and it not unfrequently happens that those very persons who were mad until they were united in wedlock, become more so to be disunited. To the first love very soon succeeds coldness and indifference, then follow reproaches, complaints, quarrels, and finally scandalous separations, nothing remaining of the first desired union but a hated impossibility of being free of the knot extremely abhorred. But from whence arises so great a disorder, so common amongst us, and so difficult to be remedied ? It arises from no other cause than that of entering blindly into a state, and only through an impulse of passion, without reflection or counsel, without the proper preparation, or serious consideration, which an affair of such importance requires. This is the real cause why, ordinarily, so many marriages end in repentance and disgust.

After having explained what marriage is in itself, both as a natural contract instituted and blessed by God in the beginning of the world, and as a sacrament of the New Law, I now proceed to speak of what ought to precede the entrance into that holy state, that is to say, the dispositions, both remote and proximate, required.

The first disposition—remote—is to consult God, so that you may know whether you are really called to

that state. God calls all without any exception to
eternal life, but not all by the same way; some by one
way, others by another. God is the absolute Master of
all, and He wills to be served by all according to
the designs of His providence. From this general law
why should we make marriage an exception? All
agree that for the ecclesiastical state a particular vocation is required, but for the married state few believe
there is the same necessity. And yet, if there is a state
or condition of life that ought not to be entered into
without a manifest call from heaven, it is certainly that
of marriage. Marriage is a state that brings with it
the most weighty obligations to fulfil, trials difficult to
bear, and dangers regarding the eternal salvation.
Observe these three things if you wish to form a just
idea of that state. First of all the grave obligations
you have to fulfil towards not only the person whom
you wish to take as an inseparable companion, but
also towards the children you naturally expect to have.
With regard to the person chosen, under every circumstance there ought to be a loving respect, tender, faithful, patient, and persevering. How many contradictions
and difficulties will not a love of this kind endure? On
the part of the children, what and how great is the
charge undertaken? They are to be fed, provided for,
and above all, to be brought up in piety and the fear of
the Lord. A married person is responsible before God
for the soul of its companion and of the children, hence
it is there is an obligation of leading an exemplary and
Christian life. Now to do all that certainly great diligence and labour are necessary.

In the second place, marriage is a state of great and
many crosses and trials; besides the fulfilling of the
above-mentioned obligations, there may, and do arise,
on the part of the one or other, a coldness and a want
of apparent affection and kindness, dissensions and
quarrels, jealousy and infidelity. What a martyrdom
it must be for two persons to live together whose
maxims and principles are opposed to each other?
How many sacrifices must be made in order to preserve

294 FAMILIAR INSTRUCTIONS ON THE SACRAMENTS.

peace and harmony ? But without that who is there that does not know that marriages well considered beforehand have their disagreements, since there is nothing in the world perfect ? A husband, though wise and prudent, may not be so at all times and in all things. Wives, though very good and much esteemed, they also may be wanting in something. It is not possible that everything should go on smoothly, a difference of inclinations and fancy very easily arises between the married persons, and is that not sufficient to put on trial their patience ?

What shall I say of the most trying cares and solicitudes that must necessarily accompany the education of children, giving them a truly Christian direction and placing them in a suitable position. Very often the means are wanting to place the children in that state which they desire, and unfortunately sometimes it happens that the children are either deformed or of weak intellect, and incapable of anything, or, what is worse, depraved and wicked, and badly repay the anxieties of their parents. Nor does all finish here.

In the third place, I mentioned the dangers of the eternal salvation, leaving aside those that result from the things already mentioned. Every state of life has its difficulties and its dangers, yet I do not know if you have ever observed that marriage, unlike every other state, implies the union of three things most difficult to combine together. Firstly, the use of rights without violating obligations. It would be an error to suppose that every thing may be allowed or permitted between the conjugated. Marriage has its laws and certain rules determined by God, which cannot be overlooked without sin. For this reason the Fathers of the Church distinguish three kinds of continency : virginity, widowhood, and conjugal. This last, though the less perfect, is, in a certain sense, the more difficult. In fact, the man addicted to drink is better able to refrain from placing the glass to his lips, than he would be, were he to taste the liquor, to keep from taking the contents of the glass. Without any further explanation I shall be understood by those who have need of understanding me. If, then, in this matter there be an excess or abuse is it not true that marriage becomes a continual occasion of sin ?

Again, married persons are to be united in the care and study to please each other with an inviolable fidelity to God. But how easy it is for too great a love to cause them to transgress by a sinful complacency in condescending to the wishes, caprices, and passions, and thus to the prejudice of that fidelity, which, in the first place, you owe to God—which leads you to fear more the displeasure given to your partner than that you give to God. Adam did eat of the fruit by God forbidden, this he did not to displease Eve—both sinned and drew all their descendants into the same ruin. Would to God they were not imitated by many married persons in our day !

Finally, there ought to be a union and a singular care of temporal goods, using economy, especially if there be a family to provide for, having at the same time the heart disengaged and detached, so that by the attention and care given to it there be no obstacle in the way to the fulfilling the obligations of a Christian, and the obtaining of those spiritual and eternal blessings. But is it easy to have this ? The care of temporal affairs very frequently causes those who are not married to forget God, the soul, and its salvation, how much easier it is for those who are married to cover over the neglect of their soul and their God with the plausible pretext of having a family to provide for ?

The matrimonial state, then, is a formation of obligations, crosses, and dangers, which, for the sake of brevity, I have simply noticed ; and these obligations, crosses, and dangers, are not transitory, but permanent and perpetual, even as the marriage bond is permanent and perpetual. What is, then, the consequence to be deduced ? Not that which the apostles did when they heard intimated by our Lord the laws of marriage:

"If the case of a man with his wife be so, it is not expedient to marry." But Jesus Christ answered them: "All men take not this word, but they to whom it is given." That is to say, perpetual chastity is not a virtue for all. When, therefore, I spoke of the matrimonial burden, it was not with the object of withdrawing you from entering into that state, but only to make known to those who are called to it that they ought to reflect well before doing so upon the great obligations annexed to that state, and that they ought not to embrace it unless they feel themselves called by God to it, since it is only to a divine vocation are annexed helps and graces, without which you cannot fulfil, as you ought, the obligations, and bear, in a Christian spirit, the crosses, and defend yourselves from the dangers that accompany it. And as God wills that we should serve Him in that state to which He has called us, so He has assigned to every one those graces necessary to that state to which they have been called. From which it is clearly manifest that if you enter into a state through some caprice of your own, you lose the right to those graces and place yourself on the road to perdition. This principle regards every state of life, but speaking in particular of marriage, I ought to mention another circumstance most important, and it is that you ought not only to consult the divine will in the choice of this state, but also in the choice of the person whom you wish to make an inseparable companion, for the nature of this contract is dissolved only by death. I have already told you in the former Instruction that from the time Jesus Christ raised matrimony to a sacrament, it has acquired and maintains such firmness that there is no one who has the power on earth to break or dissolve the sacred bond, it is stronger than any promise, contract, oath, or even a vow solemnly made in the profession of a religious. All these are not so binding upon persons but that they may be dissolved either by an authority or by private consent; but it is not so with the marriage bond, for it is of such a nature that no human power can break it, according to what our Lord has said: "What God has joined together, let no man put asunder." Although a separation may be granted, yet the marriage bond broken—*never*.

From which it follows that should the husband be a cruel and savage man, or vile and avaricious, or extravagant and wasteful, or impious, disorderly, and licentious, this for the wife would be a great trial, but this trial must be endured till death; or, should a man be united to a woman passionate, ungovernable, capricious, a lover of vanity, trifles, and pleasures, this would be for a husband an insufferable affliction, but during the lifetime of his wife there is no escape from it, and however great the trial may be he will have to bear it.

Supposing, then, that marriage is a state becoming you, nevertheless, the person whom you may wish to be associated with may not be suited for you. Therefore, it is of the greatest importance not to err on this point, for it will be one for which there is no remedy; and it is very easy to err, and the danger is greater, of making a mistake in this state, more so than in that of the religious state, because there is no novitiate of trial. It is not sufficient to be called by God to the married state, but it is also necessary that the choice of the person should be determined by Him. It may be asked by some what they have to do by way of investigating and finding out what may be the will of God, so that they may not make a false step? I answer that without expecting from God a direct revelation, you will be able to ascertain the step you ought to take, should you faithfully put in practice the advice that I shall give in the next Instruction. All that I shall at present say is, that when a person wishes to deliberate upon a point of the gravest importance, he ought not to allow only temporal and human motives to guide and direct him, but he ought chiefly to take into consideration the interests of his soul and its salvation, to which all else ought to be directed, and upon that, above all, the resolutions are of the greatest consequence. When you have well examined your own conscience, and the proper dispositions, proceed to secure that which seems to you the most safe and convenient, and with that in view recommend your-self to God, and from Him will come light that will enable you to know, with security, the road you ought to walk in.

XXXIII.

ON THE DISPOSITIONS FOR MARRIAGE—*continued.*

You have been already told that, before entering into the married state, the first thing that you ought to do is to ascertain, in the manner I pointed out to you, whether you have been indeed called by God to that state. Supposing, then, that you believe yourselves called by God, you ought, in the next place, to pray fervently to Him that He would give His aid in disposing for you a suitable person ; for the Holy Ghost says—" If a man finds a good woman, he has found a good portion." " Who shall find a valiant woman ? Far and from the uttermost coasts is the price of her." Now, what means these expressions of the Holy Ghost ? They mean more than you suppose. They mean, to be happily united, it is not sufficient to use your own dilligence, or take the advice of your parents, or make an investigation, or ask of information concerning the person whom you wish to marry : but to meet with one to whom you may be happily united, is a most singular grace, coming down from heaven. Consequently, if you wish to receive this grace, you must pray to God from your heart, since it is of faith that prayer is the way to obtain the graces necessary for us.

But if we pray, will God hear us ? Most certainly He will. Listen to the words of the Holy Ghost— " Happy is the husband of a good wife ; she shall be given in the portion of them that fear God to a man for his good deeds." This, then, is the secret : if you wish to have God's aid and His blessing, it is necessary that you be devout and fear God, that you perform good deeds, that you lead a Christian life. " A good woman shall be given to a man for his good deeds." Also, if the woman desires God's aid in obtaining for her a wise and prudent husband; if she wishes God to bestow upon her the grace of a worthy and happy marriage—then it is necessary for her to be prudent, modest, devout, and retired; that she guard herself from certain dangers, from certain occasions; that she lead a Christian life. Otherwise, against her own will, she will remain unmarried, or she will make an unhappy marriage, which will render her whole life one of misery, sorrow, and affliction. For as it is true God gives to the man a good wife for his good deeds, so also it is true a good husband is given to the woman for her virtue, piety, and devotion.

But do the most part of young people perform good deeds? Are they pious? Do they fear God? Do they prepare themselves for the married state as Christians ought to prepare? On the contrary, they do nothing but add sin to sin. And can they expect God to bless their marriage, and bring them to a favourable end? The Holy Ghost declares they are not to expect it, because a good woman shall be given to a man for his good deeds. Let us consider the life of the greater part of young men and women before marriage. Scarcely have they arrived to the use of reason when they begin to be irreverent in Church, disobedient to parents, negligent in learning what pertains to faith and the duties of a Christian. They begin life by teaching malice and committing sin; and when they grow older, the young women given to pride, wish to follow every fashion that appears, running after every worldly amusement, speaking to this one and to that one, standing at the door or window all day long, or reading the dangerous and pernicious publications of the day; and their pious mothers, not wishing to displease their daughters, either consent to all these things, or they do not apply a proper remedy—and, therefore, these mothers are accountable before God for many sins. How many of such young women go on for years immersed in thoughts, desires, in conversations, in looks, and in acts that are sinful? How often they promise this one, and that one, and then others, without

asking their parents' consent; and then it often happens
the question is forced upon them, Who will have us ?
or they make a most unhappy marriage!   How many
become mothers, and then find themselves cruelly deceived, plunged into misery, laughed at even by those
who had given such fair promises, rejected and discarded
by their own, end their lives in disappointed hope
and the pangs of a wounded conscience!   Who can
enumerate the number of sins committed by these foolish
daughters of Eve ?

The young men, as they grow up, go in search of
pleasure, such as a wicked and corrupt world offers
them, absenting themselves from the bosom of their
parental home, giving themselves. up to gambling, and,
in the midst of companions more wicked than themselves, listen to and join in conversations that ought
not to be named as becometh Christians.   If they go
to Church, it is for the purpose of seeing this or that
person; seldom or never hearing Mass with attention
or devotion, or listening to instructions with profit to
themselves; neglecting the sacraments or receiving them
without the proper dispositions; taking pleasure in
deceiving persons, and rejoicing in their iniquity.
They disregard advice, lose all respect for their father,
bruise the heart of their mother, and when the
promise is given, they consider lawful what is forbidden.   And with a life so vicious—a life with such
a chain of sins, connected one with the other—they
go forth to receive the Sacrament of Matrimony,
and then expect God to give them a good portion,
and make their marriage a prosperous and happy one.
This is a presumption, because the Holy Ghost declares
that a happy marriage will be given only to those who
fear God.   The ordinary chastisement God visits upon
such in this life is, when they do marry, their marriage
will become an unfortunate one, either by reason of the
little affection that will exist between the husband and
wife, or by reason of the jealousy, discord, and disunion
that there will be always in the house, or by reason of the
miseries, sufferings, injuries, and cruelty that will have to

be undergone. In fine, unhappy will be the marriage of those who have led a bad life before entering into that state, for one or other of these causes—yes, that young man who never allowed a day to pass before his marriage without visiting his spouse; and now that she is in the house, he can no longer endure the sight of her, and does nothing else but abuse and ill-treat her. Oh, how many unhappy marriages there are in consequence of sins before marriage!

Then, if you desire God's assistance, if you wish Him to give you the happiness of making a suitable choice and union, it is necessary for you to lead a good life: and then God will hear your prayers, give you help and light to make this choice. And here you may wish to know what is to guide you in this choice?

In making the choice of a person with whom you wish to be united in marriage, after you have recommended it to God, it will be necessary for you to be on your guard, and use the greatest precautions, for it is very easy to be led astray. The Holy Ghost, upon this subject, has given golden rules, specially for young men, but which are also applicable to young women. And with regard to these, and in general to all women, should I now have to say what may not be pleasant to them, I hope they will excuse me, since it is not I who speak but the Holy Ghost, whose words I give. What, then, are the golden rules given by the Holy Ghost to young men, that they may be happily united in marriage? The first is this—"Look not upon a woman's beauty, and desire not a woman for beauty." That is to say, young men, be on your guard against looking only to beauty, and against forming the resolution of choosing such an one only because she is handsome and graceful in form. Would you not consider that man a fool who would take a house, with the obligation of living in it during his lifetime, only because the external appearance of that house is beautiful—for it might be that the house itself inside may be filthy and unfit for habitation? Thus it is also with a young man of little judgment who espouses for his lifetime a young woman only because he sees she is a fine beautiful woman : for although she may have a handsome face and a graceful form, it may be that within her there is a wicked and malicious spirit, a capricious disposition—it may be that she is full of vices and defects. And if so, to be constrained to live with such an one a lifetime, with a creature so formed, would be a great cross! "It would be better," says the Holy Ghost, "it would be more agreeable, to abide with a lion and a dragon, than to dwell with a wicked woman." And again—" It is better to dwell in a wilderness, than with a quarrelsome and passionate woman." Therefore, the first and principal thing you have to look to, young men, is not so much to beauty, but that the person whom you desire to marry has a good disposition ; that she has been well brought up; that she be modest, retired, devout, filled with the fear of God, and attentive to her duties—and if you find one having these qualities, take her, make her your wife, and your marriage will be a happy one. But if she is not adorned with these gifts, although she may be more beautiful than the sun, take her not : remove far from her, look not upon her, desire her not—otherwise you will draw down upon yourselves an affliction that will last till death. What has been said with regard to young men may equally be applied to young women. They ought to regard not so much the comeliness of the young man—that he be daring, dexterous, and prosperous : but whether he be good and virtuous—whether he be a young man of tried virtue and good qualities. Yet it not unfrequently happens that a young man is good, possessing all the qualities requisite for a good husband, but because he is not handsome and brave, as some others, that ambitious woman refuses to have him. Yes, you will refuse him, and you will remain as you are, or you will meet with one who will soon take out of your head all those foolish fancies.

I am prepared to meet the objection that some of you are ready to make against what has been said. "It is all very well, but the eye ought to have its part in making a choice of an inseparable companion." Yes, perfectly true; but the judgment and the intellect demand their part, and, indeed, the best part, because these are the true guides of all human actions. Be convinced that a man of sound judgment gives the preference to virtue and good dispositions, for he knows and foresees that should he take to his house a handsome bride, but of little discretion, one with an empty head, or capricious, or foolish, a hundred eyes will not be sufficient to keep such an one from the window, or from company and amusements, and an immense and useless labour will be required to induce her to forsake her foolish ways, so that the patience of Job will be necessary to bear with her. Therefore I say to you who are called to the married state, and wish to be happily associated, look not only to beauty, but have in view the virtues and good qualities of the person. "Look not upon a woman's beauty." If, however, there is together with beauty also virtue, oh, then, it is certainly more agreeable; for the Holy Ghost says: "As the sun riseth to the world, so is the beauty of a good wife for the ornament of her house." But it will be always true, treating of two persons, one handsome, but of little good, the other good, but not handsome; this last is to be preferred to the first, because beauty is a thing that quickly passeth away, like a flower that cometh forth in the morning, and in the evening fadeth away. That which makes a woman worthy of esteem is, says the Holy Ghost, her piety and her fear of God. "Favour is deceitful, and beauty is vain, the woman that feareth the Lord, she shall be praised." The first rule, then, laid down by the Holy Ghost for those who are called to embrace the married state is to look to the inward beauty, that is to say, the virtues and good dispositions of the person. "Look not upon a woman's beauty, and desire not a woman for her beauty."

The second rule given by this same divine Spirit is to be on your guard in your choice that you do not espouse "a woman foolish and clamorous, and full of allurements, and knowing nothing at all;" that is a woman but little or no good, or such that appears kneaded with rage, who has always a bad temper that vexes and torments her—that resents like a viper, having always something to complain of, never contented, and over whom neither attention, kindness, nor the most agreeable treatment has any influence ; obstinate, inflexible, incorrigible, so that neither threats nor the certainty of the severest chastisements are able ever to produce a change in her.   From such a woman, says the Holy Ghost, turn away your face ; because to be yoked with such an one would be the greatest affliction, more agreeable it would be to be in the desert with the bear and the lion, than to have a woman of that sort.

The third rule given by the Holy Ghost is this. "Turn away thy face from a woman dressed up." Be on your guard against one who is ambitious, who wants to appear always elegantly dressed, who no sooner has she got one dress than she wants another—always buying or spending, and running after the newest fashions—from such weak heads turn away thy face, otherwise your marriage will be unhappy, and you will have in your house a woman that will be your ruin and that of your family.   The words used by the Holy Ghost "dressed up" signify also one that has been reared with too great a delicacy, with too much care, with too much pleasure, accustomed to follow her own will in everything, whose parents did not dare so much as to speak to her, and who gave her all that she desired. A woman of such a stamp you ought absolutely to avoid, because she will not suit you, for she is of that class that is never contented—who begins to cry and fret at everything, having always something to complain of, and of little or no use—if such an one has children, either she will not know how to bring them up, or like herself they will be badly trained, putting the whole house into disorder, and the marriage will have an unhappy end.   "Turn away thy face from a woman dressed up."

The fourth rule given by the Holy Ghost is this—To be happily married it is necessary to avoid "a woman that hath a mind for many." What means this word many? Who are these changeable and inconstant women? They are those weak-minded, inconstant women like a leaf moved by every wind, to-day one fancy, to-morrow another—that say one thing and then withdraw their word—will and then will not, having always new ideas; now all serene then disquieted for a time—they are those who are always on the move, either with the body or with the mind, having a thousand desires, without ever being guided by a decisive will—they have their heads filled with fancies, revolving from one desire to another—from one thing to another, without ever being satisfied or contented with anything—without ever showing a firmness of purpose—being always governed by a capricious, bad, and inconstant humour. Of such, says the Holy Ghost, be on your guard. "Look not upon a woman that hath a mind for many."

In conclusion I will briefly sum up what has been said. The first thing required of those who feel themselves called by God to the married state is to recommend themselves to God that He would give a great treasure, for such is a good wife. Secondly, to lead a good life, for a good wife is a good portion, she shall be given in the portion of them that fear God, to a man for his good deeds." Thirdly, to give your attention to the choice of the person, and therefore avoid being yoked with a person only on account of her beauty, when she is wicked and vicious—avoid taking into your house one who has a bad tongue and a temper ungovernable—also, avoid her whose head is filled with fashions, having an ambitious, changeable, and inconstant mind, for such an one would make your house a purgatory, and in place of assisting you in gaining heaven she would expose you to the danger of losing your soul. Were these golden rules, given by the Holy Ghost, observed by persons when they are about to make a choice of an inseparable companion, then their marriages would be made prosperous and happy.

XXXIV

CONTINUING to explain to you the manner you ought to conduct yourselves before marriage, or the way you ought to prepare yourselves, so that your marriage may have a happy end, it is necessary that I should give you an important advice, which is, be on your guard against giving a promise of marriage without first communicating and having the approbation of your parents, much less against their express will and prohibition. Were a son or a daughter to enter into contracts, buy and sell, and conduct affairs entirely without the consent of father or mother, or against their express will, is it not true that this would be wrong? And would it not be also a want of respect to their parents? But what contract is there of so great an importance as that of a promise of marriage? On the part of the parents of the daughter, the question is one of taking from them a person who is their absolute property and of giving her to another—of also taking away a part of their substance to give her a dowry; and can all this be done without making known and having the approbation of the parents, or against their will? Do you not see that this would be not only a want of respect, but a manifest injustice? If, on the other hand, it regards the father of the young man, the receiving into his house a bride, to consider her as his daughter, maintain and provide all that is necessary for her—can all this be done without his approbation and consent, or against his express will? Do you not see that this also would be another fault, another injury more serious?

I know some will say, "Has not God given liberty to children to marry whom they please?" No, God has not given them that liberty any more than He has given them liberty to be wanting in respect to their parents. No, He has never granted that liberty—He has taken it entirely away from them by having commanded children to honour their father and mother, that it may be well with them, and may be long-lived on earth. Hence it is we find in the Mosaic law children allowed themselves to be entirely under the will of their parents with regard to their marriages, so that the father and mother chose for them the person and gave them away in marriage. The Sacred Scripture gives us the example of Esau, who married according to his own caprice, and without the consent of his parents; but the Scripture tells us that he was a wicked son, and that his marriage was not a happy one. We also find the Angel Raphael exhorting Tobias to espouse Sara, but he did not tell him to go and do so without the consent of her parents, but that he should go and ask her of her father, and "he will give her thee to wife." Whence it is the apostle says—"Therefore, he that giveth his virgin in marriage, doth well: and he that giveth her not, doth better." What mean these words? It appears that the apostle wished to indicate the deference that children ought to show to the will of their parents. We also know that the natural, ecclesiastical, and civil law have always declaimed against the promise of marriage being given without the consent of parents or against their will, and we know also that such marriages are declared unlawful and sinful; yet how many promises are given, how many marriages are made by young people without the knowledge and against the will of their parents! It is sufficient for a young man or woman to know that their parents wish them to discontinue the company of such an one, and, in place of doing so, he or she becomes more desirous of speaking, and of promising that one. It is sufficient for the parents to show their displeasure at their son marrying such an one for him to show more his determination and obstinacy in wishing to marry her. And on these occasions there are always those who are ready to become a medium of iniquity, who are ready to give bad advice to them, telling them to take no notice of their parents, to do what they think fit, and when the marriage shall have taken place, then everything will be happily settled. Yes, do you wish to know how it will be settled? By being an unhappy marriage, either by reason of sufferings that will have to be undergone, or there will be discord and dissensions in the house, or sickness or perhaps an untimely death to the husband or wife—in many ways the marriage will be an unhappy one, as shown in the former instruction. In fact, how can you expect God to make marriages happy and prosperous that have been contracted with such bad dispositions, and with such bad preparation, and with a conscience burdened with sins? The apostle says—"Honour thy father and thy mother, that it may be well with thee, and thou mayest be long-lived upon earth." Then it is the same as if he had said that those children who are wanting in respect to their parents will not be happy or long-lived upon this earth, and consequently their marriage will, without doubt, be unfortunate

It is true, and I know it to be so, that sometimes parents are indiscreet and unreasonable, and, as it were, tyrants over their children, wishing them and using every possible force to induce them to marry against their own will some one for the sake of a little of this world's substance, or preventing them from making an honest and suitable match. Yes, this is true: and such parents will have to render a rigorous account to God for it. But in these cases there is a remedy. Let such children recommend themselves to God, turn to their superiors, act according to the advice given them, and without being wanting in respect to their parents, and they will easily find a way to overcome every inconvenience. And if these children cannot find a remedy, let them comfort and arm themselves with patience, never be wanting in respect to their parents, trust in God; and rest assured that He knows how to prosper, bless, and console them.

Another advice I ought to give you in disposing

yourselves for a happy marriage, is this—not to allow a long time to intervene between the promise and the marriage itself, as some do, who, after the promise has been given, remain two or three years before celebrating the marriage. The inconveniences and disorders* arising from the promise being given so long beforehand, are so grave, that we ought not to disguise them. The promise having been made, the parties enter into a greater trust, a greater familiarity, and intimacy with each other; and the parents, animated with the hope that the promise having been made the marriage will take place, have no longer that careful watchfulness over them that they had before, and leaving them to remain alone, they incautiously open the way to a thousand disorders. Hence it is by that miserable reasoning, "You are mine, and I am yours," they do and say things that are not permitted, and thus they pass insensibly from lesser things to what is more sinful, and look upon such as lawful and innocent. In this manner grave sins are committed, which are either not confessed before marriage, or, if confessed, without sorrow, without repentance, and consequently they begin by committing a sacrilege in the confession, another in receiving Holy Communion, and a third at their marriage, from which causes arise so many unfortunate and unhappy unions.

Worse still it is when the promise is made so long before the time, and made with an oath: for it often happens that the promise is not observed, and, after so many fair expressions, they change their mind and will—then they are guilty of rash oaths: and with sin they dispose themselves for an unhappy marriage. Therefore, to avoid this danger, and dispose yourselves to contract a good marriage, it is better not to make the promise till a short time before the marriage; and when the promise is made, be not too much together, much less live in the same house. Employ your time in thinking over your affairs, in making a preparation for a good confession, so that you may receive worthily the Sacrament of Matrimony, with all its effects.

It now remains for me to give you a third admonition for the well-disposing yourselves for the holy state of marriage, and it is one of the greatest importance. It is this—have a good, right, and holy end in view; because, should you enter into the married state having a holy end in view, you may hope that God will grant you a happy end to your marriage; but if the end is bad, you must not expect anything but misfortune and adversity. The young man that wishes to be married for the sake of a large dowry, a rich property, or that he may have dominion over some estate, that he may be connected with a wealthy family, whose patronage may be useful to him in some future time; would such an one be animated with an honest and good end? No, this would be a human, worldly, and base end, which of itself alone is unworthy, and, consequently, a marriage formed for that end, would be badly formed, and it would have a bad end. The young woman who dislikes obedience, dependence, subjection, and who is wanting in respect to her parents because they never allow her to be out of their sight, who is displeased at not being allowed to go out when and with whom she chooses, who is not allowed to have all the dress she wishes, and it seems to her that married women have it all their own way at home, can command and do what they please; smitten with this appearance, tormented with this idea, she also desires to be married, but her principal end is that she may make a figure in the world and enjoy all the vanity of it, in fine, to do what other married women do. Is this a good end? No, it is a bad end she has in view, from which nothing but an unhappy marriage can be derived. That young man or woman that desires to be married, having for the principal end the satisfying of the passions, the enjoyment of pleasures, the delight of sensual pleasures, would this be a good end? No, this would be an irrational end, from which no blessing could follow.

What, then, are the motives, the end which persons ought to have in view in entering into the married state? The Church, in the Roman Catechism, tells us. "The first, then, is this very society of the other sex, sought by the instinct of nature, entered into with the hope of mutual aid, that each, assisted by the help of the other, may the more easily bear the ills of life and support the weakness of old age." Adam was alone in the terrestrial paradise. The three persons of the Holy Trinity in the creation said: "It is not good for man to be alone;" and then woman was formed in the manner before described and presented to Adam; he took her for his companion and formed an inseparable society.

Another end and motive which you ought to have in view is, "the desire of procreation, not so much, indeed, with a view that heirs be left to one's property and wealth, as that of professors of the true faith and religion be brought up, which, indeed, as sufficiently appears from the Sacred Scriptures, was the principal object the holy patriarchs proposed to themselves when they married." And this should be the end of every good Christian in marrying if he wishes God to give a happy end to his marriage. Hence it is, we can understand how culpable are those who, entering into the married state, have no other end in view but that of satisfying their disordinate passion. Hence it is, we can understand how wicked are those who, after marriage, do not wish to bear the burden of that state, seeking by every means to prevent them from having children, either by unlawful remedies, or by preventing conception, or by abortion, or by doing what is directly opposed to the principal end of that state, for which God has instituted the marriage bond, and thus render themselves guilty of homicide.

The third motive for marriage is that it may be a remedy for our corrupt nature, that has been made so by original sin, and is always inclined to evil; so that he who feels that he is unable to combat with and resist the flesh, may find in marriage a remedy, and thus avoid the commission of many sins. Listen to the Apostle: "But for fear of fornication, let every man have his own wife, and let every woman have her own husband."

These, then, are the three ends, just and holy, which persons may have in view for entering into the married state, namely: to have the society of a faithful companion, with the hope of mutual aid and assistance to bear more easily the ills of life, to desire the procreation of children, that they may be professors of the true faith, as a remedy for the passions and a preservative against sin. If, then, in marrying you have not in view these ends, or, at least, your principal end is not one of the three named, your marriage will not be pleasing to God, and not being pleasing to Him, it will not be blessed by Him. But if your principal end is one of these three, although you may have with it other motives, as, for instance that you may have heirs to your property, the receiving of a dowry, showing a preference for that one rather than to another, because more pleasing to you, and things similar; in that case there will be nothing wrong, for the principal end is good and just. In fact, Jacob, joined to the good end he had in being married to Rachel in preference to her sister, was because she was more beautiful, and the Scripture does not reprehend him for so doing.

And now-a-days, let us speak to ourselves in confidence, are there many who, in getting married, have in view a good end, such as ought to rule and govern them? Oh! no, the number is very small. The end that the many have is a worldly one—the principal end by which they are animated is solely the satisfying of their disordinate passions. Is it then to be wondered at that so many marriages have an unhappy end? We ought rather to wonder that there are any of them blessed by God. How is it possible that marriages can end happily that are contracted with a bad end in view, without the fear of God, without any thought of God's glory? That you may be convinced of this, listen to what is recorded in the Sacred Scripture: Tobias, a good young man, the son of a virtuous father, obedient, wise, modest, and fearing God, he being of an age to marry, whilst on his way, by the command of his father, to a distant part of the country, was accompanied by a beautiful young man, who was the angel Raphael. When on the road the angel spoke thus: "Tobias, thou must take Sara to wife, she is rich, all her substance is due to thee, ask her, therefore, of her father, and he will give her thee to wife." Tobias answered: "I hear she hath been given to seven husbands, and they all died. Now I am afraid lest the same thing should happen to me also." Then the angel said to him: "Hear me, and I will shew thee who they are, over whom the devil can prevail. For they who in such manner receive matrimony as to shut out God from themselves and from their mind, and to give themselves to lust, as the horse and the mule, which have not understanding, over them the devil hath power. But you, Tobias, shall take her, and with her give some time to prayer, take her with the fear of God, have a right end in view, and fear not, nothing shall happen to thee, thou shalt take the virgin with the fear of the Lord, moved rather for love of children than for lust, that in the seed of Abraham thou mayest obtain a blessing in children." Tobias did as he was told, and he took Sara to wife, and the marriage was blessed by God and made happy.

Therefore, do you wish God to give you a good portion—do you wish His help, His grace, that your marriage may have a happy end? Remember well what I have said to-day and on last Sunday, and try to put it into practice. The first thing is, recommend yourselves fervently to God; secondly, lead a good life; thirdly, choose a person that has the fear of God and of good conduct; fourthly, have respect for your parents; fifthly, avoid the dangers and occasions, particularly after the promise has been given; sixthly, have a good and right end in view; lastly, do all things in the fear of the Lord.

XXXV.

MIXED MARRIAGES.

WHEN a marriage takes place between a Catholic and a non-Catholic, it is called a mixed marriage. By a non-Catholic is meant either a heretic or Schismatic; that is, one who is out of the one true Church, and who professes to belong to some sect or schism bearing the name of Christian. This kind of marriage is forbidden, unless a dispensation has been obtained from the Pope, who alone can give it, and then only under certain conditions, by which the faith of the Catholic party and that of the children is sufficiently insured. This dispensation can never be lawfully given unless there are just reasons, and subject to these conditions. *Firstly*, that all the children that may be born of the marriage shall be baptised and brought up Catholics. *Secondly*, that the Catholic party shall have full liberty for the practice of the Catholic faith. *Thirdly*, that no religious ceremony shall take place elsewhere than in the Catholic Church.

These promises are exacted in compliance with the dictates of the divine and natural law, which forbid us to place ourselves or those committed to our charge in danger of losing our souls by heresy or any other sin. Should, however, a marriage take place otherwise than subject to these conditions, experience shows that great injury is done to religion.

The Church has always disapproved of mixed marriages, and has employed her influence and authority to prevent them, and rightly so, for such marriages are not in accordance with the natural or divine law. For by the natural law we are bound to avoid whatever may be dangerous to the faith or injurious to the soul.

That there is danger in mixed marriages experience leaves us no room to doubt. The hatred in which non-Catholics hold the true faith, the disregard they have for fasting, abstinence, confession, and other things commanded by the Church—the Catholic party not being allowed, or only under great difficulties, full and free profession of the faith, make it extremely difficult to find one so strong-minded as to resist a continual opposition to the practices of religion. Instances are daily brought under our eyes in which Catholics, owing to these marriages, have ceased to care for their religion, and for the salvation of the souls of their children. The dangers to which Christians are exposed by intermarrying with pagans, and which are given by the Fathers of the Church in order to deter Christians from such marriages, may be equally applied to mixed marriages.

The first thing to be looked to in marriage is religion. For the Holy Ghost says: "With the holy, thou wilt be holy, with the perverse, thou wilt be perverse." If, then, it is so in other things, how much more so in marriage, where there is one flesh and one spirit? How can there be true love where there is difference of faith? There is another very grave danger, that of the perversion of the children by the non-Catholic party—also the danger of divorce, which may at any moment take place on the part of those who believe in the dissolubility of marriage.

By the divine law the Jews were forbidden to intermarry with those that were not of the faith, and the same reason for this prohibition has place against mixed marriages. "Neither shalt thou give thy daughter to his son, nor take his daughter for thy son: for she will turn away thy son from following me."

The Apostle St. Paul lays down a rule for Christian marriage in these words: "Let her marry to whom she will: only in the Lord." Now, these words, "Only in the Lord," signify to marry him who belongs to the Church of Christ: and unless we observe this rule, given by the Apostle, we expose ourselves to the danger of losing our souls and those of our children. Hence the wisdom of the Church in disapproving of mixed marriages, and using all her authority to prevent them.

By some it may be said that the dangers I have mentioned arising from mixed marriages do not always follow, and that these dangers can be easily avoided— since the greater number of non-Catholics are indifferent about religion. To which I reply, the same reason holds good in marriage that has place in every moral action, and which of its own nature brings with it a grave danger of sinning, in which case the natural and divine law forbid us to risk our eternal salvation, according to the sentence of the Holy Ghost, " He that loves the danger shall perish therein." Nor can it be denied but that in mixed marriages there is this danger, though absolutely they do not lead to sin : if, however, we look to the nature of such marriages, and to what usually follows from them, we shall be forced to confess that there is that danger, and therefore such marriages ought to be avoided. For it is the duty of every Catholic to listen to the voice of the Church, which declares her disapproval of mixed marriages, and we are not obedient children of that Church unless we follow her teaching. The evils we have mentioned do not always follow, but such cases are exceptions, very rare, and only prove the general rule.

True it is, many non-Catholics are indifferent about religion, that is, they are indifferent about what religion they themselves profess, nevertheless they are not ashamed at using means most unjust in order to prevent those around them from becoming Catholics, or practising the Catholic faith, in this sense they are not indifferent. And only those who have interested motives in view, or who have never given any serious consideration to the subject, can advocate a union between persons of different religious opinions which is so unlikely to promote the happiness or spiritual welfare of either party. That mixed marriages become the fruitful sources of many and great evils is a sad truth. The years of bitterness and sorrow endured by those who, disregarding the warnings of all who have a right to advise, are continually being brought under our eyes, ought to deter those who, unhappily, wish to contract these marriages. But, notwithstanding the evils so numerous, the dangers so great occurring from these marriages, the strong disapproval of the Church, who, when induced to grant the required dispensation, omits the prayers giving solemnity to the marriage, and conveying the nuptial blessing, thus avoiding every act that might seem to imply her approval of such marriage, and wishing her children to share her horror and disapproval. How sad it is to see Catholics seeking to be associated in a marriage the end of which is too frequently the loss of connubial peace and concord, followed by strifes, contentions, and quarrels, exposing themselves to the danger of being deprived (as many have been even after the most solemn promises have been made by the non-Catholic party) of practising their faith in life, and of receiving its consolations at the hour of death.

Again, more deplorable is the conduct of those who, disregarding the laws of the Church, enter into a state that is holy in itself, but which they sacrilegiously profane by seeking to be joined together either in a church, as by law established, or by a civil functionary, whose condition and calling of life render him the last person to whom a Catholic, believing in the sanctity of marriage, should go.

Reflect well, then, upon what has been said in this and in the former instructions, you who are thinking of entering into the married state—consider its first institution by God in the terrestrial paradise, or of its being raised by Jesus Christ to a sacrament; from these considerations you will see that such a state of life ought not to be embraced, unless with a holy end in view, using holy means and having holy dispositions becoming the holiness of that state. Consult God with regard to that state, and the choice of the person whom you desire to have as a perpetual and indivisible companion. Look not upon marriage as a worldly affair of which religion and your eternal salvation form no part. Let

religion be the basis and foundation of all your actions
—religion in your maxims, but above all in your example. If you have religion and piety you will listen
to and obey the commands of God and His Church—
you will make yourselves fully acquainted with the
duties and obligations of the married state before entering therein, and if God has called you to that state,
follow what He makes known to you by His Church,
avoiding an alliance with those who are not of the
household of the faith. "For we are the children of
saints, and we must not be joined together like heathens
that know not God," that thus you may obtain the
blessing of God and His holy Church, and have in your
state peace and happiness in this world, and eternal
life in the next.

With this I bring to a conclusion my instructions on
the great and holy Sacrament of Marriage; and though
little or no fruit may follow from them, to me there will
be this gain, that of having done my duty towards you
by speaking to you on this sacrament. True, many
things might have been better said, but I have spoken
according to the power that is in me, and I have spoken
through a love of the truth, and in defence of Catholic
doctrine. As to the rest, should I have on this or any
other occasion spoken with a freedom not pleasing to
all, let such bear in mind that there is nothing in a
minister of the Divine Word more displeasing to God,
or base in man, than that of not speaking boldly and
freely the truths which he has been commissioned to
teach. What, then, I have said, through love for Holy
Church and the salvation of your souls, it is your duty
to observe, and so render yourselves doers and not
hearers only of the law. Should your future conduct
show that you have been only hearers of the law, that
you have allowed yourselves to be blinded by passion or
worldly interest in making a choice, and that your choice
should fall upon one not belonging to the faith, and the
evils of which I have spoken come upon you—"then
the words I have spoken to you shall judge you at the
last day." There is a responsibility upon you and upon

me—upon you, that you be not, by neglecting to hear the Church, as the heathen and the publican ; upon me, that I preach the Word to you. And in so doing, " If I yet pleased men, I should not be the servant of Christ," and thus I should become a castaway. Oh, happy, thrice happy, will you be, if you follow the teaching of the Church, for at such marriage-feasts there will be invited Jesús, and Mary His Mother will be there.

XXXVI.

ON VIRGINITY.

Up to the present I have instructed you on those things regarding the married state. I now take up an entirely different subject—a subject that deserves to be treated of, and one that merits your attention, and it is that of virginity, of purity, of chastity. In the instructions on the Sacrament of Matrimony I said that marriage is a good and holy state—that far from it having been invented by the devil, as some heretics have said, it is a state instituted by God Himself in the terrestrial paradise, and finally raised by Jesus Christ to the dignity of a sacrament. So that the Apostle St. Paul not only calls marriage holy and honourable, but declares it to be a "great sacrament in Christ and in the Church." Now, I undertake to show you that a state of virginity is far superior to that of marriage: that virginity, purity, chastity, is one of the most beautiful of moral virtues—a virtue most dear and pleasing to God.

And it is most evident from what God has said by the Apostle St. Paul, who begins by saying that he "would all men were even as himself." Speaking to the unmarried and widows, he says: "It is good for them if they so continue, even as I"—"because," he goes on to say, "because he that giveth his virgin in marriage doth well, and he that giveth her not doth better." Attend to the reason, showing that the state of virginity is superior to that of marriage: "He that is with a wife is solicitous for the things of the world, how he may please his wife, and he is divided." He says the same of the married woman: "She that is married thinketh on the things of the world, how she may please her husband." On the contrary, "He that is without a wife is solicitous for the things that belong to the Lord, how he may please God: and the unmarried woman and the virgin thinketh on the things of the Lord, that she may be holy in body and in spirit." Upon this the Council of Trent declares, that "If any one saith that the married state is to be placed above the state of virginity, or of celibacy, and that it is not better and more blessed to remain in virginity, or in celibacy, than to be united in matrimony, let him be anathema." If it is thus, let those hold their peace who are so ignorant and so carnal as to think that all our happiness should consist in the pleasures of sense, and who never cease to contemn and despise those who observe virginity, and declaim against celibacy. Let such open their eyes to the truth, confess and acknowledge that virginity, purity, chastity, is a virtue that has always been most esteemed and dear to God.

In fact, who can deny but that virginity has always been held in great esteem, when we know from history that it was always respected and venerated, not only by Christians in every age, but also by pagans themselves? Are not those martyrs to be esteemed who were respected even by the most ferocious beasts? The ancient Romans, who boasted of giving the just weight to everything, held in great esteem the state of virginity. They esteemed it so great, according to the testimony of St. Jerome, that not only the great and the nobles of the city, but the emperors themselves, when they met a vestal virgin, immediately gave place to her, as a mark of the great esteem and respect in which they held her. And this was not only an external demonstration, but a true and real one: for if by chance a virgin was walking in the street, and were to meet a prisoner who had been condemned to death, through respect for her, they considered themselves obliged to absolve him from the sentence of death, as if the sight of a virgin were sufficient to render him innocent. If, then, virginity was so esteemed by pagans themselves, who were led only by a natural light, imagine in what esteem it has been held since Jesus Christ has come upon this earth and made

known to us its preciousness? That you may understand this, listen to what the fathers of the Church have
said of it. St. Ignatius, writing to the Bishop of
Antioch, tells him " to have care of the virgins, as so
many most precious jewels of Christ." Then writing to
another, he tells him " to have in esteem the virgins, as
so many ministers of Christ." St. Cyprian says that
"virgins are the most illustrious portion of Christ's
flock." St. Gregory, that " virgins participate of a virtue belonging to the Divine nature." St. John Chrysostom, that " virgins are to be esteemed as so many
angels in human flesh." St. Ambrose and St. Augustine assert that they " may be compared to the angels
in heaven." And St. Bernard goes further, and says
that, in a certain sense, "they are to be preferred to the
angels," because "the angels though more happy, virgins are more wonderful." What more can be said to
show how much virginity is to be esteemed? St Anthony, to indicate the worth of virginity, says that "all
Christian souls are spouses of Jesus Christ, but the souls
of those who observe purity and chastity are in a particular manner spouses of Jesus Christ." For this reason
St. Agnes replied to him who desired her for his spouse,
" that he was not to think of her, because she was the
spouse of Jesus Christ, Whom angels serve."

In fact, that souls pure and chaste have always been
most dear and beloved of God, that virginity has always
been that virtue most loved and esteemed by God,
Jesus Christ Himself has given us many proofs. He
willed to have for His mother a virgin, for His adopted
father St. Joseph, the most chaste among men, for His
precursor, St. John the Baptist, the most pure among
creatures; amongst His apostles He willed to have a
beloved disciple in the person of St. John, wholly dedicated to a perfect virginity; before His death He willed
to destine one who should have the special care of His
Virgin Mother, but in preference to all the apostles He
chose St. John, because He was a virgin in body and
in spirit. Finally, Jesus Christ permitted Himself to
be tempted and calumniated in many ways, but He

never allowed Himself to be tempted or calumniated against virginity ; all these are signs, clear as the noonday sun, that there is not a vice so displeasing to Jesus Christ as that of impurity, so there is not a virtue so pleasing to Him as that of purity and chastity.

From what the Fathers have said with regard to virginity, even to prefer it to the angelical dignity, from what we are able to imagine of it, we have not been, nor shall we ever be able fully to understand how estimable is this virtue. As long as we are in this world it is not possible for us to know its value, but we shall know it in heaven. Ah ! there it will be seen so resplendent as to enrapture with admiration all the happy citizens of that place. It is sufficient for us to know that virgins in heaven follow the Lamb whithersoever He goeth ; it suffices to know that they have the name of the Father written on their foreheads, that they sing to God a hymn that the other saints may hear, but are not allowed to join in, they are the firstfruits to God and to the Lamb, as the first-fruits of the earth are more esteemed, so are virgins more esteemed than all the other saints in heaven. Finally, it will suffice to say that in reward of their virginity they are docorated by a distinctive and special mark, besides the crown common to the other saints, they will have one more resplendent. No, we are unable to explain or imagine how estimable is the virtue of holy purity. God Himself has said : " No price is worthy of a continent soul." Place on one side all the princes of this world, and on the other side a virgin poor in this world, and if she is truly a virgin, both in body and in spirit, she is infinitely more to be esteemed than all the married united together, with all their riches and greatness. Oh, how greatly is to be praised a soul chaste and pure, not only before man but before God ! " O how greatly is the chaste generation with glory, for the memory thereof is immortal ; because it is known both with God and with men." And holy Church cries out in these words : " O holy virginity, I know not what flowers of praise to give you !"

And if it is thus, oh, how much to be deplored is the blindness of those who make no account of this virtue, of a pearl so precious! Oh, how much to be deplored is the blindness of those who, before they have scarcely arrived to the use of reason, seem eager only to taint their souls by words, thoughts, desires, and actions, contrary to a virtue so beautiful! How much to be deplored is the blindness of those of Eve's daughters, who consider it a disgrace because they cannot be married, who consider the state of virginity one of disgrace, and who permit that which ought not to be so much as named amongst us, with the vain hope of marriage, and for the most part the end is the loss of esteem and reputation, amongst all! Putting aside these reproofs, let us pass on to make an observation more pleasing, that we may be more convinced of the greatness of this virtue.

You know, that before the coming of Jesus Christ into this world, the Archangel Gabriel came from heaven to announce to the Blessed Virgin that she was chosen to be the Mother of God, and for that to obtain her consent. It might seem to us that the Blessed Virgin ought at once to have given her consent. But no, the announcement troubled her. Now why was she troubled? Was it at the presence of an angel? The sacred text tells us that she was troubled at his saying and not at his presence. Perhaps she was troubled on hearing it declared to her that she was full of grace and that the Lord was with her. No; for this had been always the only object of her desire. What, then, was the motive of Mary being troubled? St. Bernard tells us it was in hearing that she was blessed among women, which she had always desired to be among virgins, and she feared that by becoming the Mother of God it would be prejudicial to her virginity; for this reason she was troubled. Let us try to imagine the anxiety with which the souls detained in Limbo and the angels in heaven, and even God Himself, awaited the consent of Mary, that there might be effected the most wonderful of works—the Incarnation of the Son of God, the redemption of the human race. On hearing the will of God so manifestly made known to her—on hearing that her Son would be the Son of God, the Saviour of the world, so long desired by the patriarchs, foretold by the prophets, one would have supposed that she would have at once given her consent, and yet she gives it not until every doubt is removed, and fully assured how it is to be done—" How shall this be done, because I know not man." But when she was assured by the angel that she should become a mother and remain a virgin, then, and not till then, did she give her consent —" Behold the handmaid of the Lord : be it done unto me according to Thy word ;" as if she had said—" Let the Son of God be born of me, that the world may be redeemed, that souls may be freed from Limbo, that the devil may be bound down ; let there be joy in heaven ; yes, I give my consent, but under this express condition, that I remain a virgin—otherwise to have for a son the Son of God, to become Queen of heaven and earth, would not remove from my mind the anguish for the loss of my virginity."

If, then, the Blessed Virgin preferred, as it were, her virginity to the birth of the Son of God, to the salvation of the whole world, we are constrained to believe that virginity, purity, chastity, is a virtue without its equal, a pearl of great price, one of the most noble of the angelical prerogatives. And, now, where are those who think so little of this virtue, who despise it, who throw it away as if it were of little or no value ? Where are those weak and foolish ones who expose themselves to every danger, to every occasion, and part with it for a vain promise ? The Blessed Virgin was troubled at the salutation of an angel ; and you are so careless, as not to fear conversation indelicate, unworthy friendships, counsel and instigations of devils in human form, who are continually laying in wait to rob you of this priceless treasure ! Ah, foolish and neglectful you are ! Attend to what I have yet to say, for I wish to show you that this virtue, so much despised by you, has always been esteemed by Lucifer himself. In fact, the

devil has always sought to be worshipped by virgins.
Besides the vestal virgins of Rome, of which I have
spoken, we read that the devil had in India a temple in
which he was worshipped by a multitude of virgins, who
were so rigorously bound by his laws, that should they
have violated them, they were doomed to be burned
alive, together with their accomplice and their relatives.
This fact proves the esteem in which the devil holds
this virtue, even to chastise with the utmost rigour
whosoever should transgress it. If, then, the devil has
led pagans to have an esteem so great for the virtue of
chastity, what esteem will he make of it in Christians?
Not only has he an esteem, but respect for it, and he
fears it extremely. In the history of the Church we
read of a devil being cast out of a person by the presence
of a poor, humble virgin—giving us to understand that
virginity alone was sufficient to put him to flight.

Having now briefly shown you how much the virtue
of chastity is esteemed : that it is so much appreciated,
not only on earth and in heaven, but even in hell—who
is there that ought not to be ashamed for having hitherto
thought so little of a virtue so great, for having openly
despised and perhaps violated it in body or in spirit ?
Who is there that will not resolve to preserve it with
the greatest jealousy in the future ? But how is a virtue
so precious, so dear to God, to be preserved ? Here are
two remedies considered to be most efficacious. The
first is, to fly from the proximate occasion, for he who
exposeth himself to the danger will perish therein.
The second is prayer, for says the Holy Ghost—" As I
knew that I could not otherwise be continent except God
gave it, I went to the Lord and besought Him." I have
said these are the two best remedies, without mention-
ing others that are necessary and efficacious, such as
keeping a guard over the senses, particularly that of the
eyes, tongue, mortification of the appetite, and meditating on the four last things, the Passion of our Blessed
Lord. Prayer, however, is the great remedy—" As I
knew that I could not otherwise be continent, except
God gave it, I went to the Lord, and besought Him."